This series aims to provide a comprehensive space for an increasingly diverse and complex area of interdisciplinary social science research: gender and education. Because the field of women and gender studies is developing rapidly and becoming 'internationalised' – as are traditional social science disciplines such as sociology, educational studies, social geography, and so on – there is a greater need for this dynamic, global series that plots emerging definitions and debates and monitors critical complexities of gender and education. This series has an explicitly feminist approach and orientation and attends to key theoretical and methodological debates, ensuring a continued conversation and relevance within the well-established, inter-disciplinary field of gender and education.

The series combines renewed and revitalised feminist research methods and theories with emergent and salient public policy issues. These include pre-compulsory and post-compulsory education; 'early years' and 'lifelong' education; educational (dis)engagements of pupils, students and staff; trajectories and intersectional inequalities including race, class, sexuality, age and disability; policy and practice across educational landscapes; diversity and difference, including institutional (schools, colleges, universities), locational and embodied (in 'teacher'–'learner' positions); varied global activism in and beyond the classroom and the 'public university'; educational technologies and transitions and the (ir)relevance of (in)formal educational settings; and emergent educational mainstreams and margins. In using a critical approach to gender and education, the series recognises the importance of probing beyond the boundaries of specific territorial-legislative domains in order to develop a more international, intersectional focus. In addressing varied conceptual and methodological questions, the series combines an intersectional focus on competing – and sometimes colliding – strands of educational provisioning and equality and 'diversity', and provides insightful reflections on the continuing critical shift of gender and feminism within (and beyond) the academy.

More information about this series at
http://www.springer.com/series/14626

Rachel Thwaites • Amy Pressland
Editors

Being an Early Career Feminist Academic

Global Perspectives, Experiences and Challenges

Editors
Rachel Thwaites
Canterbury Christ Church University
United Kingdom

Amy Pressland
Human Resources
DB Cargo UK
United Kingdom

Palgrave Studies in Gender and Education
ISBN 978-1-137-54324-0   ISBN 978-1-137-54325-7   (eBook)
DOI 10.1057/978-1-137-54325-7

Library of Congress Control Number: 2016950455

Cover illustration: © Gary Waters / Alamy Stock Photo

Printed on acid-free paper

This Palgrave Macmillan imprint is published by Springer Nature
The registered company is Macmillan Publishers Ltd.
The registered company address is: The Campus, 4 Crinan Street, London, N1 9XW, United Kingdom

ACKNOWLEDGMENTS

We would like to say a huge thank you to our contributors for their insightful and inspiring work, which has opened up many spaces for feminist conversation. We would also like to thank everyone who attended and spoke at our BSA Early Career Forum event in Birmingham in April 2016, which extended some of these conversations and gave us hope for change. We would especially like to thank Yvette Taylor for her support of this project.

Many thanks also go to the team at Palgrave—most especially Andrew James and Eleanor Christie—for their ongoing support and the calm way in which they provided guidance from initial idea to completed book.

Our thanks also go to Adam Gorrill for his creative skills, which can be found on the front cover, and to Neil Smith for the initial title idea suggestion of 'Feminist Beginnings'. Rachel would like to thank Neil for all his ongoing enthusiasm for the book. And Amy is very grateful to her family for their continual support for her professional endeavours.

Finally, our joint thanks go to the Centre for Women's Studies at the University of York, where we completed our PhDs. Not only did it bring us together and provide the support we needed to conduct and complete our doctoral projects, it also afforded a 'bubble of safety' for two early career feminist academics.

CONTENTS

LIST OF FIGURES AND TABLE

NOTES ON CONTRIBUTORS

Sophie Alkhaled is a British-Syrian Lecturer at Lancaster University. She received her PhD in management studies from the University of Aberdeen, funded by The College of Arts and Social Sciences and the Federation for Women Graduates. She previously held a teaching fellowship at the University of Aberdeen and a postdoctoral research fellowship at Stockholm University, funded by the Swedish Research Council and Stockholm School of Entrepreneurship. Her interdisciplinary research interest is feminism in the Middle East, particularly the question of women's emancipation and political activism through entrepreneurship. Her doctoral research, entitled "Women entrepreneurs in Saudi Arabia: Bargaining within a patriarchal society", examined women's entrepreneurship and boundary negotiation in the context of Saudi Arabia. She has presented her work at a number of international conferences and was subsequently invited as the first woman keynote speaker at the 5th International Conference of Faculty of Economic and Administrative Sciences in Amman, Jordan, where she discussed issues related to women, work, and political participation in the Middle East in the wake of the Arab Spring. Alkhaled is currently engaged in research on Syrian women refugees' informal political activism through entrepreneurship in Jordan.

Agnes Bosanquet is Early Career Researcher and Lecturer in Higher Education at Macquarie University in Sydney, Australia. Her PhD in cultural studies performed an autoethnographic response to Luce Irigaray's philosophy of sexual difference, transcendence, and the mother-daughter relation. From her background in cultural studies, Bosanquet values critical theory and creative methodologies, which she applies to her research in education on changing academic roles and identities, academic writing, and graduate attributes.

Emily Cooper is Lecturer in Human Geography at University of Central Lancashire. Her interests lie in the interaction of sex, space, and society, with a particular focus on the experiences of living in close proximity to the sex industry. Cooper's doctoral research (completed at the Lancaster Environment Centre, Lancaster University, in 2014) explored the impacts of brothels on residential communities in Blackpool. Other general research interests include the following: conflict and deviance in urban space, the geographies of stigma and exclusion in everyday life, liminality, and visual/cultural criminology. She is also a member of the Sex Work Research Hub.

Muireann Crowley is a PhD candidate in English Literature at the University of Edinburgh. Her doctoral research examines authorship in Romantic Irish literature; more broadly, her research interests include feminism, women's writing, and intellectual history.

Irina Gewinner is a lecturer and research assistant at the Institute of Sociology, University of Hanover, Germany. She is currently working on her PhD on transition to work in Russia and a project on career choices of Russian youth in Germany. Her research interests include social inequality in education and the labour market, as well as gender equality in tertiary education.

Helena Goodwyn teaches in the English department at Queen Mary, University of London, and completed her PhD in 2015. Her research interests include nineteenth-century British and American literature, print culture, women's literature, book and media history, and transatlantic literature of the nineteenth and twentieth centuries. She is co-editor of the 2015 essay collection *English Studies: the State of the Discipline, Past, Present, and Future.*

Emily Hogg teaches in the English department at Queen Mary, University of London, and completed her PhD in 2014; it explored the relationship between contemporary women's writing and contemporary discourses of human rights. With Clara Jones she co-edited the collection *Influence and Inheritance in Feminist English Studies* (Palgrave Macmillan, 2015), to which she also contributed a chapter, and she has written articles or reviews in *English Studies, New Formations,* and *Alluvium.*

Marjaana Jauhola is an Academy of Finland Research Fellow in Gender Studies, University of Helsinki, Finland, and holds a PhD in international politics from Aberystwyth University, UK (2010). Her works include the monograph *Post-Tsunami Reconstruction in Indonesia: Negotiating Normativity through Gender Mainstreaming Initiatives in Aceh* (2013), and she is currently working on a digital monograph with documentary film *Scraps of Hope* (scrapsofhope.info/aceh), which is based on her street ethnographic life narrative research in the city of Banda Aceh. She is interested in politics of post-disaster and post-conflict landscapes as a site of political and social struggle that provoke norms in relation to gender, class, ethnicity, sexuality, and religion, through normative calls for gendered piety and propriety.

Olga Marques is Assistant Professor in the Criminology and Justice programme at the University of Ontario Institute of Technology in Oshawa, Ontario, Canada. She received her PhD in criminology from the University of Ottawa in 2014. Her dissertation research focused on women who use sexually explicit materials for their own sexual pleasure, and centred on the inter-relationships between social norms, social control, and resistance, in an area where questions of deviancy, regulation, and censorship continue to surface. Her research and teaching interests include sexual labour, constructions of sexualized deviance, as well as the examination of regulation and justice as they relate to both sex/sexuality/gender and race/ethnicity.

Misato Matsuoka has been a part-time lecturer at Tokai University (Japan) since April 2016. Prior to that, she was an associate fellow at the Institute of Advanced Study (IAS) at the University of Warwick and an early career fellow at the same institute. Before her doctoral studies at Warwick, she completed an MA in global studies and a BA at the Faculty of Liberal Arts at Sophia University (Japan). During her undergraduate years she studied at the Peace and Conflict Studies Center at the University of California, Berkeley, for one year as an exchange student, and during her postgraduate years was an intern at the Northeast Asia Team, Department of Political Affairs (DPA) at the United Nations (UN), working as a research assistant. Her completed PhD is entitled "Moving Beyond (Traditional) Alliance Theory?: a Neo-Gramscian Approach to the U.S.-Japan Alliance". Her research interests include theories of international relations (IR), security studies, Japanese foreign policymaking, regionalism in the Asia-Pacific and domestic politics in Japan (including gender issues). She has written online articles including "Transforming IR Education in Japan" (E-International Relations).

Lara McKenzie is a research associate in Anthropology and Sociology at The University of Western Australia, where she received her PhD in 2013. Her PhD research focused on age-dissimilar romantic relationships in Australia, exploring themes of gender, age, difference, love, autonomy, and relatedness. Her dissertation was recently published as a book, *Age-dissimilar couples and romantic relationships: Ageless love?* (Palgrave Macmillan, Studies in Family and Intimate Life Series, 2015). She has also undertaken research on e-learning and inequalities in education, internationalization at home, and is currently conducting a study on recent PhD graduates' experiences of looking for stable academic work.

Órla Meadhbh Murray is a PhD student and tutor in Sociology at the University of Edinburgh conducting an institutional ethnography of UK higher education. Her research focuses on how neoliberalism and structural inequality operate in everyday interactions in higher education, specifically how people perform legitimacy through their reading and use of texts. Her broader interests include the following: feminism, intersectionality, identity, performance, work/labour, power, epistemology, and theatre and the arts.

Katherine Natanel is Lecturer in Gender Studies at the University of Exeter's Institute of Arab and Islamic Studies. She received her PhD in Gender Studies from SOAS, University of London, and was also previously a postdoctoral associate there. Her recent research focuses on the gendered production of political apathy among Jewish Israelis and is published by University of California Press under the title *Sustaining Conflict: Apathy and Domination in Israel-Palestine* (2016). Her research interests include political participation and mobilization, feminist and gender theory, conflict and political violence, political emotion, and gender in the Middle East.

Klara Regnö holds a PhD in industrial economics and management and is employed as a researcher at the National Secretariat for Gender Research, Gothenburg University, and as a senior lecturer at Mälardalen University, Sweden. Her research interests concerns gender, management, gender equality, and organizational change. She has been involved in a number of research and change projects on gender and organization and is the co-writer of three government-commissioned inquiries into gender equality in the private sector. Her award winning doctoral thesis focuses on management, gender equality, and diversity in women-dominated organizations.

The Res-Sisters are a feminist collective of nine early career academics. They are Jessie Abrahams (Cardiff University); Kim Allen (University of Leeds); Victoria Cann (University of East Anglia); Laura Harvey (University of Surrey); Sumi Hollingworth (London South Bank University); Nicola Ingram (Lancaster University); Kirsty Morrin (University of Manchester); Helene Snee (Manchester Metropolitan University); and Annabel Wilson (Cardiff University). The group's collective interests include challenging inequality both within and outside of academia, resisting the neoliberal agenda, and making space for alternative voices to be heard.

Saara Särmä is a feminist, artist, and researcher. She is the co-founder of Feminist Think Tank Hattu and the creator of "Congrats, you have an all male panel!" Särmä currently works as a postdoctoral researcher at the University of Tampere, Finland, where she received her doctorate in 2014. Her doctoral dissertation in International Relations titled "Junk Feminism and Nuclear Wannabes – Collaging Parodies of Iran and North Korea" focused on internet parody images and developed a unique and innovative art-based collage methodology for studying world politics. She is interested in the politics of visuality, feminist academic activism, and laughter in world politics. Currently she is working on developing the visual collage methodology further as both a research and a pedagogical tool and experimenting with collective possibilities of collaging. Her postdoctoral project focuses on the role of memes and online image circulation in global politics. Her artwork can be seen at www.huippumisukka.fi.

Anna Tarrant is a Leverhulme Trust funded early career research fellow in Sociology and Social Policy at the University of Leeds. Her current project is a qualitative longitudinal study that examines the lived experiences of change and continuity in men's care responsibilities when living on a low income. This study builds on research interests in men and masculinities, family life and care, and poverty.

Lena Wånggren is a research fellow in English Literature at the University of Edinburgh, where she also teaches. Her research concerns questions of gender in late nineteenth-century literature and culture, as well as feminist theory, pedagogy, and the medical humanities.

Introduction: Being an Early Career Feminist Academic in a Changing Academy

Rachel Thwaites and Amy Pressland

This book comes at a time of dramatic change in higher education (HE) around the globe; some of the fundamental principles underpinning HE are being questioned, forcing academics and the wider public to begin to ask what higher education is for and what the purpose of research is in society at large (for example, Collini 2012; Small 2013), as well as where work such as teaching or 'citizenship' duties fit within the wider scheme of an academic career and the methods by which this career should be judged and, increasingly, measured (Collini 2012: 37; Small 2013: 10). Within academia the pressures to perform exceptionally across all levels of teaching, research, and administration grow, yet, with research remaining the most prestigious part of the three main areas of an academic role, syphoning off teaching and administrative roles to academics who are earlier in their careers and often on short-term or hourly paid contracts is becoming more common, with highly negative results for the wellbeing and career progression of early career academics as well as the quality of teaching provided to students in HE (as the collection of essays from the *Times Higher Education* makes clear: Anon, Leathwood and Read, and Else, all 2015).

R. Thwaites (✉)
Canterbury Christ Church University, Canterbury, Kent, UK

A. Pressland
DB Cargo UK, Doncaster, Yorkshire, UK

© The Author(s) 2017
R. Thwaites, A. Pressland (eds.), *Being an Early Career Feminist Academic*, DOI 10.1057/978-1-137-54325-7_1

1

The casualization of HE is increasingly being discussed in academic literature (Lopes and Dewan 2014: 29) and in the public domain: in the UK context, a recent article in *The Guardian* mentions statistics from the Higher Education Statistics Agency (HESA) which suggest that over a third of academics in the United Kingdom are on fixed-term, temporary contracts (Fazackerley 2013). These statistics actually mask the work being done by those on zero-hours contracts who are not recorded by HESA, leading Lopes and Dewan to argue that University College Union statistics are perhaps closer to representing the true picture of casualization in HE: 'University College Union (UCU) estimated in July 2013 that 47% of "teaching-only contracts" are in fact zero-hour contracts' (Lopes and Dewan 2014: 30).

This casualization of the workforce is a part of the growing neoliberalisation of higher education. As Mudge argues (2008: 704, 705), neoliberalism is an intellectual, political, and bureaucratic system which elevates the market above all else and encourages the use of the market as an organiser of people and institutions. Education, once seen as something that ought to be free from the influence of the market, is now increasingly coming under and being heavily influenced by this neoliberal rhetoric and agenda (Mudge 2008: 704). As the 'common sense' narratives of personal risk, individual responsibility, competition, and decentralisation take hold, the academy is shifting in profound ways, which have extensive impacts upon the lives of academics. Furthermore, as the cost of degrees rises across many parts of the world, consumerism creeps into the academic arena: the value of academic endeavour comes under ever-closer scrutiny; and, indeed, actual measurement, often with little regard for the way in which academic research is carried out or the differences between subjects, disciplines, and methods. Researchers and teachers find themselves having to justify their work and meet student, funder, and university demands in new and pressing ways. This, for many 'early careers' on short-term contracts, hourly paid contracts, or even zero-hours contracts, is all happening while their own security within the institution becomes ever more precarious.

This precariousness is an increasingly common part of the early career stage, and in fact, early career academics are becoming an ever-larger part of what Standing has termed 'the precariat' (Standing 2014). A class of people living in unstable and untenable conditions, the precariat is a group evolving out of an increasingly neoliberal political ideology. Although, as Standing makes clear, the precariat is a heterogeneous group (Standing

2014: 13) much of what brings them together is 'a sense that their labour is instrumental (to live), opportunistic (taking what comes) and precarious (insecure)' (Standing 2014: 14). For early career researchers there may well be a sense of building a career and using this insecure period to get somewhere better or higher, which might suggest that they do not fit within this new class grouping. However, early careers fit within many of the categories Standing outlines as defining the precariat (however loosely). For example, with fewer opportunities available, fierce competition for what jobs there are, and much ambivalence about remaining within academia (as our contributors discuss) any sense of definite upward mobility is challenged. Early careers often have little control over where they must live and work due to the scarcity of jobs, and may have little autonomy within their roles due to their lower status (Standing 2014: 10).

Also, Standing argues (2014: 11) that precarious income and patterns of income are features of the precariat: many early careers work from one short-term contract to the next, scraping a living together. They may have little employment or job security, as they are not full employees and do not necessarily receive benefits such as sick pay, holiday pay, or even build up a pension; they may not know if their hours will be renewed term-on-term or if they will be redeployed to a suitable contract once their current contract comes to an end. This temporariness leads to a sense of being outside the profession, and indeed management and employment procedures can reinforce this idea or actually make it a reality: with a very limited collective voice early careers lack representational security (though unions in the United Kingdom, for example, have recognised and are trying to tackle casualization; see the *University and College Union* website) (Standing, 2014: 10). Inequality is becoming normalised and taken for granted within academia globally.

As the HE sector shifts in response to these changes (and reiterates them), inequity grows. As mentioned earlier, teaching may fall disproportionately on the shoulders of early career academics as mid- and later-career academics move to meet the demands of their own career stages. The intensity of teaching and the time it involves can mean that early career academics find their research plans very much on hold. Simultaneously, teaching is being subjected to the professionalization which other areas of academia have undergone, and the need to 'demonstrate capabilities' and do well in student surveys are significant parts of showing teaching ability and thereby improving prospects for promotion. Though there are positives to this professionalization and increased training and scrutiny, the rhetoric is similar to the increasingly pressurized and monetised arena of research and can reduce teaching excellence to a series of tick-boxes. With the prospect of a 'Teaching Excellence Framework' on the horizon for universities in the United Kingdom (currently only planned for England) and similar auditing and measuring tools and processes across the globe beginning to be employed, the role of early career academics in teaching may potentially become further pressured, while at the same time also further relegated to the lowest levels, with the least recognition but the greatest investment of time.

The current pace of change in HE is also unprecedented, with an acceleration and intensification of neoliberal practices. It has been fuelled by the marketisation of education, which is now the de facto model in the United Kingdom and beyond. As such, shifts have taken place at the meta-level in our fundamental understanding of HE and its role in society. At a more micro-level huge changes can be witnessed in the student body and their expectations of HE; the positive 'widening participation' agenda has led to a more diverse student makeup, with more students from all backgrounds attending university than ever before; however, the hike in tuition fees in many countries, whereby students now bear the brunt of the costs of HE as opposed to national governments, creates enhanced expectations amongst students who have become more demanding about the quality of the 'product' they now perceive themselves to be purchasing (it may also begin to push out certain groups of students who had only just begun to enter HE). Moreover, academic staff face increasing pressures to meet these student expectations whilst continuing to produce world-class, ground-breaking research, which they disseminate to niche and lay audiences in the name of public engagement. This is called 'playing the game' and it has never been more important for academics to toe this particular line; this is not necessarily about having a 'successful' career in academia, it can be simply about surviving.

Within this context, entering the HE field as an early career academic presents many challenges, as well as possibilities. Moving from the relative autonomy, and potential bubble of safety, of the PhD into teaching or research contracts, where there may be less flexibility and freedom within the institutional hierarchy, can be a truly significant change. There are more PhD graduates than ever before but not enough jobs to go around. Early-career academics frequently face the prospect of working on fixed-term contracts, with little security and no certainty of advancement, while constantly looking for their next role. Data suggest that as little as 12% of female PhD candidates want to stay in academia to work as lecturers and researchers by their final year of study (Rice 2012), which indicates that they are being dissuaded by a tough job market and/or simply cannot cope with the short-term-contract nature of the initial stages—and sometimes beyond—of today's academic working life. The contributions in this collection speak to the pressures and constraints highlighted by this statistic and the need for collective action to stem the flow of early careers leaving the profession, to make the gendered differences in experience explicit, as well as to balance the competing demands of upholding a feminist politics within a neoliberal environment.

Feminist Early Career Academics: Conflicting Identities?

Higher Education has traditionally been a male-dominated institution globally, as our contributors will show in the chapters of this collection. Historically, universities have been the preserve of men in terms of the numbers of male students and members of faculty, as well as the macho culture which has pervaded the hallowed halls of HE institutions (Savigny 2014). Malcolm Bradbury satirised this culture in his now infamous *The History Man*, a novel written in 1975, ostensibly set at a leading 1960s campus university in the United Kingdom. In Bradbury's account, the leading character, Howard Kirk, is an ambitiously ruthless sociologist who produces numerous displays of overt misogyny, bolstering the patriarchal academic hierarchy. Although fictitious, it could be argued that elements of *The History Man* are painfully close to reality in its portrayal of the macho culture present in many HE institutions.

Conversely, in the past four decades there has been exponential growth in the number of women attending HE as undergraduate students.[1] In many parts of Europe, North and South America, and parts of Asia, women outnumber men in terms of enrolment to university. However, according to the UNESCO Institute for Statistics, as soon as we consider PhD graduates and researchers working in HE, men occupy a significantly larger percentage of the academic space than women (UNESCO 2014). Furthermore, the situation worsens the higher up the university management chain one goes (Savigny 2014). Indeed, in the United Kingdom women account for 45% of academics at universities; however, they occupy only 20% of professorships. At the highest rank in universities, only 14% of vice-chancellors are women (HESA 2015). The hallowed council chambers have long been decorated with portraits of white, greying men, and although one of the oldest institutions in the United Kingdom, Oxford University, appointed its first ever female vice-chancellor recently, the record of women's advancement in this most senior and prestigious position is woefully poor.

The junior female academic thus faces an uphill battle in terms of career aspirations. Being a 'feminist' early career academic adds a further layer of complexity: maintaining one's feminist identity and politics within what has traditionally been a very male-dominated institution where few women reach the most senior positions, and within an increasingly marketising academy, where students are viewed as 'customers', may sit uneasily with a politics of 'equality for all', collectivity, caring, and transformatory politics. Feminist values and practices can provide a means of working through some of these challenges, but may also bring complications as different ideologies collide. Some of these complications will be explored in this book.

As feminist researchers and teachers ourselves, we feel that the impact of trying to live out a feminist politics that involves another set of priorities that affect the way we think about the everyday and overarching experience of an academic career. This political outlook can lead to transformative events but can also create difficulties in a non-feminist department or a research climate that does not take gender seriously.

We have both come from a Women's Studies centre, where we completed our respective PhDs. In this 'safe' environment, feminism was taken as the guiding force for our individual and collective endeavours both in our postgraduate projects and beyond the walls of HE through activism. Although there were varying interpretations and ways in which students and staff embodied their feminist selves, the political climate of the centre meant that our collective identity was 'feminist' and embraced all bifurcations of feminism. It was only upon leaving this feminist bubble that we became cognisant of how 'unsafe' non-feminist HE institutions can be for early career feminist academics. Since completing our PhDs we have been employed as Research Fellows and Lecturers at 'good' universities in the United Kingdom. However, our journeys to this point have been neither linear nor simple, which mirrors some of our contributors' stories of gaining post-PhD employment. Moreover, we struggle to grapple on a daily basis with some of the themes of this book (i.e., our feminist identities, how to live out our feminist politics in the classroom, finding spaces to do feminist work, and so on).

It is important to highlight that this book is written and edited by feminists; however, not every chapter is specifically 'about' feminists. In conceptualising the idea for this book we decided that we wanted to give space to a range of early career scholars who self-identify as feminist and who see gender as the most important category for analysis. In this way this collection of empirical, personal, and theoretically driven pieces take a feminist 'approach'. As mentioned earlier, we are cognisant of the existence of numerous ways in which to 'be' feminist and live out our feminism. Academically speaking, despite numerous explorations (Harding 1986, 1987; Scraton and Flintoff 2002; Humphries and Truman 1994; Ramazanglu and Holland 2002; Bryman 2008), there has been no consensus on a singular, distinctive method of feminist inquiry. Ramazanoglu and Holland (2002: 13) state, 'feminist methodology is one set of approaches to the problems of producing justifiable knowledge of gender relations … [and] always entails some theory of power.' Feminist methodology, as an academic area of research, began in response to feminist researchers challenging existing methods—which created exclusively masculine knowledge—and thus critiquing existing understandings of gendered social relations (Ramazanoglu and Holland 2002; Stanley 2013). There are a myriad of feminist methodologies and debates about what these entail, however, in this collection our contributors use feminism as a guiding concept in research, providing a framework in which to operate. That is to say, the stimulus, research design, analysis, and theoretical framework for conducting research as a feminist are distinctive and driven from each author's feminist identity.

Much has been written about the often subjective nature of feminist research; Stanley (2013) argues that this is a strength of the field as it engenders the ability to understand peoples' lived realities. Harding (1987) goes further to suggest that as feminists our standpoint provides a privileged position from which to investigate, understand, and analyse the lives of women. Stanley (2013) describes this as the 'power' that feminists have in interviewing women. Although we do not aver that this is universally the case, our contributors are arguably in a privileged position in terms of being able to provide detailed accounts and insights into their experiences of HE as early career feminist academics. However, they occupy less privileged positions within the academy more widely. We therefore seek to think of the interactions between power, feminist research, and feminist researchers themselves as complex and not to approach them naively (Taylor 1996: 121).

Defining 'Early Career'

There have been an increasing number of academic publications dedicated to the discussion of gender at work in HE institutions (Blackmore 2002; Deem 1998; Johansson and Sliwa 2014; Kelan 2010; Lafferty and Fleming 2000; Lee and Won 2014; Peterson 2015; Savigny 2014; Thompson 2015). However, the vast majority of these focus almost exclusively on the people who occupy the upper echelons of the academic workforce. It is clear how to demarcate this group; senior management is a less ambiguous group to understand than 'early career'.

In the initial stages of conceptualising this book we thought long and hard about how we understood the term 'early career academic'. After much discussion between ourselves and our colleagues, we defined early career academics as those who are within five years of having been awarded their PhD. The term 'early career', however, is contested in HE and is laden with politics, particularly in the current neoliberal era of university management. 'Early-career academic' is a cumbersome title with particular expectations attached to it, but often little benefit or prestige. Indeed, 'early career' is often associated with a heavy teaching workload, no successful grant reputation, a myriad of obscure administrative roles, and a lack of job security. Although we tie the term 'early career' to the achievement and award of the PhD, we recognise that there are many academics who have been working in HE for many years prior to completing a doctorate, and numerous more who do not and will not study for a PhD, but are still academics. Thus the term 'early career' is also not tied to a specific age bracket, as one of our contributors will discuss, nor even necessarily to the award of the PhD, as doctoral students are increasingly encouraged to professionalise themselves and take on some of the tasks of faculty. We are interested in how the award of the PhD and subsequent transition to academic employment for newly qualified feminist academics plays out and are experienced by individuals in the context of the marketised university.

Global Perspectives

In bringing together chapters from early career feminists from around the world we faced a number of challenges in bridging cultural differences, but were both pleased and disheartened, in equal measure, to see the similarities in experiences around the world. We are both UK-based and many of our examples within this introduction are drawn from events there;

however, this book is intended to provide a much more global perspective, and hence contributors speak to their own social and cultural situations. These, in a globalised and neoliberalising world, have many resonances across cultures and geographical boundaries. We do wish to note, however, that the majority of these perspectives are from what is more widely termed 'the West' (though this term is not monolithic and is highly debatable), and we are aware therefore that gaps remain. Extant research on women's experiences of HE institutions globally is severely lacking, particularly from developing countries and the global South. As women begin to occupy more senior positions in universities, and in many cases female undergraduate students outnumber males, we hope that more analyses will be conducted to explore women's evolving and expanding roles in HE institutions globally.

To use the contexts of two of our own contributors though, two noteworthy studies to mention here demonstrate how systemic structures can have oppositional impacts on gender equality in universities globally. Peterson (2015) conducted a qualitative study of senior women academics in Sweden. Government control over the governance of universities has been pivotal in Swedish academia: 'The government appoints university boards using equal representation policies which means that women and men are often equally represented in these boards' (Peterson, 2015: 57). These tightly monitored recruitment practices have led to a significantly increased visibility of women on university boards. Peterson (2015) argues that these policies created the impetus for change; however, senior female academics must also become gender-equality change agents. She argues that awareness is not sufficient to engender real change and that a critical mass of women with enough authority are required to create tangible and visible change for themselves and other, more junior, female academics.

Conversely, Lafferty and Fleming (2000) detail how the erosion of the public sector by the implementation of neoliberal policies in Australia has had profound effects on the effectiveness of gender-equality policies. They argue that the shift from 'access and equity to efficiency and accountability' (2000: 257) in Australian universities has had significant long-term ramifications for academics. They state that the 'privatisation, manageralisam and restricting on corporate lines has ushered in the implementation of market-driven principles that contradict those of gender equity. The devolution of budgetary responsibility to departmental heads has also meant that the career aspirations of many staff are dependent on the decisions of (predominantly male) departmental heads' (Lafferty and Fleming 2000: 263).

Here we have two contrasting examples from Sweden and Australia which demonstrate the different ways in which governance of universities can adversely affect gender equality. Our contributors will further elaborate on the global differences and similarities of early career feminist academics' experiences of doing academic work in Russia, Finland, Japan, the United Kingdom, Australia, Sweden, Canada, and Saudi Arabia.

Johansson and Sliwa (2014) quite rightly point out that research on women who are 'double strangers' in academia (women working in a male-dominated institution and not native to the country in which they are working) is almost nonexistent. A number of our contributors fit into this unique but growing category and their perspectives add another layer of complexity to understanding the challenge of achieving gender equity in a globalising HE sector.

For the purpose of consistency and comprehension we also wish to highlight here that authors use varying terms to refer to similar ideas depending on their location. For example, in the United Kingdom it is common for the career trajectory[2] of an academic to be Post-doctoral Researcher/Teaching Fellow, Lecturer, Senior Lecturer, Reader, and finally Chair/Professor. In countries such as Australia and Canada, these career stages are named differently. The contributors of this book will elucidate these distinctions in more detail.

COLLECTIVE THREADS

Though the contexts and exact academic 'moments' and examples vary across the chapters, certain themes arose which cut across our contributors' experiences; we will spend some time elucidating these 'collective threads' before outlining the structure of the book in more detail. The first 'thread' is the use of online spaces for feminist activism and academic solidarity and resilience. Online discussions between friends and colleagues as well as the use of forums and online spaces to write, share views and research, and to organise and be active as feminists were used to provide an alternative to traditional academic spaces. This hugely positive online space was used to build friendships and to practice deeply held feminist values. The collaboration and kindness evidenced in these online interactions is inspiring, but also reveals a more negative and worrying trend within the 'traditional' academe. Contributors (and their colleagues) had to look 'outside' to find people willing to support them, share their concerns and worries, and to act as networks of resilience in patriarchal institutions which did not show support for their feminist work. As scholars of political discussion online,

Stromer-Galley and Wichowski (2013) argue, online discussion forums can provide spaces for people to speak freely to like-minded individuals in a way they may not be able to face-to-face. Though Kendall has argued that online spaces are potentially more about 'networked individualism' than 'real community' (Kendall 2013: 312), the fact that early career academics are turning to these spaces as a place of escape and to build resilience suggests they can act as genuine spaces of solidarity and change, for both the individual and the collective.

These online spaces help early career feminist academics to consolidate their sense of self in a professional 'game', which sees gender and feminist work as less important. However, the theme of identity and self cut across each chapter in varied ways. As we mentioned above the definition of 'early career' is contested, and our contributors felt this come to bear on them and how they are perceived within their institution. Doctoral students asked whether they can be counted as early career—they challenged our thinking as editors on this point too—and British PhD students in particular asked why other countries and cultural contexts would accept them as staff, while in the United Kingdom they remain labelled technically as students, despite taking on some of the work that salaried staff do. This 'in-between' moment where both staff and student identities apply caused contributors to question their place in the academy, the value of the work they do—or at least how it is valued by their institution—and at what point a career in academia 'really' begins. Work, the different kinds and different values attributed to it, will be investigated in more depth throughout the book.

Other facets of identity also came to the fore for some contributors: gender, race/ethnicity, age, and motherhood. For all of our contributors, being a woman created particular battles to be faced within the academy. Working within a male-dominated institutional setting means that women are often placed as 'outsiders' and a gendered division of labour is maintained, with women taking on the less prestigious roles (Acker 1990: 146). Women find they take on the bulk of the 'emotional' work (Hochschild 2003) and the work which is less significant or which focusses on smoothing over the social or interactional workings of the department or school—for example, organising the seminar series, the wine receptions, the social events, and dealing with student crises, as the chapter entitled, 'Feminist Work in Academia and Beyond' will outline. Furthermore, as found by Drago et al. (2008), female academics are seen as 'more likely' to be caring for dependents at home and to need to take time off and are therefore constructed as less than ideal workers in the academic sphere.

When presenting oneself as a particular gendered subject is part of the everyday presentation of self and successful assimilation into society (Budgeon 2003) it should come as no surprise that presenting oneself as suitably gendered is a part of working life as well (Acker 1990: 147). Furthermore, expectations from colleagues and managers about what 'women' and 'men' should and can do is as important as self-presentation and has real effects on the work that is offered to staff or that they are encouraged to take on. As Acker notes (1990: 148), such managerial perceptions of work and work performance get written into the bureaucracy of the institution through performance management processes and are therefore regularly reiterated and reinforced.

Working as a woman within feminist fields or taking a feminist approach to research and teaching also creates specific tensions, where women are seen as less credible, less rational, and less worthy than their male counterparts—perhaps even especially those male counterparts working in the same areas as them, who are deemed as 'open minded' and seen to be progressive. These hierarchies of knowledge are not only about gender, and other social positionings will influence how people are perceived and their knowledge evaluated. As Patricia Hill Collins argues (1991: 3), the dominant (white, male) perspective will exclude knowledge which does not 'satisfy the political and epistemological criteria' it holds to be valuable.

The importance of social positionings can be seen explicitly in some of our contributors' chapters. Race and ethnicity were crucial intersections in the making and living of identities: one of our contributors was forced by her colleagues to confront the question, 'Are you one of us or one of them?' before they would consider her work as credible. This chapter also poses the (implicit) question of whether whiteness or those from singly Western ethnicities would be confronted in such a way by colleagues and to what extent the community of feminist scholars needs to engage more with race and ethnicity in all of its research and writings—a challenge that has been posed to white feminists for decades now and continues to stimulate debate (see for example Mohanty 1988; Friedman 1993; Aziz 1998; Carby 1998). It also reveals the complexity of intersections and the need to understand Zillah Eistenstein's argument that: 'labels reify ... hierarchies ... Silences and exclusions form the erasure' (2004: 2).

The tensions arising for feminist early-career academics embarking on their first major research project and trying to establish themselves and build up their sense of themselves as scholars are clear: other people expect these scholars to declare themselves and their allegiances before being prepared to engage with their work. This is a key debate within feminist scholarship, as it has been argued that researchers need to be aware of the influence of their own biographies on the kind of research they do, the questions they ask, and the answers they find credible (Harding 1986: 26). It has also been argued that reflexivity helps to deal with some of the potential problems of studying groups with which the researcher does not share all the same positionings (Maynard and Purvis 1995: 1). Yet, publically declaring personal biases, stories, and experiences can be challenging for scholars; and these personal narratives raise significant questions about the reflexive nature of some current feminist research and its positivity for the researcher herself. Our contributors take different approaches to this and in so doing add to the wider debate around feminist reflexivity.

With the definition of 'early career' so contested, it seemed important to include the voices of 'older' early career scholars: those who may not have followed a traditional academic path, may have come to academia late, or may have written their PhD later despite doing research and teaching within the academy for many years. Being an 'older' early career poses its own problems, as people question why one has not built up more experience and published more research over one's career, requiring justification of every career move and period of time not working in academia. Age is a significant concern for early career scholars in all its forms: the category itself includes a suggestion of younger and inexperienced, which our 'older' early career contributors problematize by their very identification with that category. However, the idea of youth and inexperience creates more room to dismiss and trivialise the work of feminist scholars, and many of our contributors find themselves navigating the categories applied to them as they try to establish a career. Ageism is an often silenced and under-researched form of discrimination, but one that suffuses education (Davies et al. 2007: 96). Recognising and tackling ageism within educational institutions, at the level of both students and staff, is important for creating an anti-oppressive curriculum and the education system more widely (Davies et al. 2007: 102).

Finally, motherhood was for one contributor a significant identity marker which she attempts to balance with her work in academia. This is a marker of identity for many women within the academy and one which has its own challenges and joys. The (constructed) pressures on academics to give themselves and their time totally to their career may conflict intensely with the gendered social ideal of mothers who give themselves totally to the rearing of their children, or indeed simply with the desire to bring balance to these life-roles. Arendell (2004: 1198), bringing together a decade of scholarship on motherhood, argues that there is often 'a high personal price' to pay for trying to achieve a positive balance between work and motherhood, including '[l]oss of sleep, curtailed leisure time, and feeling overloaded and stressed' which are 'the currencies extorted from mothers involved both in paid work and child raising'.

The emotional work of various kinds which mothers engage in is another complex and intense part of 'modern mothering' (Arendell 2004: 1196); this is clearly evidenced by our contributor as she works to negotiate and balance the intensity of rearing her children with the demands of work. These conflicting and emotive 'callings' cause particular consternation for women trying to establish themselves in their career. Feminist scholars may aspire towards a more collaborative environment where children are an accepted and welcome part of their working lives but find instead that the academic environment is still not open to this despite flexible working and parental leave.

These aspects of identity are crucial to understanding the position of early career feminists in a neoliberal academy as the 'ideal worker' comes to have an increasingly narrow definition and neoliberal attitudes towards education and scholarship force feminist and other scholarship to prove itself to have 'value', 'impact', and to be 'instrumental' in achieving particular aims, often related to applied and economic outcomes. This book focuses on those who self-define as feminist in their work and their life politics; this facet of identity is assumed. We felt that a book about HE which took feminism at the early career stage into account was needed at this point in time for many of the reasons described above. We also feel that a feminist identity within the academy can be a site of resistance towards these more instrumental institutional focuses. Being a feminist within a changing academy offers the chance to explore alternative visions of what HE institutions can be, how colleagues should work together, how work is defined and how it is valued, how research should be perceived and disseminated, what the nature of teaching should be, and what we should expect from ourselves as teachers and from our students. Feminism offers the space for a more radical, kinder, and more inclusive higher education.

This idea was also a major theme for our contributors, who in various terms referred to 'micro-activism' alongside grander acts of resistance and change. They call for feminist early career scholars to look for even the smaller things they can do to be an activist within the academy, and not to discount everyday encounters with colleagues and students as potential places for resistance. These discussions raise interesting broader questions about what activism means within a neoliberal academy and when carried out by 'double agents': scholars who hold a different politics and want to enact a different approach to education and research, but nevertheless work within the academy and to an extent necessarily 'play the game'.

Micro-activism could be seen as giving up and giving in: we turn away from grander activism to smaller, everyday acts because we have lost hope in the efficacy of more radical action. We as editors can see the potential in this argument and want to explore whether there are boundaries to what can be achieved on a grand scale within higher education. We also, however, believe strongly in the everyday and in the feminist movement's constant engagement with the everyday to raise consciousness and explore daily oppression. The everyday is not separate from the wider culture and context, but reflects and recreates it. In this sense, small acts within the everyday are powerful political moments, which challenge accepted and ingrained ways of being and working, as well as having a potential ripple effect.

In a neoliberal academy where actors become increasingly self-reflexive and self-monitoring, the ability to think and act freely becomes more difficult. One should be looking to do research projects which are perceived by funders, research quality assessment exercises, and the institution in which they work to be 'useful'— usually in monetary and 'impact' terms— or they may find themselves under pressure from the university hierarchy to justify their position; they will also find their ideas and projects harder to fund as funders increasingly turn to requiring more instrumental outcomes from research. This closes off spaces of thinking and writing, and narrows what is deemed important and useful work within higher education. As a neoliberal agenda encroaches on the higher education sector, we cut ourselves off from ways of knowing, understanding, and engaging with the world. In such a constricted space, micro-activism becomes vital and necessary.

The conflicts for feminist early career scholars over their position as 'double agents' are complex, but vital. We have to recognise our position within the academy and the privileges this brings, as well as the collusions with the overarching neoliberal agenda. We hope this book brings some of these debates to the fore, and we invite the reader to engage with them as presented here and in their own (working) lives. Interrogating and facing up to these collusions is important, not only for our sense of ourselves as feminists and the furthering of a more inclusive and kinder academy, but also as a starting point for questioning these collusions and seeing where different actions can be taken, be they micro or macro. This is not an easy task, but it is one which must be constantly undertaken to ensure that we do not lose our foundational sense of the need for change and equality in higher education, and elsewhere.

What strikes us also, as we write this introduction and review the contributions to this book, is the amount of emotional investment involved in maintaining an academic career and not leaving the 'game' entirely. The conflicts of working as a feminist—which as an academic discipline encourages the use of reflexivity and engagement with emotions—and working within disciplines which may look for 'objectivity' and detachment are clear. Emotion is a constant and important reminder that we care about our work and feel invested in what we do. To suppress these emotions seems strange and false; a working on our selves and emotions which suggests a great deal of surface and deep emotional labour (Hochschild 2003). We are pleased that this book can be a space to express these emotions and show how central and valuable they are to being a teacher and scholar.

Having looked at several of the underlying themes of this book, we will now give an outline of the overall structure. The book is organised so that it can be read from start to finish, each section progressing to build a wider picture of feminist early career academic life, or dipped into for readers to look at specific sections and concerns.

BOOK STRUCTURE

In the ensuing chapters we offer a collection of original essays, some based on empirical research and others on personal experience, to highlight the experiences of feminist early career researchers and teachers from an international perspective. In so doing, we aim to open up debate on the marketisation of the academy and the significant changes which are taking effect in the HE sector across the globe. This is an important debate for academics of all career stages but has a particular impact on those just entering the profession, who are faced with huge competition for jobs and a much changed approach to research and teaching. It offers a new angle on a significant and increasingly important discussion on the ethos of higher education and the sector's place within society. The sheer number of abstracts and positive responses we received responding to our call for papers showed us the interest and significance of this early-career moment, especially when dealing with the often conflicting positions of being a feminist looking to work with colleagues ethically on creating a more equal world and an academic committing oneself to teaching 'customers', drumming up money for 'business', and creating 'impact' with outside partners.

Being an Early Career Feminist Academic is divided into five parts. The first part, 'Introducing the Early Career Experience', begins with 'A Precarious Passion: Gendered and Age-Based Insecurity Among Aspiring Academics in Australia', Lara McKenzie's exploration, using empirical qualitative research, of precarity and gender among aspiring academics in Australia. McKenzie interviewed 12 early-career academics in the arts, humanities, and social sciences to explore their experiences and practices as aspiring academics. The work was carried out in Perth and Adelaide, and McKenzie examines critically the experiences of precarity from a gendered perspective, focusing in particular on power relations among university staff at different levels. The chapter includes an exploration of interviewees' emotional, social, and personal responses to these relations of power, including fear, silence, and competitiveness, on the one hand, with collegiality, resistance, and anti-competitiveness on the other. The gendered outcomes of acting in a certain way are highlighted and feminist scholarship is used to contextualise the narratives. In the process, early career experiences of academia are explored using their own words, further scrutinizing the themes of precarity, power, and control, while utilising a feminist lens.

Olga Marques' chapter, "Navigating Gendered Expectations at the Margins of Feminism and Criminology", examines the issue of how to maintain one's feminist self in the classroom during the early career stage. Marques argues that as a result of the historic neglect of both women and feminism, the discipline of criminology is male-centric. When feminism is highlighted in the curriculum, it is often within the context of studying women as offenders and victims. Indeed, courses in criminology are gender-marked asymmetrically, with the study of women and criminality and/or victimization treated in separate courses, identified by the title 'women', with a lack of corresponding courses specifically titled 'men' and criminality and/or victimization. The message to students is thus that feminism is about women and criminology about men—and perhaps 'for' these respective groups also. Given these realities, imparting a decidedly feminist slant to the discipline of criminology by gendering crime to explore the implications of masculinity and femininity on understandings of criminality and deviance is a difficult task. The societal relevance of gender and sex is also being undermined beyond academia, making inclusion of these subjects in courses more difficult for students to accept. This is especially true for an early career feminist criminologist, like Marques, who studies sexual regulation, sex work, and pornography—topics that are seen as at the margins of importance and not taken seriously—from a sex-positive feminist lens, much to the chagrin of a discipline that often places these topics under the rubric of degradation and exploitation. Therefore, in this chapter Marques addresses the question of who is seen as a knowledgeable and credible teacher and whether it is the topic or the teacher which is the main issue for students.

The second part is entitled, 'Affect and Identities: Negotiating Tensions in the Early Career', and it contains three chapters which provide explorations of the academic self combined with other identity markers that have often been problematic in the context of the neoliberal academy. The first, Agnes Bosanquet's 'Academic, Woman, Mother: Negotiating Multiple Subjectivities During Early Career', looks at the multiple subjectivities that some early career female academics face when they enter motherhood 'and' academia. Boasanquet argues that the collision of academia and motherhood can further destabilise career trajectories and subsequent track records. This chapter examines the voices of academic mothers in two ways: first, it presents findings from a survey of early career academics in three Australian universities. Second, it offers an auto-ethnographic account of combining motherhood and feminist academic work, documenting Boasanquet's experience of researching Luce Irigaray's philosophy, and the disruption occasioned by the birth and illness of Boasanquet's daughter. The chapter concludes by offering an account of the fluid, messy, and multiple subjectivities negotiated by early career academic mothers.

The second chapter, 'Room for Confidence: Early Career Feminists in the English Department', by Helena Goodwyn and Emily Jane Hogg, focuses on a discipline frequently perceived as 'feminine': English. As with many disciplines in universities, it now includes more female undergraduates than male, but there is a steep drop-off through postgraduate education and into an academic career. Goodwyn and Hogg consider the challenge of being a female in an English department by drawing on statistical analysis of English Studies enrolment and completion rates and use their personal experience of reading and teaching Virginia Woolf's canonical, feminist essay 'A Room of One's Own'. They argue that the position of PhD students is very specific: in research and teaching practice they are a member of the academic community, and yet they remain simultaneously a student. Embodying feminist politics in the classroom and in one's research practices whilst in this transitional stage is fraught with anxieties and concerns. For example, in an increasingly casualised workforce, PhD students and early career academics are required to shoulder responsibility for teaching without the academic staff member's traditional resources—without, for example, private offices in which to hold student consultations, plan seminars, or mark work. Moreover, Goodwyn and Hogg argue that where jobs are scarce, connections and networking seem to become ever more important, and yet, a dearth of successful women in management positions in universities is a dispiriting fact for ambitious young women entering the academic sphere. In this provocative piece Goodwyn and Hogg provoke and answer the questions, How much 'anger and bitterness' is allowable, advisable or useful? and How might identifying as a feminist in an English department help one to find ways to develop the 'imponderable' but 'invaluable' confidence Woolf describes?

The final chapter in this section, '"Are You One of Us, or One of Them?" An Autothnography of a "Hybrid" Feminist Researcher Bridging Two Worlds', by Sophie Alkhaled, is a personal piece, which also draws upon academic research and feminist theory regarding the themes of this edited collection. Using an evocative auto-ethnographic approach, this chapter discusses the intersectionality of 'opportunities' and 'boundaries' faced by Alkhaled as a 'hybrid' British/Syrian feminist researcher (focusing on the intersections of gender, age, nationality, and ethnicity) during her PhD studies in the United Kingdom and her fieldwork in Saudi Arabia. In this chapter Alkhaled reflects on her doctoral experiences and how she began to cope with and resist some of her peers' hostility towards herself and her research. Alkhaled problematises being a feminist researcher in higher education across various cultural and organisational contexts, in a historically male dominated discipline and in researching 'the Other', as well as delving in a personal way into how one can maintain a feminist identity whilst continuing to bridge two worlds where the nuances of patriarchy vary explicitly and implicitly.

The third part of this collection, 'Exploring Experience Through Innovative Methodologies', contests traditional research methods to analyse and discuss the challenges that early career feminist academics face in a number of European HE settings. First, in 'Exposing the "Hidden Injuries" of Feminist Early-Career Researchers: An Experiential Think Piece About Maintaining Feminist Identities', Anna Tarrant and Emily Cooper use a dialogic style of writing to expose the 'hidden injuries' incurred by early career feminist academics trying to maintain their feminist identities. Since completing their PhDs they have held five and three (respectively) fixed-term positions in academia (at times held concurrently with jobs outside of academia), some teaching-focused and some research only. While it is not necessarily indicative of every early career academic's experience, they argue that this number reveals the extent to which working on fixed-term contracts and changing jobs frequently (with its attendant upheaval) has become normalised in the early career stage, which offers little security and no certain prospect of advancement. Both authors aspire to the 'holy grail' of combining research and teaching into one role: the Lectureship. Both aspire to job security and some recognition that their institutions, their colleagues, their students, and their research audiences value the work they do.

By adopting an innovative methodology, Tarrant and Cooper are able to represent how they experience and negotiate daily struggles as young, feminist early career researchers and to provide examples of the way in which their identities and practices as young female scholars are commented upon and subjected to critical attention by others. This chapter also includes an exploration of how regular online conversations are key, according to Tarrant and Cooper, to strategies of resilience and have become part of their personal support networks, in which they discuss and work through the often-tricky and affective qualitative experiences of the contemporary academy.

Marjaana Jauhola and Saara Särmä's 'Reflecting Realities and Creating Utopias: Early Career Feminists (Un)Doing International Relations in Finland' follows Tarrant and Cooper's lead by also utilising an innovative methodological style to explore the discipline of International Relations (IR) in Finland. Despite a rich tradition of feminist scholarship over the past 30 years aimed at 'shaking up' the discipline of IR, Jauhola and Särmä argue that IR in Finland is still male-dominated, sexist, and misogynist. As such, the discipline could be considered to mirror the gender politics of the practice of international relations. Most of the scholarship examining this male dominance has emerged from the English-speaking sector of IR, although international relations are studied and theorized about at campuses all around the world; and thus this chapter provides new knowledge about the position of early career female academics in an understudied subject. The chapter draws from a collective-memory process carried out by young feminist IR researchers in Finland and offers insights into the politics and analysis of power of the discipline from a feminist perspective. The collective collaging and critical memory work produces documentation of 'subjugated knowledges' on IR in two ways: (1) collection of lived and embodied experiences of being a feminist scholar, and (2) envisioning feminist utopias for alternative visions of Feminist International Relations (FIR).

The fourth part is entitled, 'Work, Networks and Social Capital: Building the Academic Career', and it begins with Klara Regnö's chapter, 'Challenges to Feminist Solidarity in the Era of New Public Management', which examines New Public Management (NPM) in academia in Sweden and the effect this is having on early-career academics in particular. NPM has been introduced into academia through various 'reforms' which have set up a quasi-market model in universities: there is a great deal more regulation, monitoring, and control, as well as a focus on the finances being brought into each department. In the face of this 'reform', certain work becomes illegitimate and unimportant, despite its having been previously perceived as an important part of an academic career. These reforms and the growth of short-term contracts have, Regnö argues, have challenged feminist solidarity within academia and are making it more difficult to challenge the male-dominated nature of the field. Inequality is deepening and early career academics are becoming increasingly dependent on more senior academics to get ahead, often living on little money and doing much of the work seen as less prestigious, including teaching. In this environment, Regnö asks what early career feminist academics can do to shore up the progress women have made at universities and within academia but also whether, and how, they can continue to promote a feminist agenda of solidarity and equality in the changing academy. In so doing, Regnö engages directly with the overall questions and themes of the book concerning the neoliberal agenda, marketisation, changing professional standards, and the restrictions placed on younger academics with a feminist viewpoint who might want to challenge these precepts and stay true to their own values, while also succeeding professionally.

In 'Inequality in Academia: The Way Social Connections Work', Irina Gewinner investigates inequality in academia in relation to the gendered nature of early career academics' participation in conferences in Russia by looking at the application process; who applies; and, crucially, who is chosen to attend and present their work. Gewinner begins her chapter by arguing that scholarly discussion on inequality and discrimination in academia often involves particularly common issues: gender inequality/

discrimination and the closely connected problem of wage inequality/discrimination. Shifting the discussion to wage inequalities, Gewinner states that recent studies have paid little attention to the inequality faced by early-career female academics regarding their participation in scientific events, such as conferences, as a source of occupational advancement and access to social networks.

Specifically, Gewinner poses two questions: (1) Are young female members of academia likely to be excluded from scientific events such as workshops and conferences? (2) What are the driving forces behind and mechanisms of exclusion employed by the gatekeepers? Gewinner analyses data from a research project conducted in Russia, using a gendered approach to analysing her data, and presents a compelling case for the need for early career female academics to actively pursue and participate in scholarly events which expose their work and enhance their networking opportunities.

The final chapter of this part, 'Feminist Work in Academia and Beyond', written by Órla Meadhbh Murray, Muireann Crowley, and Lena Wånggren, explores feminist work in academia, couching personal experiences of early career feminist academics in methodological discussions of Dorothy Smith's feminist approach to institutional ethnography. This chapter thus seeks to unite the experiential and the theoretical by integrating excerpts from the conversations that generated the chapter into the body of its argument. By using Smith's expanded notion of 'work', which includes the invisible emotional and social labour that is essential to the running of the university yet is often unpaid and underappreciated, the authors provide a feminist critique of the neoliberal university. While doing this, they identify issues such as casualisation, workload ,and preconceptions around the academic 'lifestyle' as feminist issues, especially for early career feminists in higher education.

Reflecting on their own experiences as early career feminist academics, they explore the negotiation of feminist aims within institutional boundaries. Work carried out by women, casualised staff, and postgraduate students in higher education, they argue, is essential yet often unacknowledged or not valued as 'proper' academic work. By asking who organises the post-seminar wine reception, whose shoulders we cry on, and whether or not this is considered work, they highlight the gendered, racialised, and classed hierarchies of academia and their institutional reproduction. The chapter asks readers and practitioners to consider their own situations in higher education and question what their feminist 'work' entails.

The final part of the book, 'Envisaging Feminist Futures' encourages early career feminist academics to look forward and imagine a brighter future, when the issues discussed by previous contributors are successfully addressed. Katherine Natanel, in 'On Becoming "Bad Subjects": Teaching to Transgress in Neoliberal Education', starts this part by highlighting the challenges and possibilities of attempting to teach a feminist curriculum using a feminist pedagogy. Natanel begins by drawing on her three years of experience as a Graduate Teaching Assistant and two years as a Senior Teaching Fellow in a Gender Studies department. She reflects upon the challenges facing feminist early career scholars who 'teach to transgress' (hooks 1994) in the context of neoliberalism. As recent academic articles and media accounts have highlighted, Natanel argues that HE has increasingly become a site of isolation and disenchantment for scholars who survive the rigours of doctoral study and find themselves entering a flooded job market and enduring exploitative conditions. The prospect of years spent 'patching together' employment in HE yields particular tensions for feminist scholars, Natanel argues; and through a personal account, she explores the fraught experience of practicing feminist politics and critical pedagogy within the structures of neoliberal education in the United Kingdom. Natanel argues that the challenge facing feminist 'bad subjects' is how to become agents of the very transgression they teach, actively contesting neoliberal logics as they carve out new spaces within academia.

The following chapter, written by Misato Matsuoka, 'Embracing Vulnerability? A Reflection on my Academic Journey as a Japanese Early Career Feminist Academic Abroad', explores her personal account of realising her feminist self over the course of her academic studies from undergraduate to PhD candidate. Matsuoka reflects on her academic and pedagogical experiences as an international student, which provoked many internal questions about her national identity, ethnic, and gendered self. She was born into a Japanese family living the United States and moved to Japan and then the United Kingdom during some of her most formative years. She charts her feelings of being an 'outsider', even when living in her native country of Japan. Using the concepts of vulnerability and precarity to explore and understand her identity as a feminist early career academic abroad, Matsuoka's chapter reflects her personal and academic journey through the difficulties and opportunities she has faced in her quest to become a scholar in International Relations (IR). Moreover, Matsuoka explores the contested position of feminism in the discipline of

IR and particularly how this inspired a self-interrogation regarding her own feminist awakening. This honest and highly personal account provides a fascinating display of one feminist scholar's journey through a myriad of academic and identity challenges.

The final chapter, "'I'm an Early-Career Feminist Academic: Get Me Out of Here?" Encountering and Resisting the Neoliberal Academy' was written by the Res-Sisters, who are a collective of nine early career feminist academics from UK universities (Jessie Abrahams, Cardiff University; Kim Allen, Manchester Metropolitan University; Victoria Cann, University of East Anglia; Laura Harvey, University of Surrey; Sumi Hollingworth, London South Bank University; Nicola Ingram, University of Bath; Kirsty Morrin, University of Manchester; Helene Snee, Manchester Metropolitan University; Annabel Wilson, Cardiff University). In this chapter, the Res-Sisters argue that with the increasing marketisation of higher education, the entrenchment of accountability cultures, and the normalisation of casualised labour, neoliberal imperatives permeate the academy. Such transformations demand a particular kind of academic subject: highly productive, individualised, enterprising, unattached, and able to withstand precarity. But, they ask, who exactly is the person who can play this game?

This chapter seeks to contribute to a discussion about the difficulties of carving out and sustaining an academic career. It does so by drawing on the lived experiences of nine early career feminist academics. As feminists and sociologists, they are acutely aware of gender inequality and how this interacts with other identity categories to produce different experiences of in/exclusion. Ironically, they find themselves confronted with these very same forces within contemporary academia. In the spirit of feminist politics and tradition of feminist consciousness-raising, this chapter is a purposely 'collective' endeavor. They draw, verbatim, from excerpts from a recorded group discussion by 'the collective', which are theorized and set within relevant literature on neoliberalism, academic labour, class and gender identities, and feminist practice and politics.

We hope that this book will provide revealing accounts of the lived experiences of early-career feminist academics. We also hope that the following chapters pose provocative questions with which feminist academics and university management teams alike can engage. This global account from feminists in the early stages of their academic careers aims to fill a (cavernous) hole in academic literature so that we might understand, adapt, challenge, support, and move forward in order to address the situation of women in academia and the status of equality more generally across higher education.

Notes

1. According to a report by UNESCO, the number of female students in tertiary institutions has grown almost twice as fast as that of men since 1970. See more at: http://www.uis.unesco.org/Education/Pages/women-higher-education.aspx#sthash.USwUme3I.dpuf
2. This is a common career trajectory in the Social Sciences, from which most of our contributors stem. However, we are cognisant of other disciplines in HE that vary from this path and that different institutions/countries have different terms for job roles.

References

Acker, J. (1990). Hierarchies, jobs, bodies: A theory of gendered organizations. *Gender and Society, 4*(2), 139–158.

Anon. (2015, June 4). A day in the life of a temporary lecturer. *Times Higher Education*. Available at: https://www.timeshighereducation.com/content/few-crumbs-of-comfort-in-a-temporary-lecturers-day. Accessed 24 Mar 2016.

Arendell, T. (2004). Conceiving and investigating motherhood: The decade's scholarship. *Journal of Marriage and Family, 62*(4), 1192–1207.

Aziz, R. (1998). Feminism and the challenge of racism: Deviance or difference? In H. S. Mirza (Ed.), *Black British feminism: A reader* (pp. 70–77). London: Routledge.

Blackmore, J. (2002). Globalisation and the restructuring of higher education for new knowledge economies: New dangers or old habits troubling gender equity work in universities. *Higher Education Quarterly., 56*(4), 419–441.

Bradbury, M. (2000). *The history man* (2 ed.). Oxford: Picador.

Bryman, A. (2008). *Social research methods* (3 ed.). Oxford: Oxford University Press.

Budgeon, S. (2003). *Choosing a self: Young women and the individualization of identity*. Westport: Praeger.

Carby, H. V. (1998). White women listen! Black feminism and the boundaries of sisterhood. In H. S. Mirza (Ed.), *Black British feminism: A reader* (pp. 45–53). London: Routledge.

Collini, S. (2012). *What are universities for?* London: Penguin Books.

Davies, M. R., Hirsch, J., & Graves Holmes, G. (2007). Conversation: Unearthing hidden curriculums. *Counterpoints, 315*, 95–103.

Deem, R. (1998). 'New manageralism' and higher education: The management of performances and cultures in universities in the United Kingdom. *International Studies in Sociology of Education, 8*(1), 47–70.

Drago, R., Colbeck, C., Hollenshead, C., & Sullivan, B. (2008). Work-family policies and the avoidance of bias against caregiving. In A. Marcus-Newhall, D. F. Halpern, & S. J. Tan (Eds.), *The changing realities of work and family* (pp. 43–66). Chichester: Wiley-Blackwell.

Eistenstein, Z. (2004). *Against empire: Feminism, racism, and the West.* London: Zed Books.

Else, H. (2015, June 4). Zero points: The persistence of temporary measures. *Times Higher Education.* Available at: https://www.timeshighereducation.com/content/few-crumbs-of-comfort-in-a-temporary-lecturers-day. Accessed 24 Mar 2016.

Emslie, C., & Hunt, K. (2009). 'Live to work' or 'work to live'? A qualitative study of gender and work-life balance among Mena and women in mid-life. *Gender, Work and Organisation, 16*(1), 152–172.

Fazackerley, A. (2013, February 4). Why are many academics on short-term contracts for years?. *The Guardian.* Accessible at: http://www.theguardian.com/education/2013/feb/04/academic-casual-contracts-higher-education. Accessed 8 Mar 2016.

Friedman, S. S. (1993). Relational epistemology and the question of Anglo-American feminist criticism. *Tulsa Studies in Women's Literature, 12*(2), 247–261.

Harding, S. (1986). *The science question in feminism.* Milton Keynes: Open University Press.

Harding, S. (Ed.) (1987). *Feminism and methodology.* Milton Keynes: Open University Press.

Higher Education Statistics Agency (HESA). (2015). Academic staff. Accessible at: https://www.hesa.ac.uk/stats-staff. Accessed 29 Mar 2016.

Hill Collins, P. (1991). *Black feminist thought: Knowledge, consciousness, and the politics of empowerment.* London: Routledge.

Hochschild, A. (2003). *The managed heart.* Berkeley: The University of California Press.

hooks, B. (1994). *Teaching to transgress: Education as the practice of freedom.* London: Routledge.

Humphries, B., & Truman, C. (Eds.) (1994). *Re-thinking social research.* Aldershot: Ashgate.

Johansson, M., & Sliwa, M. (2014). Gender, foreigness and academia: An intersectional analysis of the experiences of foreign women academics in UK Business Schools. *Gender, Work and Organisation, 21*(1), 18–36.

Kelan, E. (2010). Gender logic and (Un)doing gender at work. *Gender, Work, and Organisation, 17*(2), 174–194.

Kendall, L. (2013). Community and the Internet. In M. Consalvo & C. Ess (Eds.), *The handbook of Internet studies* (pp. 309–325). Chichester: Wiley-Blackwell.

Lafferty, C., & Fleming, J. (2000). The restructuring of academic work in Australia: Power, management and gender. *British Journal of Sociology of Education, 21*(2), 257–267.

Leathwood, C., & Read, B. (2015, June 4). The young and the not so young alike are feeling the pinch. *Times Higher Education.* Available at: https://www.timeshighereducation.com/content/few-crumbs-of-comfort-in-a-temporary-lecturers-day. Accessed 24 Mar 2016.

Lee, J., & Won, D. (2014). Trailblazing women in academia: Representation of women in senior faculty and the gender gap in juniour faculty's salaries in higher educational institutions. *The Social Science Journal, 51*, 331–340.

Lopes, A., & Dewan, I. (2014). Precarious pedagogies? The impact of casual and zero-hour contracts in higher education. *Journal of Feminist Scholarship, 7*(8), 28–42.

Martin, P. (2006). Practising gender at work: Further thoughts on reflexivity. *Gender, Work and Organisation, 13*(3), 255–276.

Maynard, M., & Purvis, J. (1995). Doing feminist research. In M. Maynard & J. Purvis (Eds.), *Researching women's lives from a feminist perspective* (pp. 1–9). London: Taylor and Francis.

Mohanty, C. (1988). Under western eyes: Feminist scholarship and colonial discourses. *Feminist Review, 30*, 61–88.

Mudge, S. L. (2008). What is neo-liberalism? *Socio-Economic Review, 6*, 703–731.

Peterson, H. (2015). "Unfair to women?" Equal representation policies in Swedish academia. *Equality, Diversity and Inclusion: An International Journal, 34*(1), 55–66.

Ramazanoglu, C., & Holland, J. (2002). *Feminist methodology: Challenges and choices.* London: Sage.

Rice, C. (2012, May 24). Why women leave academia and why universities should be worried. *The Guardian.* Accessible at: http://www.theguardian.com/higher-education-network/blog/2012/may/24/why-women-leave-academia. Accessed 9 Mar 2016.

Savigny, H. (2014). Women, know your limits: Cultural sexism in academia. *Gender and Education, 26*(7), 794–809.

Scraton, S., & Flintoff, A. (2002). *Gender and sport: A reader.* New York: Routledge.

Small, H. (2013). *The value of the humanitites.* Oxford: Oxford University Press.

Standing, G. (2014). *The precariat: The new dangerous class.* London: Bloomsbury.

Stanley, L. (Ed.) (2013). *Feminist praxis: Research, theory and epistemology in feminist sociology.* London: Routledge.

Stromer-Galley, J., & Wichowski, A. (2013). Political discussion online. In M. Consalvo & C. Ess (Eds.), *The handbook of Internet studies* (pp. 168–187). Chichester: Wiley-Blackwell.

Taylor, K. (1996). Keeping mum: The paradoxes of gendered power relations in interviewing. In E. Burman, P. Alldred, C. Bewley, B. Goldberg, C. Heenan, D. Marks, J. Marshall, K. Taylor, R. Ullah, & S. Warner (Eds.), *Challenging women: Psychology's exclusions, feminist possibilities* (pp. 106–122). Buckingham: Open University Press.

Thompson, B. (2015). Succumbing, surviving, succeeding? Women managers in academia. *Gender in Management: An International Journal, 30*(1), 397–413.

UNESCO. (2014). Education: Gross enrolment ratio by levels of education. Accessible at: http://data.uis.unesco.org/index.aspx?queryid=142&lang=en. Accessed 29 Mar 2016.

PART I

Introducing the Early Career Experience

A Precarious Passion: Gendered and Age-Based Insecurity Among Aspiring Academics in Australia

Lara McKenzie

In recent years, a significant interest in the career prospects of aspiring academics has emerged,[1] with articles and studies frequently appearing worldwide, especially in the online news media (Kendzior 2013; Luzia 2014). This has led to a growing research interest in the lived realities of this group. Yet while some of the research undertaken in Australia has been qualitative (Brown et al. 2010; Laudel and Gläser 2008), or has included qualitative elements (Bazeley et al. 1996; Gottschalk and McEachern 2010), the majority has been quantitative (Bexley et al. 2011; May 2011; May et al. 2013a, b). Moreover, these studies have focused almost exclusively on casually employed academics,[2] or academics on short-term contracts, with a particular emphasis on those in teaching roles (May 2011;

My heartfelt thanks go to all the people who participated in this research. I found it both profoundly comforting and deeply disturbing that your experiences so closely mirrored my own. Thanks also to those who read and provided feedback on earlier versions of this manuscript, especially the editors of this volume. This research is unfunded, and was not conducted as part of my paid (part-time, fixed-term) academic work.

L. McKenzie (✉)
The University of Western Australia, Perth, Australia

© The Author(s) 2017
R. Thwaites, A. Pressland (eds.), *Being an Early Career Feminist Academic*, DOI 10.1057/978-1-137-54325-7_2

May et al. 2013a, b). There has been little recognition that aspiring academics might seek employment beyond academia, albeit temporarily.

In this chapter, I consider aspiring academics' gendered and age-based precarity, offering qualitative insights into their understandings and experiences of seeking academic careers. Yet, rather than specifically addressing feminist early career researchers, as others in this volume have done, here I adopt a feminist approach to academic precarity, which encompasses the experiences of both women and men. I draw on 17 semi-structured interviews, carried out in three universities in Perth, Western Australia, and in Adelaide, South Australia. Interviewees were primarily educated and worked within disciplines encompassed by the Arts, Humanities, and Social Sciences. Some were, or had been, insecurely employed by universities to undertake academic work, while others had not.

The vast majority of my interviewees used words such as 'unstable' and 'insecure' to describe their work and lives. In particular, they referred to their job security, career prospects, financial situation, the location of their work, and, as a result, their relationships with others, as characterised by uncertainty. Interviewees' shared understandings and experiences of this precarity were informed by gender- and age-based expectations and practices. In this chapter, utilising scholarship on gender, employment, and higher education, I explore how precarity had different consequences for men and women, as well as according to age.

I begin by outlining the current context of Australian academia, including research on the academic workforce, as well as trends towards casualisation and how they relate to gender and age. Although my focus is not exclusively on casually employed academics, a high proportion of this group aspire to permanent employment in academia (Australia. National Tertiary Education Union 2012; May et al. 2013a). Therefore, I find it necessary and useful to draw on this literature.

I then elucidate my interviewees' common features, as well as where and how the research was carried out. Next, I explore interviewees' understandings and experiences of precarity in relation to job security, career prospects, time management, financial considerations, the location of their work, and their relationships with others. Here, I pay particular attention to the dimensions of gender and age. I contrast interviewees' notions of and encounters with academic precarity with their ideals of permanent academic employment as potentially flexible, family friendly, and fulfilling, highlighting the tensions, contradictions, and complexities in their accounts.

I argue that the pursuit of academic employment renders domestic and personal life extremely problematic for both genders, yet men and women, and people of different ages, experienced this differently. The women I spoke with in their twenties and thirties frequently expressed concerns about how their unstable employment prevented them from having children, buying a house, and 'settling down' or about how their families and relationships impacted their academic career prospects. Although my male interviewees also expressed a number of these concerns, as did my older female interviewees, they were for the most part less concerned about having children and the possibility of moving for academic work. Yet, regardless of gender and age, notions of instability and precarity created conflicts with interviewees' passion for academic work and its possibilities.

CONTEXTUALISING AUSTRALIAN ACADEMIA

In 2008, the widely publicised *Review of Australian Higher Education* (Bradley et al. 2008), popularly known as the Bradley Review, was published by the Australian government. The review's panel of 'higher-education experts' argued that Australian universities were facing major workforce shortages due to the ageing and impending retirement of much of the academic workforce (Bradley et al. 2008). This, they suggested, was exacerbated by a shortage of young, high-quality academics (Bradley et al. 2008; cf. May 2011).

In contrast, many academics have critiqued the burgeoning casualisation of university teaching and research, arguing that younger, aspiring academics have few opportunities for career advancement in Australia and worldwide (Burgess et al. 2008; Gottschalk and McEachern 2010; Newfield 2008). University teaching, in particular, has become increasingly casualised, with recent estimates suggesting that about half of undergraduate teaching in Australia is now performed by casual staff (May et al. 2013a). More broadly, 'full-time equivalent'[3] casual academic employment is more than three times higher than it was in 1990, while there has been minimal growth in continuing and fixed-term academic employment (May et al. 2013a; see also Australia. Department of Education 2014a).

Social science research has pointed out the risks and challenges associated with casualisation, as well as significant disadvantages experienced by casual staff (May 2011). May et al. (2013a), for instance, find evidence of widespread frustration among casual teaching staff in regard to their prospects for career progression. Other issues faced by casual academics include a 'lack of access to basic facilities such as a desk and a computer, exclusion from collegial forums, high administrative burdens, feelings of isolation and poor communication from employers' (May et al. 2013a, p. 261; see also Brown et al. 2010). Moreover, in their survey and interview-based study of academic casuals, Lorene Gottschalk and Steve McEachern (2010, p. 48) found that these staff, and teaching staff particularly, were frustrated and disillusioned by the realisation that the transition to a secure, full-time job was an 'impossible dream'.

In discussions of academic precarity and permanency, gender and age are significant factors. In Australia, casual academics are disproportionately young and female: May (2011, p. 6) finds that 57 per cent of academic casuals are women, and that 52 per cent are aged 35 or younger. These are the same groups that are frequently considered to be underrepresented in more permanent positions (Jones and Lovejoy 1980; May 2011; for examples, see Australia. Department of Education 2014b; Bradley et al. 2008). Female academics tend to be employed at lower levels, for less pay, and are less likely to be in full-time employment than their male counterparts (Jones and Lovejoy 1980). Furthermore, the Australian academic workforce is a rapidly ageing one, with a high proportion of staff being in their mid-forties to mid-sixties, while academics in their twenties and thirties are comparatively rare (Hugo 2008).

Such trends are not unique to Australia (for example, see Barbezat and Hughes 2005; Sharff and Lessinger 1995), but they do have distinctive historical roots in this country. As Hannah Forsyth (2014) makes clear in her recent book exploring the history of Australian universities, these institutions have both egalitarian and elitist influences. The first universities were established in Australia in the early 1850s, and, beginning in 1881, they began to admit women, being among the first to do so worldwide (Forsyth 2014). Even before the First World War, women made up a high proportion of university enrolments: up to 50 per cent in some disciplines (Forsyth 2014, p. 10). Yet overall enrolments remained low, and universities contributed little to more widespread social mobility for women (Forsyth 2014). From the late 1940s to the late 1960s, when the number of university students was dramatically increasing, the proportion of female enrolments fell, as universities recruited males to the emerging 'technological disciplines' (Forsyth 2014, p. 40). In the 1960s and 1970s, with the rise of second-wave feminism, female students and academics became more common in Australia (Forsyth 2014). Yet today, the

Australian academic workforce remains imbalanced in terms of gender (Hugo 2008).

The age profile of contemporary academia has also been shaped by Australia's workforce history. Prior to the Second World War, the median age of Australian workers was 37 years (Hugo 2008, p. 14). Post-war increases in immigration and birth rates led to a decline in this figure (to 34 years in 1981) followed by a dramatic increase that continues to this day (to 40 years in 2014) (Australia. Australian Bureau of Statistics 2014b; Hugo 2008, p. 14). In short, the Australian workforce has aged considerably since the 1980s. Meanwhile, the expansion of universities in the 1960s and 1970s led to the large-scale employment of young academics from overseas (Hugo 2008). This resulted in a workforce that was, at the time, even younger than the national median (Hugo 2008). Following the 1970s, however, the availability of new academic positions in Australia decreased dramatically, leading to today's ageing academic workforce (Hugo 2008). Thus, Australia's contemporary academic workforce—and the location of aspiring academics within it—has distinct historical roots, related to but separate from those of other countries (Barbezat and Hughes 2005; Lopes and Dewan 2015; Sharff and Lessinger 1995).

RESEARCHING ASPIRING ACADEMICS

The interview research discussed in this chapter is part of a broader research project examining the experiences, practices, and perceptions of aspiring academics: those seeking (relatively) stable research, teaching, or teaching and research posts at universities; those who have successfully or unsuccessfully done so in the past; and current PhD students who have plans to pursue an academic career. This study focuses on aspiring academics' intended and actual research pathways into and out of academia since and prior to the completion of their PhDs; their perceptions regarding universities, university staff, academic research, and university teaching; and the personal and emotional dimensions of their experiences within academia.

Here, I examine my findings through the lens of gender, age, and precarity, drawing on 17 semi-structured interviews with female and male early career academics, carried out at three universities in Perth, Western Australia, and in Adelaide, South Australia. Interviews were conducted between January and July 2015, and interviewees were recruited through my own acquaintances as well as snowball sampling. They were between 40 minutes and two hours in length. Interviews were recorded, transcribed, and analysed thematically. The names used to refer to my interviewees throughout this chapter are pseudonyms.

Interviewees were primarily educated and worked within the Arts, Humanities, or Social Sciences disciplines. Although I did not intend to concentrate on women academics, the majority of my interviewees were indeed women: specifically, 12 women and 5 men. Most of my interviewees were young—in their twenties and thirties—with fewer being in their forties, fifties, and sixties. Those accounts that I discuss in depth here, however, are all from women and men in their late twenties or thirties. Where possible, I interviewed people from a variety of different socio-economic and cultural backgrounds, although the majority of those I spoke with were white and came from middle-class families. All were either Australian citizens or permanent residents.

Of those interviewees currently working at a university (n = 12), all were employed by the institution where they had undertaken (or were undertaking) their PhD. They worked as unit coordinators, research assistants, tutors, administrators, and in student support. Employment on casual or part-time, short-term (14 weeks to 12 months) contracts was most common for those undertaking academic work. Those employed in student support or administration generally worked full-time, most often on contracts of around 6–12 months. Those who were not working at universities were unemployed, lived off their PhD scholarships, or worked elsewhere (n = 5).

The majority of those I interviewed could be described as early career academics or researchers: they had completed their PhDs several years ago and had undertaken some paid academic work since then. In Australia, the widely used definition of 'early career researchers', provided by the Australian Research Council, describes those within five years of the beginning of their (post-PhD) research careers, who have also 'normally' been awarded a PhD within the previous five years (Australian Research Council 2014). I find this link between research and early career status to be extremely problematic, given that the vast majority of the people I interviewed were not paid to undertake research, and, when they were, it was for short periods only. I also spoke to several current PhD students (one of whom had recently received an offer of long-term academic employment). Consequently, I use the term 'aspiring academics', rather than early career researchers or academics.

Given the literature discussed above, it is not surprising that my interviewees spoke of their work and lives as 'unstable' and 'insecure'.

In the sections that follow, I discuss the notions of instability, insecurity, and precarity in relation to people's overlapping discussions of job insecurity and financial instability, their career prospects, and their relationships with others. I relate my analysis back to the categories of gender and age, and discuss tensions and contradictions in interviewees' accounts.

PRECARIOUS WORK

A number of the people I spoke with described themselves as having 'given up' on an academic career. Yet all of these people remained employed at universities, and most had plans for future publications. Katie, for instance, had completed her PhD a few years ago. Since then, she had undertaken casual work—teaching, research, and administration—at the university where she completed her studies. She told me that there were no jobs, even temporary ones, in her former department, and that she had needed to look for work elsewhere within the university. When I asked her about her financial position and employment at the moment, she responded—

Katie   The money is a big thing… I'd like to be able to afford to move out of share[d] housing. I'd like to be able to afford to have children before I'm 70, buy a house, all that kind of very white-picket fence kind of stuff. I feel like I didn't realise that I was basically signing up for [*pauses*]… you think this is what happens when you go into the creative arts. It's like, "No, I did a sensible thing! I did lots of university! I was going to become a teacher!" So that's probably naivety on my part… At the moment, there's days where I'm like, "No, fuck all this… I'm not enjoying any of this, I'm not contributing anything, and I'm not making a living wage. Why am I bothering?" So, that's where going to career sessions [for non-academic jobs] comes in.

Lara   Yeah.

Katie   Or whatever. It's just looking at different options so after I get back [from an overseas trip]… I'm planning to go see a recruiter and say, "What other jobs are out there?"…

Lara   So what do you think the attraction of academia is then? 'Cos I've wondered this about myself as well. Why do you still want to do it?

Katie   Well part of it is that you worked really hard to acquire this body of knowledge that only you have, and then suddenly it's like, 'Alright, that's just going whittle away. No one wants to know about any of that'. The days where I was in the British library just reading, great fun! I loved it! And you get all these ideas. [But I] can't live like this. And to be honest most of the people I've seen, even the ones who are tenured staff, don't look very happy! The past year in particular has been really bad for the department, financially in particular, and they're all just walking around like death warmed up. They're declaring that it's the worst it's ever been, and bursting into tears in the corridors. Is that really something I would sign up for? And knowing that the best I could hope for at this stage is that I might get a two-year post-doc. somewhere, and then I'll have to apply for another two year post-doc. somewhere, and then maybe by the time I'm 40 I will get some kind of permanent position. I just don't think that's really what I want to do at this point.

Katie's sentiments were echoed by virtually everyone I spoke with, men and women, other than those who had yet to complete their PhDs or were not employed by a university. Like Katie, most had been convinced that choosing to pursue a PhD and academic career was not a 'risky' decision, and, upon realising the difficulties of obtaining academic work, considered themselves to have been 'naïve'. Indeed, the uniformity of people's language was striking. Interviewees, on the one hand, spoke of their poor career prospects, insecure employment and money, and high levels of stress, and, on the other hand, referenced their own naïvety and the lack of 'thought' they had put into undertaking a PhD and seeking an academic career.

Daniel, who had submitted his PhD thesis about six months before we spoke, also talked about the insecurity of academic work. When I asked Daniel what he had done after submitting his thesis, he told me that he had applied for a lot of jobs, and had quickly found one in (university) student support. I asked him what sort of jobs he had applied for, and he replied:

Daniel   The jobs I applied for were all university administrative related.
Lara   Okay, so not academic?
Daniel   So not academic jobs, more professional... So my rationale behind that was that I wanted a full-time job. Whilst I really wanted to continue teaching, I didn't believe it would have given me the security that I was looking for in full-time employment.

Daniel had recently cut back his working hours, from five to four days a week, and dedicated his day off to research and writing. Although he was 'happy for the time being' in his current position, he did not want to remain there in the long-term. He added that he had not 'closed the door' on a 'traditional academic career'.

Another interviewee, Perry, was in a similar position to Katie and Daniel. He had finished his PhD several years ago; however, he had since remained working in the academic department where he had undertaken his studies. He had been employed in academic roles on a series of casual and short-term contracts. Perry and his partner rented their home, and had recently had to move. He spoke about how, to counter his sense that his life was 'unsettled', he cultivated a collection of 'portable' pot plants and antiques.

For those employed in unstable academic roles, the inability to buy a home, to remain living in one place, or to manage mortgage repayments was a common theme. Interviewees in student support or administrative roles had similar concerns to those in academic roles: although their employment was generally less short-term, they were not employed permanently, and virtually none of them wanted to remain in these roles long-term.

Overall, women's and men's accounts were extremely similar with regard to their discussions of financial and employment stability. Yet such instabilities impacted them unevenly, with women being far more likely to be in highly unstable work, on shorter-term contracts, and working for lower pay. This reality was to some extent reflected in the fact that I had difficulty finding men in unstable work to interview, but it was also evident in the types of paid positions occupied by interviewees: men tended to be in slightly more stable work and also tended to enjoy greater seniority. Furthermore, while the older aspiring academics that I spoke with appeared to be far 'less' concerned with job instability, they also tended not to be working in temporary academic positions themselves.

My observations are confirmed by previous research, which shows that young women are those most likely to be found in temporary academic employment, and particularly in casual teaching roles (Jones and Lovejoy 1980; May 2011). As a result, issues of work instability are especially pertinent to this group. Furthermore, young women, particularly those with caring responsibilities, are also less able to shift from casual to full-time work (Gottschalk and McEachern 2010), while casually employed men tend to have better access to workspaces and financial support (May et al. 2013b).

PRECARIOUS CAREERS

Interviewees also spoke about their career prospects as uncertain and of their inability to 'find time' to pursue their academic goals. Once again, Perry's account illustrates this well. As outlined above, he had been employed in academic roles on a casual or short-term basis for several years. Although he was paid to work only part-time, for the most part his contracts did not reflect the actual amount of work required of him. In the exchange that follows, he discusses the possibility of leaving academia.

Lara   Why do you want to work as an academic?
Perry   I don't know if I do anymore. Late last year I had a bit of a...I wouldn't say it's an epiphany...it's more my attempts to try to find a job in academia have not really come to all that much. And I spent a lot of time last year writing. I didn't write a huge number of applications but I wrote probably about eight or something like that. And I didn't get an interview out of any of them. At first I was just thinking, "Oh well, you know, I just need to publish more", but then after a while I thought, "Well there's a kind of trap there", which is that you think that all you need to do is a little bit more of this and then something will happen next time around.

Later in our interview, he continued:

Perry   Part of what people tend to do that really shits me, in terms of [continuing or tenured] staff, is that say you're really busy one day. You've just maybe got a sense of achievement about having done a good lecture or done something in regard to teaching or something like that. And you're like, "Yeah, that's great", and then someone comes in and goes, "Oh yeah, that is good. You really need to publish", you know? And it just takes the wind out of your sails really badly. So no matter how good it is, "Oh you just need to publish", you know, "publish more"...
Lara   Why do [you think] they say it to you?
Perry   ... It's probably because even though I've published a heap I haven't actually published [much from my thesis]. I always find some excuse to not finish it. And then, normally, it's actually that I've taken the work, you know, the short term, "I need to survive and make money so that I can pay the rent". And I end up putting a lot of time and effort into that.

These problems were common among those I interviewed: publishing was deemed desirable and necessary, but there was also a great deal of ambivalence concerning academic writing and the pressure to publish. In Perry's case, his academic employment made it difficult for him to 'find time' to write, something for which he was not paid, while he was also applying for more permanent jobs. This was an extremely common experience among those employed as short-term-contract or casual academics. Those employed in student support and administration faced a similar challenge: their work was generally full-time, and they found spending their weekends and evenings writing and applying for academic work to be both difficult and undesirable.

My interviewees' ongoing struggles to gain long-term, academic employment are accounted for in the existing literature, which suggests that the 'establishment and pursuit of a successful research career' is contingent on 'secure, non-exploitative employment in one's field of expertise' (Bazeley et al. 1996, p. 34; see also Laudel and Gläser 2008). Virtually none of my interviewees had access to such employment. Yet, despite such circumstances, to most of them academic work was extremely alluring. When asked why they wanted to work in academia, interviewees cited a 'love' or 'passion' for teaching, research, writing, academia's collegiality, and the ability to engage in intellectual discussions with one's colleagues. For instance, Tamara, who had completed her PhD several years ago, and now worked in an administrative and student support role at a university, told me:

> I loved being in the classroom, I got energy from them. Being an introvert, I fed off their energy. And they seemed to respond and every day I would think of different activities, and they would say that the units were much better than they expected. And so I seemed to be okay at it, and also it was fun. And I would have loved to continue researching as well, at the same time, so I think it could have suited me, part of it, could have suited me. And then I realised, talking to academics and stuff, about the other side: of working weekends, working nights. I started to see people burn out, friends didn't get work. [And] when they did get work, you would never see them again.

Furthermore, as discussed above, those in academic roles found themselves with little time for research and writing, and many complained that they were not given adequate time or resources to teach. Those currently

working outside of academia or undertaking PhDs tended to be more optimistic, citing academic freedom, time and resources for intellectual pursuits, and flexible working hours as some of the virtues of academia. Yet, overwhelmingly, my interviewees were dissatisfied with their academic career prospects and with the structure of universities in Australia and worldwide.

Although such perspectives appeared throughout interviewees' accounts, they impacted men and women of different ages in distinct ways. In their study of casual academics, May et al. (2013a) have found that those most dissatisfied with their academic career opportunities were people with PhDs, those in the Humanities and Arts, and women. They developed the 'frustrated academic index', which reported the proportion of respondents who would like to be working as academics in five years' time, but did not expect that this would be the case (May et al. 2013a). They found that about half of casuals 'aspiring to an academic position were "frustrated academics"' (May et al. 2013a, p. 271). Other research conducted in Australia has found high levels of dissatisfaction among younger academics, with a high proportion of them planning on leaving the sector (Bexley et al. 2011; May 2011; May et al. 2013b). Reasons for wanting to leave included poor job security, low pay, a lack of research funding, and dissatisfaction with the 'culture' of the sector and their institution (Bexley et al. 2011).

These reasons featured prominently in my interviews, but were balanced by feelings of responsibility to one's students and department, a 'passion' for teaching and research, and the notion that leaving after years spent in academia would be a 'waste'. Although many of my interviewees spoke about wanting to leave academia, and gave compelling reasons as to why this would be the right decision for them, most were still working in universities when I spoke with them and had plans to continue publishing their research and applying for more permanent academic positions. Once again, there were few differences between men's and women's accounts. Yet, as outlined previously, men were much more likely to be successful in moving from casual to full-time academic work (Gottschalk and McEachern 2010).

To date, only a small amount of research has focused on the emotional and personal impact of precarious academic labour. For instance, in Jagna Sharff and Johanna Lessinger's (1995, p. 2) interview research on un- or under-employed anthropologists in the United States, interviewees' remarks evoked 'the personal humiliation, economic emiseration, intellectual isolation and wastage of this system'. Sharff and Lessinger (1995, p. 3) argue that 'the continuing (and striking) concentration of women in the temporary, nontenured underclass' and the 'discouragingly high ratio of applicants to jobs' leads to the systematic exploitation of this academic 'underclass'. These observations are in keeping with my interviewees' accounts, which reveal a (largely static) gendered and age-based academic hierarchy.

PRECARIOUS PERSONAL RELATIONSHIPS

Interviewees' personal relationships were the area where the most obvious differences between men and women emerged, especially in relation to age. In line with previous research, I found that childrearing commitments and support from partners or families significantly impacted interviewees' experiences of precarity (see also Bazeley et al. 1996; Laudel and Gläser 2008). The men I spoke with tended to view their non-academic partners as sources of emotional and financial support.[4] For instance, Perry, whose account I have drawn on above, referred to his long-term girlfriend as a much-needed source of 'stability'. When I asked him whether he would move elsewhere for academic work, he told me yes, as his partner also wanted to move and was able to work from most places. Perry continued:

> Last year I applied for a heap of jobs: some of them would work for us, some of them wouldn't now, but we said we'll talk about whether or not I would take it [later]... But there'll be points where I think we'd either have to do a bit of a long-distance thing for a while, which we did for a year anyway, so it's not a big issue. But it's not really ideal.

Interestingly, it was largely men who proposed or enacted long-distance relationships, with one woman complaining that moving her husband and child across Australia had prompted an extremely negative reaction from others, including her husband. The alternative, she said, was to divorce and take the child with her, alone.

Indeed, women frequently spoke of their partners as misunderstanding the nature of academic work and tying them to their current residences (or trying to), especially if they had children. Janine, for instance, had finished her PhD a few years ago. She had had a baby with her partner shortly after completing her thesis. I asked her whether her family and friends had been helpful, or not, in her pursuit of an academic career. She said—

Janine   Well my family keeps me here so that's a major factor, I think, if I don't apply for anything outside of here. So that's probably the biggest drawback. I would have been keen to work overseas, but I have a family. [So I] can't really go anywhere.

Lara   Is your partner working here as well?

Janine   Yeah… he's very bound to [here].

Yet Janine, and several other women, also spoke of how financial support, from their partners and families, had facilitated their academic careers, particularly during their PhDs. She said that her partner had supported her for years, and that 'we had all these dreams of doing stuff but I was not making any money and my scholarship had ended'. As such, she had sought work outside of academia almost immediately after submitting her thesis. Janine now worked four days a week, while her partner worked full-time. Toward the end of our interview, she spoke about how this had impacted her academic aspirations:

> It's really challenging, not just working, but having a baby as well. Because time is really limited and I'm trying to work, to write, to manage a household, to look after my son, and to spend time with my family. And I'm doing some quite serious work here as well so it's not just like I come in and do my work from nine to five. So it's quite challenging once you kind of throw a family in to the mix. Which kind of adds to the allure of working for the university, because it seems to be flexible and family-friendly. Not that it isn't here, but it's just that you seem to be able to come and go more as you please than you do anywhere else.

Thus, it appears that, for women, having a family or partner while seeking an academic career was experienced as both productive and restrictive. Women who were unmarried or single generally described themselves as having 'no responsibilities', but were also less able to share the financial burdens associated with seeking an academic career.

Another significant concern of women was the impact that their financial situation had on their ability to have children. When I asked Evelyn, who had recently completed her PhD and had since been employed on short-term academic contracts in her department, about having children, she responded:

It's on my mind a lot, and something I've really, my partner and I have talked a lot about. I would love to have kids: we've been together 11 years now, and we both really would love to have kids. But I honestly don't see a way to do that at the moment. Financially, emotionally probably as well, having that insecurity in life, I just don't feel audacious enough to do it. I mean people have done it for so long, and in all sorts of conditions, perhaps I'm being spoilt here, but I do feel like I can't really commit myself to something like that. And I have noticed that my colleagues are waiting for permanent positions within academia, then having children, which at some point gets to be very complicated because of their age... We were renting since I came here, so for probably six years, and that got too expensive, and at that stage we bought a house. But that was basically with the help of [my partner's] parents. We can pay the mortgage, but for me that's probably more that half of what I get at this stage. So yeah, it's difficult.

Evelyn's experience was mirrored by several other women that I interviewed. Interestingly, none of the men mentioned children as a problem, although one man had two mature children who had left home. This may, in part, be due to the difference in men's and women's ages when they have their first child: in 2013 the median age for women and men being 30.8 and 33.0 years old, respectively (Australia. Australian Bureau of Statistics 2014a). Moreover, research conducted in the United States suggests that family formation impacts both women and men's academic careers, but at different stages, with women being affected earlier (Mason et al. 2013) and therefore potentially for a longer time. Furthermore, '[n]ot only did academic women have fewer children than did women doctors and lawyers, but academic men experienced a similar gap' (Mason et al. 2013, p. 3).

Both men and women raised concerns regarding the impact of academic work on their personal and domestic lives. Issues raised included the problems of relocating with a partner or child, troubles maintaining a work–life balance, and financial difficulties, which prevented people from buying a house or having children. Yet academia was also valued by women for its potentially flexible working hours (a virtue that was never commented on by men). Moreover, while men tended to identify their female partners as supportive, both emotionally and financially, women spoke of their male partners as both restricting 'and' supporting their academic careers.

The Contradictions and Complexities of Academic Precarity

As I have made clear throughout this chapter, there are significant problems facing the academic workforce in Australia today. The aspiring academics that I interviewed for this research frequently used words such as 'unstable' and 'insecure' to describe their work and lives, in particular critiquing the precarity of their jobs, career prospects, and the impact of this on their personal relationships. Interviewees' understandings and experiences, however, were informed by their gender and ages, and, as a result, academic precarity had different consequences for different people. For instance, 'finding time' to write was made more difficult by full-time work or having a young child at home. Yet ideals of permanent academic employment—as potentially flexible, family friendly, and fulfilling—were held in tandem with notions and experiences of academic precarity.

Men encountered similar, though not identical, circumstances of precarity as did women. In seeking academic careers, young women with partners experienced obligations to remain proximate to their partners and children, and this appeared to influence men's career choices to some extent as well (Rosaldo 1980). Furthermore, as previous research shows, the most precarious roles in academia—those characterised by casual or short-term contracts—are overwhelmingly those performed by young women (Jones and Lovejoy 1980; May 2011). This emerged clearly, even among my relatively small group of interviewees. Thus, academic precarity is a gendered phenomenon, which is also informed by age and relationships. Older women with grown children, as well as single women, encountered very different versions of precarity to those with partners and small children. Regardless of gender and age, however, notions of instability and precarity conflicted with interviewees' passion for academic work and its possibilities. Still, men and women's prospects of gaining long-term academic employment remained unequal.

Notes

1. When using the term 'aspiring academic' I refer to those who seek stable, usually full-time, academic employment. While some of my interviewees referred to themselves as 'academics', most spoke of

unstable academic employment as a possible means to an 'academic career'.

2. Casual work, in the Australian context, is characterised by payment at an hourly rate as well as a lack of employment rights, including protection from unfair dismissal and benefits such as leave (Burgess et al. 2008; May 2011). While insecure employment characterises the university sectors of many countries, such employment tends to be fixed-term or part-time (May 2011). In Australia, however, academic work is increasingly paid at an hourly rate (May 2011).

3. It has been estimated that one full-time equivalent staff member equals approximately seven or eight casual staff members (May 2011, p. 6).

4. Of those I interviewed that were in couple relationships, only one was in a homosexual partnership.

REFERENCES

Australia. Australian Bureau of Statistics. (2014a). *Births, Australia, 2013.* Canberra: Australian Bureau of Statistics (Cat. no. 3301.0).

Australia. Australian Bureau of Statistics. (2014b). *Labour Force, Australia, Detailed, Quarterly, Feb 2014.* Canberra: Australian Bureau of Statistics (Cat. no. 6291.0.55.003).

Australia. Department of Education. (2014a). *2014 staff full-time equivalence.* Canberra: Department of Education and Training (ED14/015204).

Australia. Department of Education. (2014b). *Staff appendix 1—Actual staff FTE.* Canberra: Department of Education and Training (ED14/015202).

Australia. National Tertiary Education Union. (2012). *Casual teaching and research staff survey 2012: Summary of key results.* South Melbourne: National Tertiary Education Union (Document 2568).

Australian Research Council. (2014, July). *Early career researcher.* Available from: http://www.arc.gov.au/applicants/researcher_early.htm. Accessed 10 June 2015.

Barbezat, D. A., & Hughes, J. W. (2005). Salary structure effects and the gender pay gap in academia. *Research in Higher Education, 46*(6), 621–640.

Bazeley, P., Kemp, L., Stevens, K., Asmar, C., Grbich, C., Marsh, H., et al. (1996). *Waiting in the wings: A study of early career academic researchers in Australia.* Canberra: Australian Government Publishing Service.

Bexley, E., James, R., & Arkoudis, S. (2011, September). *The Australian academic profession in transition: Addressing the challenge of reconceptualising academic work and regenerating the academic workforce.* Available from: http://www. cshe.unimelb.edu.au/people/bexley_docs/The_Academic_Profession_in_ Transition_Sept2011.pdf. Accessed 10 June 2015.

Bradley, D., Noonan, P., Nugent, H., & Scales, B. (2008). *Review of Australian higher education: Final report,* September 2011. Available from: www.mq.edu. au/pubstatic/public/download.jsp?id=111997. Accessed 10 June 2015.

Brown, T., Goodman, J., & Yasukawa, K. (2010). Academic casualisation in Australia: Class divisions in the university. *Journal of Industrial Relations, 52*(2), 169–182.

Burgess, J., Campbell, I., & May, R. (2008). Pathways from casual employment to economic security: The Australian experience. *Social Indicators Research, 88*(1), 161–178.

Forsyth, H. (2014). *A history of the modern Australian University.* Sydney: NewSouth Publishing.

Gottschalk, L., & Mceachern, S. (2010). The frustrated career: Casual employment in higher education. *Australian Universities' Review, 52*(1), 37–50.

Hugo, G. (2008, November). *The demographic outlook for Australian Universities' academic staff.* Available from: http://www.chass.org.au/wp-content/ uploads/2015/02/PAP20081101GH2.pdf. Accessed 15 June 2015.

Jones, J. M., & Lovejoy, F. H. (1980). Discrimination against women academics in Australian universities. *Signs, 5*(3), 518–526.

Kendzior, S. (2013). Academia's indentured servants. *Aljazeera,* 11 April. Available from: http://www.aljazeera.com/indepth/opinion/2013/04/ 20134119156459616.html. Accessed 4 July 2015.

Laudel, G., & Gläser, J. (2008). From apprentice to colleague: The metamorphosis of early career researchers. *Higher Education, 55*(3), 387–406.

Lopes, A., & Dewan, I. A. (2015). Precarious pedagogies? The impact of casual and zero-hour contracts in higher education. *Journal of Feminist Scholarship, 7*(8), 28–42.

Luzia, K. (2014, December 8). Prelude to a 'career conversation'. *CASA: A home online for casual, adjunct, sessional staff and their allies in Australian higher education.* Available from: https://actualcasuals.wordpress.com/2014/12/08/ prelude-to-a-career-conversation/. Accessed 4 July 2015.

Mason, M. A., Wolfinger, N. H., & Goulden, M. (2013). *Do babies matter? Gender and family in the Ivory tower.* New Brunswick: Rutgers University Press.

May, R. (2011, February). *Casualisation; Here to stay? The modern university and its divided workforce.* Available from: http://issuu.com/nzteu/docs/robyn_ may_airaanz_casualisation_paper_2011. Accessed 15 June 2015.

May, R., Peetz, D., & Strachan, G. (2013a). The casual academic workforce and labour market segmentation in Australia. *Labour and Industry, 23*(3), 258–275.

May, R., Strachan, G., & Peetz, D. (2013b). Workforce development and renewal in Australian universities and the management of casual academic staff. *Journal of University Teaching and Learning Practice, 10*(3), 1–24.

Newfield, C. (2008). *Unmaking the public university: The forty-year assault on the middle class.* Cambridge: Harvard University Press.

Rosaldo, M. Z. (1980). The use and abuse of anthropology: Reflections on feminism and cross-cultural understanding. *Signs.* 5(3), 389-417.

Sharff, J. W., & Lessinger, J. (1995). The academic sweatshop: Changes in the capitalist infrastructure and the part-time academic. *Anthropology of Work Review, 15*(1), 2–11.

Navigating Gendered Expectations at the Margins of Feminism and Criminology

Olga Marques

While conducting my doctoral dissertation research on women's use of sexually explicit and pornographic materials for their own sexual pleasure and exploring how interview participants negotiated their active engagement with these materials vis-à-vis the taboo, stigma, and deviancy still surrounding them, as well as their own conceptualizations of self, gender, sex(uality) and identity, one participant used the phrase coming to her 'feminist consciousness.' By using this phrase, she was speaking to her awareness that 'there's not the dichotomy, like the whore and the Madonna and that kind of thing.' While all research participants spoke of the tensions they experienced reconciling the version of feminism reiterated throughout either their post-secondary education or by the media with how they experienced their own sexuality, their engagement with pornography, and their position as women within a patriarchal society bound by rigid gender boundaries, norms, and double standards, the concept of arriving at one's 'feminist consciousness' resonated with me. Like this research participant,

Olga Marques is an Assistant Professor in the Criminology and Justice program at the University of Ontario Institute of Technology (Canada). She received her Ph.D. in Criminology from the University of Ottawa in 2014.

O. Marques (✉)
University of Ontario Institute of Technology, Oshawa, Ontario, Canada

© The Author(s) 2017
R. Thwaites, A. Pressland (eds.), *Being an Early Career Feminist Academic*, DOI 10.1057/978-1-137-54325-7_3

51

I did not arrive at my feminism all at once. It was a process that I formally embarked on during my undergraduate education, one marked with both external pressures to reject the label (Was I going to start looking like a 'feminist'? Didn't I want to get married? Did I want to be part of a 'socialist, anti-family political movement that encourages women to leave their husbands, kill their children, practice witchcraft, destroy capitalism and become lesbians'?[1]) and inner turmoil that what I felt, experienced, and believed about women, men, sex, sexuality, sex work, and so on, did not match the feminism that I was learning. Yet it was a process that culminated—after I was encouraged by one of my undergraduate professors to do my own research—in my finding that there existed a growing body of feminist scholars (e.g., Bruckert 2002; Butler 1990; Chapkis 1997; Rubin 1992) that were writing about these topics in a way that made sense to me.

However, this chapter is not about my journey into feminism; although it is a topic that undergraduate students have asked me about as they negotiate their own journeys. It is about the challenges and tensions I experience as an early career academic navigating both feminism and criminology at the margins of both fields. Having for some time been interested in sex (acts as well as visual depictions of acts), sexuality, and gender, and how these are governed, rendered deviant, and deployed as technologies of power and regulation, I have heard at various junctures that I am not 'criminology' enough, as my research interests do not neatly align with stereotypical areas within the discipline. Similarly, as a result of my particular feminist stance—one that can be found at the interstices of labels such as pro-sexuality (Butler 1990; Rubin 1992), sex-positive (Glick 2000), pro-porn (McElroy 1995; Smith and Attwood 2013), and pro–sex work as work (Chapkis 1997; Parent et al. 2010; van der Meulen 2012)—I have been told (including in response to my comments to a prominent anti-porn feminist at a public talk in 2012) that I am not feminist enough, if indeed, I am even feminist at all. Hence, my research and teaching interests—straddling criminology, as well as women/gender, cultural, and sexuality studies—often exists at 'disciplinary boundaries' (Fuller 1991). Being at the margins of these fields simultaneously represents a locus of frustration (e.g., for those students who do not understand what sex[uality] and gender have to do with criminology) and contradiction (e.g., for those students who have only learned about 'the' feminist position on the topics I teach, as opposed to feminism as a 'cacophony of voices' [Sylvester 1995]) but also presents immense potential and opportunity as well.

Spurred by a comment submitted to me by an anonymous student, this chapter commences with a reflection on understandings of gender broadly—the tacit acceptance of un-gendered language as being 'objective' or 'neutral,' the embeddedness of gendered expectations and subsequent bias faced by women academics, and the continuing trivialization and backlash against feminism. Following this, the chapter highlights the specific ways in which the type of research and teaching I am engaged in, as highlighted above, exists at disciplinary margins. Navigating these disciplinary tensions, this chapter concludes with a discussion of how I challenge these boundaries pedagogically in the classroom.

Embeddedness of Gendered Expectations

I hate your class and think it is a waste of time, clearly you are a lesbian because you don't shut up about your man complaints. This isn't a class that should be taught anywhere because feminism is a load of shit. I think you should be fired and you shouldn't be teaching [;] period.

This statement was typed over and over again in a three-page paper submitted by an anonymous student (a pseudonym was used on the assignment cover page) in an introductory course on gender, sex(uality), and the connection with justice. Given that the assignment was completed by all students registered for the course, this paper must have been submitted by a student who also prepared another paper that followed the instructions provided and was marked accordingly. Interestingly, while it was the teaching assistant who came across this submission and subsequently wrote me a high-priority email expressing concern and panic, I was decidedly nonchalant about it. By this I do not mean to imply that I did not care, or that I did not think this was a serious act of misconduct but, rather, that such sentiments and misperceptions of feminism and feminists were somewhat expected, particularly given the manner in which feminism is both trivialized and vilified in mainstream media. While it is tempting to think that the backlash against feminism is a relatively recent phenomenon, particularly as a result of the pejorative term 'feminazi' popularized by conservative U.S. radio talk-show host Rush Limbaugh in the early 1990s, such negative narratives have plagued the women's rights movement, commencing during the late nineteenth and twentieth centuries with anti-suffragette propaganda in the form of postcards attacking those campaigning for equal rights for women (McConnaughy 2013). Similarly, both Douglas (1994) and Faludi (1991) have traced the history of media-sustained dissent against the women's rights movement since the 1960s. Given this history, during the completion of my Ph.D. as well as the start of my academic career, I of course had many conversations with colleagues about experiences teaching feminism or teaching as a feminist. Women colleagues recounted accusations by disgruntled students of their being lesbian man-haters and offered me tips, while male colleagues regaled me with stories of how students were impressed with how sensitive to women's issues they were.

Commonly espoused sentiments in classrooms—which I have heard in my own classroom—include beliefs that sexism and gender inequality no longer exist, are not serious problems, or that they perhaps exist but only in those countries 'over there', and that in Western countries it is men that are facing inequality; these views are the result of patriarchal entrenchment. Not only do we consider it 'normal' to hold women/single mothers/feminism responsible for all of society's ills (e.g., dissolution of marriage, youth deviancy, incarceration rates of boys, rape, etc.)—incorrectly attributing to feminism what are, in fact, by-products of patriarchy (e.g., when men are unfairly treated in custody trials it is because patriarchy assigns parenting and nurturing 'naturally' to women)—but we have also learned that ungendered language is 'objective.'

As a feminist scholar who is not only interested in sex, sexuality, and gender, but also in the intersections of race/ethnicity with justice, I frequently hear these sorts of assertions decrying the lack of 'objective' language in discussions of race—where internet commentators frequently (incorrectly) assert that talking about race is itself racist. As if the words, concepts, ideas, and theories that we ascribe as 'objective' do not already have a predetermined invisible actor behind them. Similar to the notion advanced by critical race theorists that colour-blindness, in fact, serves to contribute to racism by delegitimizing and rendering invisible the experiences and lived realities of people of colour (Johnson 2005), gender-blindness does the same to perpetuate and entrench sexism.

This idea that gender-blind language is 'objective' presents a challenge to a feminist professor in the classroom. That is, if we are talking about women or explicitly highlighting men, feminist professors are charged with being 'sexist,' 'unfair,' 'militant,' and 'biased against men' (Copp and Kleinman 2008). But when we are teaching around the unnamed and implicit norm (i.e., the people we are talking about when we think we are talking about no one in particular—white, cis-gendered, hetero-sexual, men) we are somehow being 'objective'. Of course, this narrative of 'objectivity' obscures the reality that we are not all equally positioned in society. Race matters. As does sex, gender, sexual orientation, geography, able-bodiedness, attractiveness, and class, as well as other markers of societal privilege. Words are not neutral. More than that, the society that we have created is also not neutral. We have ordered society along gendered lines—feminine and masculine—where, and this is something that I adamantly impart to my students, the terms 'feminine' and 'masculine' do not necessarily have anything to do with male or female bodies (with respect to genitalia). We consistently and continuously gender everything—food, writing instruments, tools, colours, toys, clothing, emotions, actions, physical as well as personality traits, behaviours, and so on. While one can eat yogurt, be a vegan, use skin moisturizers, and cry easily, and possess male genitalia, this does not negate that all these behaviours are coded feminine in the media. The fact that companies have either emerged (e.g., specializing in 'man' cupcakes, candles, yogurt, etc.) or created product lines (e.g., moisturizers or other body-care items repackaged in 'man'-friendly sleek, black bottles) specifically for men, demonstrates how messages about gender are embedded into the social fabric. A social fabric rooted in a narrative of equality tends to stymie discussions of inequality. Because if we are equal, as we are constantly told, then how can inequality exist? Such (often unconscious) messages serve to shape our experiences, interactions, and interpretations of situations, people, and contexts.

The extant literature documents that while 'unprecedented numbers of women [that] have entered the male-created and male-dominated university professoriate' (Baker and Copp 1997, p. 29), women faculty members have encountered a 'chilly climate' (Hall and Sandler 1984) and have had to deal with the complexities of navigating the gendered expectations of students, peers, and the university as a whole. West and Zimmerman (1987) note that women professors are evaluated by students by their gender performance first, and by their teaching ability second. Statham et al. (1991) found that students expected female professors to display more sympathy, concern, and leniency when compared to their male counterparts. Similarly, examining course evaluations from three different terms of the same course on feminism, taught by the same woman professor, Baker and Copp (1997) found that students' contradictory reactions depended on her ability to fulfill their gendered expectations. MacNell et al. (2014)

found that students in an online course gave better evaluations if they thought the instructor was a man. Gender bias in students' expectations of professors not only manifests itself in evaluation ratings, but also in the words used when describing men and women professors. Benjamin Smith of Northeastern University created an interactive database based on the descriptive words used in 14 million reviews on the popular website *Rate My Professor*, which reveals by discipline how common any particular word was in reviews. For instance, 'genius' was used more in reviews of male professors in all 25 disciplines which the database covered, while words such as 'stylish' or 'frumpy' were more often used for women.[2]

While feminists (professors or otherwise) will need to continue to respond to, and account for, anti-feminist critique and backlash, Faludi (1991, p. xxii) notes that:

> Backlash against women's rights succeeds to the degree that it appears to not be political, that it appears not to be a struggle at all. It is most powerful when it goes private, when it lodges inside a woman's mind and turns her vision inward, until she imagines the pressure is all in her head, until she begins to enforce the backlash, too – on herself.

Thus, criticism does not come only from men, and as feminist scholars we must be attuned to how women students internalise sexism and gendered expectations. In the classroom, I have seen students—especially female students - (a) challenge the notion that sexism and sexed/gendered discrimination still exist; (b) argue that women are in fact privileged, and that 'real' sexism is practiced against men; or (c) declare that they enjoy 'patriarchy' and a 'women's rightful place,' and that they want to remain 'women,' whatever that means. For instance, I have come across the following statements while marking assignments submitted on the topic of the social construction and justice implications of rigid gender binaries:

> 'The reason why several relationships fail is because the man is in a feminine state and the woman is in a masculine state.'

> '... [need to acknowledge] the beautiful way that women were meant to behave to attract the opposite sex.'

> 'A strong a [sic] sustainable relationship occurs when a female is sympathetic, compassionate, warm and gentle; and when the man independent, decisive, assertive and dominant.'

'Although equality in the workplace has increased in the last few years, it is essential that patriarchy remains in society.'

Such thought patterns are not uncommon among university students, and as Sharp et al. (2007) found, students tend to 'endorse strong beliefs about traditional family/gender and have a tendency to resist some human development/family studies and women's studies material' (p. 533). It can also be noted that in patriarchal society women are taught to bargain with patriarchy (Kandiyoti 1988), that is, to accept gendered rules that serve to disadvantage women as a whole in exchange for whatever power one can gain from this acceptance.

As a feminist scholar—particularly an early career feminist scholar who is not so far removed generation-wise from my own students—I understand how these ideas come to be naturalized, as they are persistent throughout patriarchal society. While I unpack and challenge all of these narratives within the classroom, I constantly reflect on why they are so seductive in the first place and how I am positioned within them myself as an individual, as well as a criminologist, which is to what this chapter now turns.

DISCIPLINARY BOUNDARIES: GENDERING AND SEXING CRIMINOLOGY

Classrooms represent a microcosm of larger society, where gendered roles, expectations, and knowledges manifest themselves. To understand why students come into the classroom with particular gendered and sexed 'common sense' beliefs, we must reflect not only on how such thoughts are embedded within our culture and within the wider anti-feminist patriarchal rhetoric, but also too how they are permeated within the disciplines themselves. As higher education was historically reserved as a male space, many disciplines—including the methods of knowledge production themselves—also developed in this manner (Hesse-Biber 2011; Oakley 1981).

As a result of the historic neglect of both women and feminism, the discipline of criminology has been posited as traditionally male-centric (Chesney-Lind 1988; Comack 2006; Naffine 1997). Tracing the trajectory of feminism into and within criminology, Comack (2006, p. 22) asserts that '[d]espite the use of generic terms—such as 'criminals,' 'defendants,' or 'delinquents'— criminology has historically been about what men do, so much so that women have been invisible in mainstream criminological theory and research.' When feminism and gender are highlighted, it is often within the context of studying 'women' as offenders and victims—as if men are genderless. Indeed, the study of women and criminality and/or victimization is treated in separate courses, identified by the title 'women,' with a lack of corresponding courses specifically titled 'men' and criminality and/or victimization. The message becomes, as Naffine (1997, p. 2) highlights, that 'feminism is about women, while criminology is about men.'

Given these realities, imparting a decidedly feminist perspective to the discipline of criminology by gendering crime—that is, exploring the implications of masculinity and femininity on understanding criminality, victimization, and deviance—is a difficult task. While constructs of sex, sexuality, and gender underscore our very understanding of criminality, victimization, and deviance, among other social phenomena, such topics are often marginalized by being taught in specialized courses, and/or are relegated to gender- or women-studies programs. Constructed as something innate, natural, and 'common sensical,' gender, sex, and sexuality are frequently treated as outside of popular discussion and critique (Crawley et al. 2008). As a result, underscoring the role of rigid and dichotomous gendered and sexed roles and expectations in not only our understandings of current events, but also in how we rationalize and respond to these events, is often absent in mainstream narratives. This absence has been noted particularly in discussions surrounding criminality and victimization.

For example, following the school shooting in 2012 at Sandy Hook Elementary School in Newton, Connecticut, when 20-year-old Adam Lanza fatally shot 20 children and 6 staff members, media and popular debate turned its attention to—as it consistently does in cases of mass shootings – gun regulation, mental health, and prominent displays of violence in video games, movies, and music. However, amidst these debates existed another discussion[3] focusing on one aspect that consistently remains unspoken: namely, that of the 62 mass murders that occurred within the United States in the 30 years preceding the Sandy Hook incident, only one shooter was a woman (Follman et al. 2012).[4] As Murphy (2012) highlights, 'A thousand conversations. None of them about men.' Similarly, with respect to victimization, Jackson Katz, scholar and anti-sexism educator, states in his TED Talk 'Violence Against Women—It's a Men's Issue' (2012)[5], that while domestic violence is framed as a problem of women, often eliciting the victim-blaming narrative of 'Why did she stay?', one aspect of this type of victimization consistently remains unspoken. Amongst all the dialogue surrounding domestic violence, and how to best support victims/survivors, conversations surrounding masculinity and the embeddedness of aggression and other violent behaviours in gendered constructions of manhood are lacking, or when presented, silenced.

Amidst the growing anti-feminist men's rights activist (MRA) backlash on social media, the popularity of #ImNotAFeminist, and the stereotypes and lack of understanding of feminism as a whole (Douglas 1994), questioning constructs of sex and gender, evaluating the implications of privilege and justice, and imparting all this information into a traditionally masculine discipline is a challenging task. This challenge is heightened when we consider that the students who study criminology often want to enter careers in the traditionally masculine profession of law enforcement, and, at least in Canada, have largely grown up in a cultural context surrounded by media oversaturation and sensationalization of crime events at a moment when overall crime rates have declined (Boyce et al. 2014), panic surrounding 'stranger danger' persists even though criminological data suggests that any given individual is most likely to be victimized by someone they know (Walklate 2007), and tough-on-crime and anti-immigration political rhetoric are at the fore.

These challenges are especially salient for me, a feminist criminologist who studies topics that are already at the margins of academia and frequently treated as frivolous or non-intellectual from a sex-positive feminist perspective, much to the chagrin of a discipline that groups these under the rubric of degradation and exploitation. Bringing gender into discussions is challenging even when the topic at hand is one that neatly falls within disciplinary boundaries. For instance, in my seminar course on human trafficking, I challenge students to question why a) human trafficking is treated synonymously with sex trafficking, neglecting the realities and economic/consumer perpetuation of labour trafficking and largely rendering invisible the existence of organ trafficking and b) why in discussions of sex trafficking (and of crime, more generally), the victim is always implicitly envisioned as a girl or woman and the offender as a man—unless explicitly denoted otherwise. How have we discursively coded 'victim' as feminine, and 'perpetrator' as masculine? What are the implications of this? I am constantly encouraging the students to see criminality and victimization through a gendered lens.

What I find more interesting in doing this type of research and speaking on these sorts of topics within the classroom, however, is the response of students towards me as an individual. I have had several students comment—mostly positively—on the ease with which I use proper names for genitalia, or openly discuss the dominant cultural construction of sex, sexuality, sexual orientation, and virginity, etc., and their justice implications. Others have questioned why, as a woman, I was interested in doing my doctoral dissertation research on pornography, a topic generally asserted to be a male domain. Many students—mostly women—have asked how my parents feel about what I teach and study. Such comments have led me to reflect on my own positioning as one that disrupts gendered expectations. Despite claims of the 'pornification' of Western culture, pornography, and sex more broadly, is still considered deviant, taboo, and something that polite society does not talk about (Sigel 2002)—especially not women. The fact that I am a woman is considered as important as the content of my analytic work on sex, sexuality, pornography, and gendered sexual regulation.

In class, as well as in life, not only do I examine deviance as performative through sexually explicit texts, but I am also attuned to how my own identity is socially constructed through the performance of deviation. When people—including students—find out what my research interests are, people assume that I too am deviant. Questions about how I became interested in sexually explicit content are frequently (a) underscored with conjecture surrounding my own sexual behaviours and accessibility, or (b) laden with academic moralism or elitism surrounding the 'low-brow' nature of the genre. Secondly, my deviance arises from my own positioning as pro-porn, which does not mean that I accept such content without question but, rather, that I, along with other aligned feminist pornography scholars, believe that free expression about sex and sexuality, including its representations, is central to women's continued battle for equality and sexual agency. As Nadine Strossen (2000: 14) explains, 'Women's rights are far more endangered by censoring sexual images than they are by the images themselves'. However, such positioning renders me deviant from a radical feminist as well as moral conservative point of view, which views pornography as wholly degrading, oppressive, and violent towards women. Indeed, students are frequently surprised by my stance on sexually explicit representations, and do not connect it with feminism per se. Both Sigel (2002) and Penley (2013) write about similar experiences of how, as feminist pornography scholars, their identities too are constructed within and through the performance of gendered and academic deviance - the same arena of deviance within which pornography lies.

Such introspection on my own embodiment of certain ideas and deviances within the classroom; my positioning within the discipline of criminology; the gendered notions and expectations, as well as the perceptions of feminism, that students are likely to enter the classroom with, has led me to reflect upon how I navigate this terrain in a non-confrontational and engaging manner pedagogically. This is the focus of the following section.

NAVIGATING THE MARGINS

Given that feminist backlash as well as (unconscious) gender bias within the academy exists and persists, feminist professors must learn to navigate this terrain without simultaneously and unwittingly perpetuating this backlash and bias. One of the things being an early career feminist has led me to do is reevaluate the label of 'feminist': what it means to me and how my feminism translates into my own pedagogical approach. It is important to remember that just like feminism, feminist pedagogy is not a singular discourse. There are multiple feminist pedagogies. Despite ideological differences, all feminisms and feminist pedagogies challenge the normative and encourage feminist scholars to reflect on the contradictions of our own practices and theory. My thoughts on this can be organised as follows:

No, I Don't Hate Men...

When I first started teaching, I will admit that I used these words to position myself and my lecture content. However, to me this statement is fraught with much ambivalence. On the one hand, I understand why several of my female colleagues feel the need to make this assertion at the outset of any talk on feminism. In a patriarchal society, any discussion of sexism, gender inequality, or gendered violence is seen as an assault on men, as highlighted earlier. Furthermore, given that we are taught that gender-neutral language is objective, any explicit mention of men (as opposed to the general 'people') is also interpreted in similar ways. On the other hand, by commencing with this statement we are just reiterating and perpetuating sentiment that there exist at least 'some' feminists that are 'male-bashing' (Markowitz 2005). In order to alleviate these tensions within my classroom, I follow Naffine (1997: 2), who questions why the discipline of criminology believes itself to 'be free from the effects of gender when in its proper form'. That is, why do we speak about criminality and victimization in gender-neutral terms, reserving discussions of gender, in general, and women, in particular, to specialized courses? I ask students why they think there are courses with titles like 'Women in the Criminal Justice System' but no courses similarly entitled, 'Men in the Criminal Justice System.' Who do they think they are learning about in courses where sex or gender is not specified? I articulate the importance of bringing gender into criminological analysis to understand what masculinity and femininity have to do with crime, criminality, and victimization. I point out that doing so is not 'hating men' but, rather, that rendering gender constructions and expectations invisible is what is problematic.

My students and I frequently joke about my 'Olga-isms'—those statements that I have repeated often enough that my students know me by them. One such Olga-ism is the question, 'What are we not saying, when we are saying what we are saying?' This is perhaps somewhat convoluted, but the point that I am underscoring here is that language is not neutral, that certain 'common sense' lines of thought only work because they rest on unnamed and invisible assumptions. In the context of what I teach, I provide the example of the frequently asked question, 'What was she wearing?' when discussing victims of sexual assault. Students agree that this is something they often initially ask; however, I challenge them to think about what this question is actually implying. What are the narratives that make this a viable question to ask? At its base, this question only works if we hold particular assumptions about the nature of men and their (in)ability for sexual self-control. By engaging in such thought exercises, I am able to bring gender into the classroom in a critical way, without perpetuating fallacies about what feminists are like.

You Can't Challenge What Remains Unsaid

While it is often personally challenging to hear anti-woman, sexuality-shaming, victim-blaming, and rape-apologist sentiment, I encourage my students to be honest and open about the thoughts they are coming into the classroom with or with which they are struggling. It would be infinitely easier to teach the content without acknowledging popular rhetoric; however, there are few real educational benefits to this. While the line between building a safe and inclusive classroom and allowing expression of such sentiments in class is tenuous, we must remember that '[f]eminist pedagogy acknowledges that the classroom is a site of gender, race, and class inequalities, and simultaneously a site of political struggle and change' (Briskin and Coulter 1992, p. 251). Oftentimes students do not realise what they are saying, as certain language and discourse is not only popularized but normalized. To me, these are teachable moments. For instance, while articulating a reflection on global differences of how the racialized, sexualized 'other' is constructed in my course on human trafficking, a student inadvertently made a racialized remark (of the sort that homogenized and stereotyped an entire group of people) in passing. I allowed the student to continue, thanked them for the contribution to class discussion, and then indicated that before continuing on with the substance of the comment, which was focused on the rise of precarious employment opportunities on the global scale, that I wanted to unpack the language of the singular remark made. Of course the student was apologetic, indicating that they did not intend any malice, and that it was just a common idiom. However, in order to make it a teachable moment, I asked the class questions like, Where does that come from? What does it mean that it is a normalized way of speaking? I impart to my students that we need to become critical consumers of language and not just tacitly accept that words are neutral or devoid of meaning or history.

Students as Active Purveyors of Knowledge
Central to the goals of feminist pedagogical practice is the 'transformation of the student from passive recipient of 'truth' to a subject actively engaged in constructing knowledge' (Currie 1992, p. 342). On the first day of class I tell my students that I believe that learning is collaborative and that I have as much to learn from them as they do from me. My students frequently offer nuanced insights as they navigate through the assigned readings and lecture content, using them to position their own personal biographies. They 'do' theory, without knowing that they are doing so. For instance, in a lively class discussion surrounding school dress codes and the underlying notion that boys are distracted in the classroom by what girls are wearing, student comments such as, 'Let's face it, girl's bodies are sexier than boy's bodies,' were met with rebuttals such as, 'Because the media is always presenting women's bodies as sexy, and men's bodies as funny,' 'Girls are conditioned to want to be sexy, to wear makeup, to flirt,' as well as, 'I'm a woman, and I think guy's bodies are really sexy. There are things that a guy wears that are really distracting!'

Although the majority of my planned lecture was taken up by this class debate, I found it fascinating how the students were articulating theoretical ideas without realizing it.

Every semester different questions are posed, new understandings of the course materials are articulated, and my email is brimming with news, magazine, or video items that students come across, find relevant, and would like to discuss in class. Recognising students as actively engaged in the co-construction of knowledge means that I incorporate these materials into the classroom, and oftentimes centre the content of my lectures on what they find currently relevant, using the materials they bring to my attention to create theories and concepts. This is not to say that every student actively participates in this way, or is open to course content on sex, sexuality, and gender. While I acknowledge that at the outset of the course, students 'tend to experience the gender content as provocative and volatile' (Sharp et al. 2007, p. 533) and initially grapple with thinking about sex and gender in abstract and critical ways; it is inspiring to be privy to their own intellectual transformations, however small.

As I articulated earlier, teaching through a feminist lens, particularly one that is at disciplinary margins, presents a multitude of challenges and rewards. One such reward occurred at the end of the winter 2015 semester, when a student approached me on the last day of class and stated, 'I came in thinking I was a little bit feminist, but now I am a complete feminist—and that's not a bad thing. It's sad that people think it is.'

Conclusion

Based on my own experiences, I have found that teaching and researching topics at the margins of a discipline—and for my students, at the margins of gendered expectations—simultaneously involves frustration, contradiction, and potential opportunity. Given the positive feedback received from students as well as fellow colleagues, in my estimation, I have navigated this (oftentimes) contentious terrain with success. This is not to say that pedagogically I have nothing left to learn, or that I have contemplated responses to every question that will arise in the classroom setting, as with every new cohort of students comes a new set of unanswered questions or ideas to contemplate. In reality, my status as an early career feminist scholar is/was a significant motivating factor in quickly developing, and consistently reflecting upon, a pedagogical approach that would ensure I present theories, concepts, and gendered content in an engaging, provocative, yet non-confrontational manner. Equally though, as an early-career scholar, and new member of the faculty, I felt the need to be someone that students wanted to take classes with and learn from, as I realised that 'teaching evaluations are used in promotion and tenure decisions' (Baker and Copp 1997, p. 41).

Teaching from a feminist pedagogical perspective has been identified as not only empowering students and encouraging them to think critically (Copp and Kleinman 2008; Markowitz 2005), but also empowering and encouraging for feminist scholars themselves (Sharp et al. 2007). Literature also exists on how to use and foster applied feminist principles with and among students (cf. Baker and Copp 1997; Copp and Kleinman 2008), although this is underscored by discussions of how to minimise the potential professional repercussions of doing so. For instance, Baker and Copp (1997: 41) note that faculty members are often 'evaluated by teaching criteria under the presumption that they are gender-neutral, without considering that students hold different expectations of men and women'. Given this fact, faculty members involved in tenure and promotion decision-making, should consider a) the supposed 'objectivity' in gender-neutral language and criteria used in evaluations and b) the implicit gender biases students may (un)consciously rely upon when interpreting student evaluations of their professors. It is understandable, however, that early career scholars should be concerned about their career trajectories and the ability of tenure and promotion committees to properly judge student evaluations when assessing teaching performance.

Engaging in a continual process of self-reflection and relying upon the pedagogical practices I have highlighted above, I have sought to ensure that my students are able to critically think about the gendered expectations and biases that they may hold and through which they interpret the world around them. Similarly, by commencing from the students' standpoint—relying upon topics and media that are currently trending or that they themselves point out for use in the class—I have endeavoured to create an environment whereby I am engaging with, and not only lecturing to, students. While my pedagogical decision-making is guided by my genuine interest in what my students have to say about various topics, as well as my passion for the areas in which I teach and research, it is also pragmatic. While teaching is not the only factor through which my performance is evaluated, given the courses I teach (some of which are race and gender related, both rife with controversy, especially in the context of criminology), minimizing the negative biases students may already enter the lecture room with as a result of preconceived notions of 'courses on gender, class and race as more emotional and less 'rational' than other course[s]' (Markowitz 2005, p. 41), not only encourages receptive, positive, and contemplative student engagement, but (hopefully) elicits evaluations in which negative responses to personally challenging course content are not projected onto me as an individual. Thus far, though full of its own complexity, my professional entry into the academy has been overwhelmingly positive and invigorating.

Notes

1. As stated by television evangelist Pat Robertson in a fundraising letter distributed in 1992 to Christian Coalition, an evangelical organization, in opposition to proposed equal rights amendments to the Iowa Constitution.
2. At this writing, the database can be found online at benschmidt. org/profGender/
3. For instance: Christakis, E. (2012, July 24). "The Overwhelming Maleness of Mass Homicide. Why Aren't We Talking About the One Thing Mass Murderers Have in Common?" *Time*. Available from   http://ideas.time.com/2012/07/24/the-overwhelming-maleness-of-mass-homicide/ [Accessed: 30 September 2015].
4. Jennifer San Marco, a former U.S. Postal Service employee, fatally shot seven people at the mail-processing plant where she previously worked in Golotea, California on 30 January 2006.
5. Katz, Jackson (2012, November). "Violence Against Women—It's a Men's Issue." *TEDxFiDiWomen*. Available from http://www.ted. com/talks/jackson_katz_violence_against_women_it_s_a_men_s_ issue?language=en [Accessed: 30 September 2015].

References

Baker, P., & Copp, M. (1997). Gender matters most: The interaction of gendered expectations, feminist course content and pregnancy in student course evaluations. *Teaching Sociology, 25*(1), 29–43.

Boyce, J., Cotter, A., & Perreault, S. (2014, July 23). *Police-reported crime statistics in Canada, 2013.* Juristat: Statistics Canada. Available from: http://www. statcan.gc.ca/pub/85-002-x/2014001/article/14040-eng.htm. Accessed 8 July 2015.

Briskin, L., & Coulter, R. P. (1992). Feminist pedagogy: Challenging the normative. *Canadian Journal of Education, 17*(3), 247–263.

Bruckert, C. (2002). *Taking it off, putting it on: Women in the strip trade.* Toronto: Women's Press.

Butler, J. (1990). *Gender trouble: Feminism and the subversion of identity.* New York: Routledge.

Chapkis, W. (1997). *Live sex acts: Women performing erotic labour.* New York: Routledge.

Chesney-Lind, M. (1988). Doing feminist criminology. *The Criminologist, 13*(1), 16–17.

Comack, E. (2006). The feminist engagement with criminology. In G. Gillian Balfour & E. Comack (Eds.), *Criminalizing women. Gender and (in)justice in neo-liberal times.* Halifax: Fernwood Publishing.

Copp, M., & Kleinman, S. (2008). Practicing what we teach: Feminist strategies for teaching about sexism. *Feminist Teacher, 18*(2), 101–124.

Crawley, S. L., Foley, L. J., & Shehan, C. L. (2008). *Gendering bodies.* New York: Rowman and Littlefield Publishers.

Currie, D. H. (1992). Subjectivity in the classroom: Feminism meets academe. *Canadian Journal of Education, 17*(3), 341–364.

Douglas, S. J. (1994). *Where the girls are. Growing up female with the mass media.* New York: Three Rivers Press.

Faludi, S. (1991). *Backlash: The undeclared war against American women.* New York: Crown.

Follman, M., Aronsen, G. & Pan, D. (2012, July 20). *A guide to mass shootings in America.* Available from: http://www.motherjones.com/politics/2012/07/ mass-shootings-map. Accessed 8 July 2015.

Fuller, S. (1991). Disciplinary boundaries and the rhetoric of the social sciences. *Poetics Today, 12*(2), 301–325.

Glick, E. (2000). Sex positive: Feminism, queer theory, and the politics of transgression. *Feminist Review, 64,* 19–45.

Hall, R., & Sandler, B. R. (1984). *Out of the classroom: A chilly campus climate for women?* Washington, DC: Project on the Status and Education of Women, Association of American Colleges.

Hesse-Biber, S. N. (2011). Feminist research: Exploring, interrogating, and transforming the interconnections of epistemology, methodology, and method. In S. N. Hesse-Biber (Ed.), *Handbook of feminist research. Theory and praxis* (2 ed.). New York: Sage.

Johnson, A. (2005). *Privilege, power, and difference* (2. ed.). New York: McGraw-Hill.

Kandiyoti, D. (1988). Bargaining with patriarchy. *Gender and Society, 2*(3), 274–290.

MacNell, L., Driscoll, A., & Hunt, A. N. (2014). What's in a name: Exposing gender bias in student ratings of teaching. *Innovative Higher Education.* doi:10.1007/s10755-014-9313-4.

Markowitz, L. (2005). Unmasking moral dichotomies: Can feminist pedagogy overcome student resistance? *Gender and Education* 17(1), 39-55.

McConnaughy, C. M. (2013). *The woman suffrage movement in America: A reassessment.* New York: Cambridge University Press.

McElroy, W. (1995). *XXX: A woman's right to pornography.* New York: St. Martin's.

Murphy, M. (2012, December 18). But what about the men? On masculinity and mass shootings. *Feminist Current.* Available from: http://www.feministcurrent.com/2012/12/18/but-what-about-the-men-on-masculinity-and-mass-shootings/. Accessed 30 Sept 2015.

Naffine, N. (1997). *Feminism and criminology.* Oxford: Polity Press.

Oakley, A. (1981). Interviewing women: A contradiction in terms. In H. Roberts (Ed.), *Doing feminist research.* London: Routlege & Kegan Paul.

Parent, C., Bruckert, C., Corriveau, P., Mensah, M. N., & Toupin, L. (Eds.) (2010). *Mais oui c'est un travail! Penser le travail du sex au-delà de la victimization.* Montreal: Presse de l'Université du Québec.

Penley, C. (2013). A feminist teaching pornography? That's like scopes teaching evolution! In T. Taormino, C. Parreñas Shimizu, C. Penley, & M. Miller-Young (Eds.), *Feminist porn book. The politics of producing pleasure.* New York: Feminist Press.

Rubin, G. (1992). Thinking sex: Notes for a radical theory of the politics of sexuality. In C. S. Vance (Ed.), *Pleasure and danger: Exploring female sexuality.* London: Pandora.

Sigel, L. (2002). Autobiography of a Flea. In M. L. Johnson (Ed.), *Jane sexes it up: True confessions of feminist desire.* New York: Four Walls Eight Windows.

Sharpe, E. J., Bermudez, E., Watson, W., & Fitzpatrick, J. (2007). Reflections from the Trenches: Our development as feminist teachers. *Journal of Family Issues, 28*(4), 529–548.

Smith, C. and Attwood, F. (2013). Emotional truths and thrilling slide shows: The resurgence of antiporn Feminism. In Taormino, T., Parreñas Shimizu, C., Penley, C., & Miller-Young, M. (eds.). *Feminist porn book. The politics of producing pleasure.* New York: Feminist Press.

Statham, A., Richardson, L., & Cook, J. (1991). *Gender and university teaching: A negotiated difference.* New York: New York University Press.

Strossen, N. (2000). *Defending pornography. Free speech, sex, and the fight for women's rights.* New York: New York Universtiy Press.

Sylvester, C. (1995). Riding the hyphens of feminism, peace, and place in four— (Or more) part cacophony. *Women's Studies Quarterly., 23*(3–4), 136–146.

van der Meulen, E. (2012). When sex is work: Organizing for labour rights and protections. *Labour/Le Travail, 69,* 147–169.

Walklate, S. (2007). *Imagining the victim of crime.* Berkshire: Open University Press.

West, C., & Zimmerman, D. (1987). Doing gender. *Gender and Society, 1,* 125–151.

PART II

Affect and Identities: Negotiating Tensions in the Early Career

Academic, Woman, Mother: Negotiating Multiple Subjectivities During Early Career

Agnes Bosanquet

The dominant definition of "early career" in academia is a normative one. Typically five years post-PhD, the early career academic (ECA) moves from post-doctoral, tenure track or Level A to Assistant Professor, Level B, Reader and onwards.[1] This assumes steady employment and continuous research and professional development, and does not reflect the lived experience of many ECAs. Academic work, especially during the career development phase, is excessive and frequently performed outside work hours. For women, intensifiers include unacknowledged work or academic "housework," high teaching and administrative loads, and under-representation at senior levels (Grant and Knowles 2000; Probert 2005). When motherhood and early career intersect, the challenges of research and career development are further intensified.

This chapter explores ECA motherhood in two ways. First, it presents an authoethnographic account of mothering an ill child during PhD, and coping with secondary infertility and ectopic pregnancy as an ECA. Second, it examines survey data from Australian women ECAs with caring responsibility for children. This combination of data provides a rich descriptive account supported by broader cross-sectional findings. Underpinning this

A. Bosanquet (✉)
Macquarie University, Sydney, NSW, Australia

© The Author(s) 2017
R. Thwaites, A. Pressland (eds.), *Being an Early Career Feminist Academic*, DOI 10.1057/978-1-137-54325-7_4

73

chapter is a critical feminist perspective on the multiplicity of subjectivity which holds that selfhood changes in relation to others and the world. For feminist poststructuralist theorists such as Kristeva, Irigaray, and Cixous, subjectivity is gendered and enmeshed in complex and unequal structures of discourse and power (Irigaray 1985; Kristeva 1986; Cixous 1991). The term "subjectivity" rather than the more straightforward "self" recognises this understanding of individual identity as part of broader social, cultural and political systems.

EARLY CAREER MEETS MOTHERHOOD

There is an extensive body of literature on ECA experiences of building research profiles, attaining job security, gaining funding and balancing competing workloads (Anderson, Johnson and Saha 2002; Bazeley 2003; Åkerlind 2005; Laudel and Gläser 2008). The impacts of neoliberalism are keenly felt, with ECAs being particularly vulnerable to the emphasis on performance measures, research outputs, impact metrics and funding targets. Hey and Bradford (2004) argue that the current higher education structure is dominated by a managerialist-audit perspective that privileges an ideal (masculine) academic subject. Specific studies of women academics demonstrate a gender imbalance in senior and executive roles; a concentration of women at lower levels and in casual and contract positions; and higher teaching workloads, slower career advancement and, on average, lower citation rates and grant funding for women (Aronson and Swanson 1991; Grant and Knowles 2000; Probert 2005; Grant 2006).

There are several experiential collections specifically on academic motherhood—including *Motherhood, the Elephant in the Laboratory* (2008), *Mama PhD* (2009), and *Mothers in Academia* (2013)—and extensive personal accounts from diverse perspectives (Castle and Woloshyn 2003; Mose Brown and Masi De Casanova 2009; Schlehofer 2012). These have removed some, but not all, of the stigma of talking about motherhood in an academic context. The empirical data is more limited (Young and Wright 2001; Fothergill and Feltey 2003). In Acker and Armenti's (2004: 13) "Sleepless in Academia," Canadian women academics reveal late night, obstructive institutional practices, and feeling "frenzied, fatigued and malcontent". Australian academics Klocker and Drozdzewski (2012) ask, "How many papers is a baby worth?" The answer, after some deliberation, is approximately 2.4 depending on previous output. Ward and Wolf-Wendel (2004) sum up the experience of American academic mothers at research-intensive universities with the phrase "dark clouds and silver linings." They identify four commonalities: (a) joy in professional and personal roles, (b) the "greedy" nature of academic and family life, (c) watching the clock, and (d) having children puts work into perspective (Ward and Wolf-Wendel 2004, p. 241). Much of the literature focuses on the ECA phase, and encompasses discussion of publication outputs; casualisation, tenure and promotion; academic workloads; and under-representation of women in permanent positions and at higher levels. While this may read as a list of negative consequences, this chapter shows that the challenges of combining academia and motherhood may actually help rather than hinder creative scholarly work.

Multiple Subjectivities

For feminist poststructuralists, subjectivity is anything but stable, distinct and autonomous. In *Democracy Begins Between Two,* Irigaray (2000: 4) writes, "We have to rethink the model of subjectivity which has served for centuries ... so that we can abandon a model of a single and singular subject altogether". Here Irigaray offers a conception of at least two— she emphasises the masculine and feminine—with subjectivity emerging in relation to the other. This model of intersubjectivity offers the potential for plurality or multiplicity that is evident when Irigaray (1993a: 60–63) writes about motherhood in *Sexes and Genealogies:* "A woman's subjectivity must accommodate the dimensions of mother and lover as well as the union between the two". For Irigaray, motherhood is the aspect of women's subjectivity that has been most compromised and discredited. In "And the One Doesn't Stir Without the Other" (1981), subjectivity "as women" is lost when the identities of mother and daughter are fused. In "Body Against Body: In Relation to the Mother," Irigaray (1993b: 86) describes the mother/daughter relationship as "an extremely explosive core in our societies. To think it, to change it, leads to shaking up the patriarchal order".

Feminist authors are shaking up the academic order by emphasising maternal subjectivities. In an anonymous blog post, S (2012) writes, "Motherhood, in a way, is the most visceral and physical act of rebellion against academia that I have committed." Barnacle and Mewburn (2010: 437) describe the patchwork identity of a PhD "enacted in the gaps of everyday life" through photographic images depicting the fractured identities of mother/aunt/domestic worker/PhD candidate. Similarly,

Bartlett (2006: 26) demonstrates that motherhood is intellectually and creatively productive with whimsical cartoons and bracketed interruptions to her critical text: "(But look at this beautiful baby; I fed her on milk and honey and Haraway)". Here Bartlett refers to Haraway's (1991) feminist subject "cyborg," a creature neither fully human nor machine but a fusion of identities, like the feminist academic mother. Bartlett writes (2006: 21), "Maternity undoes the professional, troubles the institutional and confuses the subject. Corporeality, subjectivity and ... intellectuality can be thought of as radically altered by maternity". In "Stabat Mater" (1986), Kristeva represents this altered subjectivity textually, with two columns alongside one another, one theoretical and the other poetic, in which she mothers her son. Similarly, Cixous writes (1991: 31) of the joyful physical, intellectual and emotional overflow of writing and breastfeeding: "A longing for text! Confusion! What's come over her? A child! Paper! Intoxications! I'm brimming over! My breasts are overflowing! Milk. Ink. Nursing time. And me? I'm hungry, too. The milky taste of ink!".

Two Lines of Evidence

This chapter examines the voices of academic mothers using two lines of evidence. First, it offers an authoethnographic account of feminist academic motherhood. Second, it presents select findings from a survey of ECAs in Australian universities (Matthews et al. 2014). Of 522 respondents, 128 (or one quarter) were women with childcare responsibilities. Both approaches represent a specific moment or "snapshot" in time; survey participants responded to questions about their academic work, and the authoethnography narrates critical incidents. As such, this data is not intended to represent a universal view of academia for women or mothers, nor to encompass the wide range of experiences therein, but to provide an opportunity for reflection, with implications beyond these moments.

Survey

The online survey, administered via SurveyMonkey®, took a mixed-methods approach, incorporating open- and closed-ended questions, emerging and predetermined approaches and quantitative and qualitative data and analysis. Participants self-identified as "early career" to disrupt dominant definitions that assume PhD completion and permanent academic appointment. Participant recruitment was via non-probability sampling: convenience and snowballing. There is an inherent risk of bias with such techniques, so the research focussed on three Australian universities and broadcast invitations to participate broadly and variously. As well as quantitative data, the survey included open-ended questions (the focus of this chapter), which asked participants to (a) outline their career plans, (b) describe their ideal academic job, and identify (c) the most and (d) the least important aspects of their work for career progression.

Responses to the open-ended questions by 128 women who indicated they had childcare responsibilities were analysed using QSR NVIVO Version 10, a qualitative analysis software tool. Themes and sub-themes emerged through iterative readings and coding of the data. The process of coding involved the researchers' sorting responses line by line into categories, which were further compared intra-data. The initial phase of open coding yielded a list of categories that were further refined and differentiated through iterative close readings of the selected data-sets over time to determine themes. To ensure reliability, these themes were tested with a co-researcher against the larger data set to reach intercoder agreement. The themes include career planning and promotion, workloads and work/life balance, and leaving academia. Specific word search queries ("mother" and "family") were also run for the full data set to enable counter-stories to emerge. This resulted in an additional theme: looking to the future.

Autoethnography

Autoethnography is a qualitative method that tells a story from the researcher's perspective (Ellis and Bochner 2000). An "autobiographical genre," it offers a way to write differently about academic experience—too often relegated to the cognitive domain—by supporting a creative space for describing identities, practices and ideas (Ellis and Bochner 2000, p. 739). By writing my story alongside that of other academic women, I am initiating a dialogue that is part of a larger feminist project of writing the self. In "The Laugh of the Medusa," Cixous (1981) says, "Woman must write her *self*: must write about women and bring women to writing ... Woman must put herself into the text" (p. 246).

Ellis, Adams and Bochner (2011: n.p.) note that autobiographies have a tendency to focus on "epiphanies" or "remembered moments perceived to have significantly impacted the trajectory of a person's life ... times of existential crisis that forced a person to attend to and analyse lived experience … and events after which life does not seem quite the same". The following series of critical incidents includes my daughter's birth and subsequent illness. During this time I struggled to complete my PhD. As with all authoethnographic accounts, it is an edited version and might have encompassed many alternative stories. I might have included my unexpected return to work as a casual lecturer when my daughter was four months old. I might have written of the childcare my parents provide. Or the completion of my PhD and the shift in discipline from cultural studies to higher education. Or negotiating to work only three days a week. Or fighting for carer's leave for my daughter's specialist appointments. Or the three years during which we tried to have a second baby. Or I might have written of the day that I was told my academic appointment was permanent, and I announced to my manager that I was finally pregnant again. Instead, I have chosen stories that mark shifts in my subjectivity as a mother, academic, and feminist. Earlier versions of two accounts were incorporated into my PhD thesis—"Placental Abruption" and "Epilepsy"—and have been previously published (Bosanquet 2010).

Placental Abruption

To reach you, the doctor cut through the layers of abdomen and uterus and left a wide sutured wound. During an induced labour, without breaks between contractions, many hours after the midwives had promised you would arrive in time for morning tea (lunch, then afternoon tea), your heart rate dropped to 60 beats a minute. Very quickly—and I cannot tell you how long, as time was slippery now—we were in theatre. When the doctor made the final incision and lifted you out, he found the placenta had abrupted. I was haemorrhaging and the blood was pooling behind my uterus; you were in distress. I had not known we were becoming detached from one another. When the doctor handed you to me, he kissed me on the forehead and said, "Well done." It was only later that I discovered where we had been: there are high foetal and maternal mortality rates with placental abruption. We recovered slowly. One of our first visitors in hospital was a colleague who congratulated me on publishing two papers that week.

Epilepsy

You were ten months old. As we were getting ready for work and childcare, I pressed my lips to your forehead, and came away burning. Your temperature was 38.4 degrees. Just after I gave you some paracetamol, you had a convulsion. Your legs and arms were stiff and shaking, your back arched, your eyes rolled back in your head, your mouth frothed. I called an ambulance. On the phone, I was almost incomprehensible. You went limp, your breathing was erratic, you turned blue. When the ambulance arrived, you were unresponsive. In hospital, you had another convulsion with a temperature of 38.2. You had tests— blood, urine, mucus, EEG, lumbar puncture. Everything seemed normal. The next morning in hospital, just after Dad had left for work, you had another seizure. You were unresponsive and blue. You were no longer breathing. Very quickly, we were surrounded by two doctors and four nurses—attempting to trace your heart rate, monitor your oxygen level, attach an oxygen mask, insert a cannula, take your blood sugar level, prepare a glucose drip and revive you. In the midst of the chaos, a doctor accidentally stuck a needle into his own hand. At that moment, the "clown doctors" arrived—laughing, throwing balloons, blowing bubbles, and playing silly horns. I watched a bubble settle on your bruise-coloured cheek in the seconds before a nurse screamed, "Get out!" and pushed the clowns from the room.

Twenty minutes later, you were sitting on my lap eating a bowl of pureed pear. The doctor described it as an "acute shutdown," the most extreme reaction to fever she had ever seen. Two months later, just after your first birthday, we were back. On arrival in hospital, you were taken straight to resuscitation. Once again, your system had shut down, but you didn't have a fever. Your blood sugar level was recorded as 0.8 (normal is between 4 and 8). You were in hospital for five days. Once home, Dad took your blood sugar level every morning. We held our panic close, and tried not to show each other the whites of our eyes. Four months on, another three hospitalisations and the diagnosis was uncertain. A year on, we had lost count of your hospital stays and your seizures. You have epilepsy. An MRI showed damage to your left temporal horn and temporal lobe asymmetry. On hearing of your birth, the neurologist said we were lucky to take home a live baby. We keep a hospital bag packed. You grow beautifully. You take your medicine. You are strong and joyful and fierce. I write these experiences into my PhD. My supervisor comments that this unconventional approach makes him "nervous."

Losing Irigaray

Pregnancy, birth and illness changed my PhD as much as they changed me. The thesis began its life as an "amorous exchange" with Luce Irigaray's philosophy. After you were born, my progress was interrupted. I was stuck, I had exhausted my capacity for creation. Writing meant leaving you. The physical, emotional and mental upheaval of motherhood rendered a type of theoretical trauma. I struggled to read Irigaray: her words and imagery no longer resonated with my experience. When I first read "And the One Doesn't Stir Without the Other," Irigaray showed that motherhood subsumed identity as a woman. In my re-reading, I see a daughter violently struggling to differentiate herself from her mother: "With your milk, Mother, I swallowed ice. And here I am now, my insides frozen" (1981, p. 60). The mother has no voice; she cannot respond. There is no hint of the double or plural subjectivity that is in Irigaray's "When Our Lips Speak Together" (1985: 209): "I/you touch you/me, that's quite enough for us to feel alive". In "Animal Compassion," Irigaray (2004) tells of the death of her pet rabbit while she was at boarding school and her subsequent hunger strike until she was allowed to come home. How did her mother feel? I wondered. I was adrift: where was I, who had previously located myself in this text? Later, this loss was recognized by one of my thesis examiners, who commented in the examination report on my disenchantment with Irigaray's philosophy: "the sense of despair is palpable."

Electricity

In August 2012, I had an ectopic pregnancy. I was meant to be teaching my first class of the semester on the night I was hospitalised. The surgery to remove my right fallopian tube was complicated. My uterus was perforated and I suffered extensive nerve damage, which caused chronic pain. I was on a lot of medications; to the extent that my specialist asked whether anyone at work had noticed my six-month sedation. In April 2013, I had my third lot of abdominal surgery in nine months. Yesterday I wore an academic gown in the graduation procession; today, an immodest hospital gown. I had a neurostimulator implanted in my abdomen; this runs an electric current alongside the nerve and replaces pain with a tingling sensation. I recharge it regularly. You describe me as a little like Astroboy; I prefer to live by Haraway's (1991) manifesto: "I'd rather be a cyborg than a goddess." It has been a life-returning success. Six weeks later (three years in the making), I am pregnant.

Happy Birthday

Today is your brother's second birthday. He is making a cake at campus childcare. At work I get a phone call from your new school. The woman on the line tells me that you came to the office. You complained of dizziness, wet yourself,

*and then fell asleep. She continues, "She has made a mess in the staff area."
A sound like a suppressed sigh. "You know she has epilepsy," I say. "Yes," is the
reply, "but she seemed normal." "She has had a seizure," I say. The woman
tells me, "She is asleep and wet. You need to pick her up." I am on my way.
I am angry. I cancel meetings, fire off emails, ask colleagues to take up my
slack. I have filled 20 pages of forms about your epilepsy. I wrote, "She is
likely to lose control of her bladder." I made posters, action plans, provided
resources, had appointments with your teachers. I don't want to know about
the mess you made, I want to know you are safe. On the way, I ring my husband, my mother. I rage. I ask for distraction. In the car, I silently say fuck
you to the woman who complained she had to clean up your mess. I watch the
speedometer. When I get to school, you are slow-moving, quiet and compliant,
not one bit your usual self. I speak to the woman in measured tones: "This
will happen again. She has had a seizure. This is what it can look like. She is
heavily medicated." Behind my words: "We are going to be seeing a lot more
of each other. We'd better get this right." You and I go home, snuggle on the
couch and watch an animated girl turn into a zombie. I surreptitiously send
emails and read papers. When it's over—the plot seemed to involve an absent
mother miraculously returned— we drive back to the university to pick up
your brother. When Dad gets home, we have dinner and cake, a new scooter.*

*

Themes from the Survey: "My Aspirations Compete with My Desire to Keep My Family Intact"

The critical incidents above demonstrate a feminist writing of the self
(or selves). But the aim of autoethnography is to move beyond the personal to locate individual experience within a wider context. As Ellis et al.
(2011: n.p.) put it, "The questions most important to autoethnographers
are Who reads our work, how are they affected by it, and how does it
keep a conversation going?". In the following section, this conversation
continues with survey data from 128 Australian academic mothers. The
survey questions focussed specifically on academic work, but implicit in
the responses that follow is much of the unacknowledged work of motherhood: the negotiation of responsibilities (for childcare in the case of sick
children, for instance), the "second shift" of domestic and caring work,
sleep deprivation and emotional labour. The language used in these survey
responses (with words such as "risk" and "sacrifice" recurring) articulate

the challenges many academic mothers face, but also evident is their agency in setting limits around workload, focussing on the aspects of academia that they love or seeking work outside universities.

Career Planning and Promotion

When asked about their plans, ECA mothers articulate uncertainty:

> *I am a female academic with financial responsibility for my family and carer responsibilities for a young school-aged child and my partner. I have worked in [the] higher education sector for a number of years. When I first started in this sector, my career aspirations were to climb the academic ladder, probably in about five years. My aspirations now compete with my desire to keep my family intact and for me to meet my family responsibilities.*

This gap between career expectations and reality is not specific to this study; globally, the academic workforce has changed significantly over the last few decades and is now dominated by casual or adjunct employees. The proliferation of terminology to describe ECAs who are in this position is illustrative: the "tenuous periphery" (Kimber 2003), the "frustrated career" (Gottschalk and McEachern 2010), the "post-doctoral treadmill" (Edwards, Bexley and Richardson 2010) and "academic aspirants" (May et al. 2011). Of note is the over-representation of women in casual and fixed-term academic appointments (May et al. 2011). Casualisation is not specific to mothers, but the following quotes demonstrate the combined impacts: *"No job security, at this stage of my career, means that I am forced to sacrifice time with my family for research, just to stay competitive for further opportunities."* Others expanded on this:

> *My greatest desire at this point is to secure permanent employment and no longer be on 6 month or 1 year contracts (as I have been for the last two and half years). The instability of my current situation is quite stressful (I have no idea if I'll still have a job in 6 months) and doesn't allow me, or my family, to make any plans into the future.*
>
> *I chose not to tutor while doing my PhD [due to family commitments]. In hindsight this was a huge mistake because I am not on anyone's radar for teaching opportunities, even to do an emergency fill while someone is sick.*

Other women describe putting career progression on hold while children are young: *"I would like to secure a full time Lecturer position once my family is older"* and *"I'd like to continue to be a tutor ... plus perhaps do some part-time research to keep my hand in while my children grow up then perhaps take on more."* Many women demonstrate agency around career-planning decisions, with 12 respondents referring to the possibility of part-time work. This has been my experience, but being a permanent part-time academic puts me in a minority. As one respondent commented, *"I have had difficulty negotiating a part-time appointment to allow me to juggle work with my family life (two small children)."* Another added, *"[Motherhood] require[s] part-time work which I feel is not really available to academics."*

Workloads and Work/Life Balance

The theme of workloads and work/life balance dominated survey responses, with the term "sacrifice" recurring: *"I firmly believe in a work/life/family balance and I see many academic staff sacrifice this balance due to work pressures."* Another wrote, *"Working above load says it all—to be successful you either need masses of support at home or be prepared to have no life and sacrifice your family."* For many respondents, academic work competes with the goals and achievements of parenting. Descriptions of an ideal workplace emphasised a limit on workloads. One mother wanted *"9 am to 5 pm academic (research and teaching) position."* Another expanded on this point:

> *[My] ideal job would be to teach and do research in a pleasant, collegial and intellectually stimulating atmosphere, where there was a reasonable workload and I didn't feel the pressure to give up family time evenings and on weekends to get work done.*

A binary is revealed in Raddon's (2002) analysis of the discourses of the "good mother" and "successful academic." While identifying the perceived contradictions of the two roles, Raddon (2002: 398) sounds a rare positive note: academic motherhood can be empowering and open up "new spaces of being through resistances to dominant discourses". This is consistent with my own experience, with the subjective shifts of motherhood challenging my orientation to feminist theory and the approach of my PhD, and ultimately guiding me to change disciplines. Such new spaces and ways of being are also evident in the survey findings when women challenge the model that sees academia subsuming family life. One respondent's career goal was to publish, research and teach *"without all of that threatening to take away from my family life."* Another added, *"It's important to me that my time at home is time with the kids, not time spent marking essays, or preparing classes in a panic, etc."* Another was more emphatic:

> University academic promotion processes systematically discriminate against those with young children who cannot work 60–80 hours per week required to meet all the criteria.

The lack of a clear boundary between academic work and home life is seen in the following response:

> [*I want*] *a job in which it is genuinely possible to find a balance between teaching and research, and that doesn't mean I have to take work home ALL the time. I am in this business because I love teaching and I love to research—but I want to be able to do both well (which is hard given workloads) and I now have a young family.*

Also evident in the comment above is a genuine love for academic work, something that was described by several participants with indicative comments, including *"I love the people I work with and the field that I research in"* and *"I love my job, my research, and am dedicated to … my students."*

Survey responses indicate that women ECAs consider research and publications the most important aspect of their work for career progression. Much of the anecdotal discussion of academic work for mothers emphasises a negative impact on research, and participants in this study were explicit on this point: *"[My] research has been impeded by fractional (continuing) appointment on raising three young children."* Another wrote, *"I have partially completed a PhD, but withdrew my candidature due to family responsibilities."* One respondent articulated her greatest difficulty as *"finding a way to generate significant research outputs despite being on a half-time appointment and having family responsibilities."* This mention of a half-time appointment and the frequent references to resisting evening and weekend work offer some evidence that women are making active decisions to contain workloads.

In an international comparison of research output, Aiston and Jung (2015) found that women average fewer publications than male colleagues; on the issue of motherhood, however, academic mothers produced "more" research output than women colleagues without children (although this differed across disciplines and countries). Examining why this data seems counterintuitive, they suggest that one explanation for women's under-performance as a whole lies in inequitable workloads (Aiston and Jung 2015). This is more complex than it first appears. In a study of Australian academic women, Dobele, Rundle-Thiele and Kopanidis (2014: 465) demonstrate that workloads are equitable between men and women, but inequity is evident when it comes to academic position. That is, women "outperform" men within their academic ranking, suggesting that "women are not getting promoted on the basis of workload performance". Participants in this study were well aware of this risk, showing reluctance to take on additional administrative workload: *"I do not want to be in a managerial position as it is not possible to have a family life work balance."* One respondent baldly stated, *"My family are worth more to me that university committees, mindless form-filling, convening programs, and promoting the university."*

Leaving Academia

Of the 128 survey respondents, 16 (12.5%) explicitly stated that they were considering leaving academia. Despite a perception of universities as flexible workplaces, the picture these respondents paint is of a system unfriendly to mothers:

Having taken maternity leave from the university system in late 2006 until the beginning of this year, I have subsequently been unable to return to the university in a full-time position. I consequently have no plans to continue in academia due to the restrictions placed on returning to the workforce for new mothers and ECAs.

I have just resigned from my current academic position as the University/School has not given me the opportunity for early career research. My teaching load has been too high. I plan to look for an alternative research position on a part-time basis in a different organisation.

With a keen awareness of casualisation, others referred to the possibility of abandoning academia but had not yet reached a decision:

I would like to get an on-going teaching and research position in a university ... I recognise that I am likely to work in a number of casual and short-term contract positions before that becomes a reality (if ever). As I have a family to support, I am aware that I might have to face the possibility of abandoning my plans and take work in another area or even a different sector.

There is scant empirical research on the experiences of women who choose to leave academia. In an older study, Rothblum (1988) discusses factors impacting women's voluntary resignation from academia, including high workloads and family demands. Consistent with later studies, she found no significant difference in research output between men and women, despite women reporting that they felt unproductive. More recently, Gardner (2013) looked at women's reasons for leaving one research institution, which included a systemic lack of support for maternity leave. In Australia, paid parental leave entitlements are comparatively generous for permanent and contracted academics (up to six months leave on full pay); however, the challenges of workloads and job security continue to have a negative impact, particularly for casual or adjunct staff without leave entitlements. This also affects non-mothers, as the following theme highlights.

Looking to the Future

Among those respondents who did not indicate current childcare responsibilities, several mentioned their intention to have children in the future. This demonstrates that motherhood is a consideration for women ECAs even before they become mothers: *"I hope to be able to juggle a career with starting a family."* Other comments extended this point:

> *My ideal academic job would be research only because I enjoy the applied research environment. I strongly prefer to work in teams rather than in isolation. This is very much an ideal job within the constraints I face as a woman who is already delaying starting a family by being in education so long. By the time I finish my PhD and get any kind of paid leave I will need to have children within a short period of time.*
>
> *[I would like to be a] full-time or part-time lecturer. Probably part time would be best as I would like time to do my own research and have a family too. There seems to be limited space for women to bring up families whilst also attempting to build an academic career.*

The flip side of motherhood as a future consideration for academic women is discrimination in the workforce. Cummins (2005) identifies the problem of "mommy tracking"—that is, the systemic sidelining of women academics due to caring responsibilities—and notes its pervasive impact on childless women academics, who take on caring responsibilities in the workplace. Elsewhere this is referred to as "academic housework" (Grant and Knowles 2000). In the United States and Canada, the notion of "May babies"—that is, timing motherhood around breaks in teaching —is well known. Armenti (2004) explores the parenting decisions of Canadian women academics and demonstrates a powerful perception that "mis-timing" motherhood is detrimental to an academic career. While this timing is not applicable to the Australian participants in this survey, and the phenomenon of "December babies" (our summer break) has not been reported here, the responses make clear that deferring and timing motherhood is a consideration in women's career planning decisions.

IMPLICATIONS

This chapter explores the subjectivities of academic mothers in order to shake up normative constructions of early career academia. There are commonalities between my experiences and those of survey participants. In particular, combining academic work and motherhood is described in affective terms. The language used by survey respondents makes this palpable: "miserable," "embittered," "suffering," "isolated," "worn out," "swamped," "stressed" and "dissatisfied". One respondent wrote of the *"desire to keep [her] family intact,"* which points towards significant emotional labour. When academia and motherhood are pitted against each other, terms like "interruption," "sacrifice" and "risk" recur. There is hope. Repeated studies have shown that academic mothers are more productive than they think (Aiston and Jung 2015; Dobele, Rundle-Thiele and Kopanidis 2014). There is some evidence in this study that women are successfully negotiating academia, taking control of decisions around career planning and workloads and enjoying their work. This is worthy of further investigation.

While this chapter focuses on the experiences of ECA mothers, the stressors of job security and workload have implications beyond the early career years and for non-mothers. As with all research, there are many counter-stories that could be told. The data presented here is multi-layered and represents the experiences of many women academics in Australian universities and, via the literature cited, women academics internationally. This is not an individual story. One of the complexities of qualitative research, especially a mixed-methods approach that includes autoethnography and survey responses, is the emergence of multiple subjectivities in the text. Describing such research, Connelly and Clandinan (1990: 9) write, "The 'I' can speak as researcher, teacher, man or woman, commentator, research participant, narrative critic, and as theory builder. Yet in living the [research] process, we are one person. We are also one in the writing". The use of many first-person accounts in this study draws attention to multiple and changeable subjectivities as feminists, mothers and academics.

Just as motherhood enables new ways of being (Raddon 2002), the combination of academic work and motherhood also opens up possibilities for new ways of thinking and doing. I would encourage all academics to provoke (responses, discussions, reactions, change), resist (choices, housekeeping, linear pathways, orthodoxy), and create (communities, families, passions, knowledges). Being provocative, resisting convention and creating possibilities are key tasks for feminists. In "Birds, Women and Writing," Cixous (2004) refers to opening "the back door of thought" (p. 169), a place where the unthought, the risky, and the impossible can be imagined. She suggests that writing comes from "deep inside" this space:

> It is deep in my body, further down, behind thought. Thought comes in front of it and closes it like a door. This does not mean it does not think, but it thinks differently from our thinking and speech. Somewhere in the depths of my heart, which is deeper than I think. Somewhere in my stomach, my womb (2004, p. 172).

For me, that "deep inside," the place "behind thought" that enables me to imagine differently has become the caesarean scars from my children's births and the neurostimulator that buzzes beneath my skin.

Acknowledgements The author gratefully acknowledges Kelly E. Matthews, Jason Lodge and Alana Mailey, who generously allowed me to utilise the ECA survey data.

NOTE

1. The nomenclature for academic levels differs across higher education systems internationally. For example, in the UK they are Lecturer, Senior Lecturer, Reader and Professor. In Australia, the roughly comparable levels are Associate Lecturer, Lecturer, Senior Lecturer, Associate Professor and Professor.

REFERENCES

Acker, S., & Armenti, C. (2004). Sleepless in academia. *Gender and Education,* *16*(1), 3–24.

Aiston, S. J., & Jung, J. (2015). Women academics and research productivity: An international comparison. *Gender & Education, 27*(3), 205–220.

Åkerlind, G. S. (2005). Postdoctoral researchers: roles, functions and career prospects. *Higher Education Research & Development, 24*(1), 21–40.

Anderson, D., Johnson, R., & Saha, L. (2002). *Changes in academic work: Implications for universities of the changing age distribution and work roles of academic staff.* Canberra: Commonwealth of Australia.

Armenti, C. (2004). May babies and posttenure babies: Maternal decisions of women professors. *The Review of Higher Education, 27*(2), 211–231.

Aronson, A. L., & Swanson, D. L. (1991). Graduate women on the brink: Writing as "outsiders within". *Women's Studies Quarterly, 19*(2/4), 156–173.

Barnacle, R., & Mewburn, I. (2010). Learning networks and the journey of 'becoming doctor'. *Studies in Higher Education, 35*(4), 433–444.

Bartlett, A. (2006). Theory, desire, and Maternity: At work in academia. *Hecate: An Interdisciplinary Journal of Women's Liberation, 32*(2), 21–33.

Bazeley, P. (2003). Defining "early career" in research. *Higher Education, 45,* 257–279.

Bosanquet, A. (2010) An image carnal and divine: Angels playing with placentas. *Outskirts: Feminisms Along the Edge 22.* Available from: http://www.outskirts. arts.uwa.edu.au/volumes/volume-22/bosanquet

Connelly, F. M., & Clandinin, D. J. (1990). Stories of experience and narrative inquiry. *Educational Researcher, 19*(5), 2–14.

Cummins, H. (2005). Mommy tracking single women in academia when they are not mommies. *Women's Studies International Forums, 28,* 222–231.

Castle, J., & Woloshyn, V. E. (2003). Motherhood and academia: Learning from our lived experiences. *Journal of the Association for Research on Mothering, 5,* 35–46.

Cixous, H. (1981). The laugh of the Medusa (K. Cohen & P. Cohen, Trans.). In E. Marks & I. de Courtivron (Eds.), *New French feminisms: An anthology* (pp. 245–264). New York: Pantheon Books.

Cixous, H. (1991). *Coming to writing and other essays.* In D. Jenson (Ed.), S. Cornell, D. Jenson, A. Liddle & S. Sellers (Trans.). Cambridge: Harvard University Press.

Cixous, H. (2004). Birds, women and writing (S. Cornell & S. Sellers, Trans.). In M. Calarco & P. Atterton (Eds.), *Animal philosophy: Essential readings in continental thought* (pp. 167–173). London: Continuum.

Dobele, A. R., Rundle-Thiele, S., & Kopanidis, F. (2014). The cracked glass ceiling: Equal work but unequal status. *Higher Education Research and Development, 33*(3), 456–468.

Edwards, D., Bexley, E., & Richardson, S. (2010). *Regenerating the academic workforce: The careers, intentions and motivations of higher degree research students in Australia, Findings of the National Research Student Survey (NRSS)*. Canberra: Department of Education Employment and Workplace Relations.

Ellis, C., Adams, T. E., & Bochner, A. P. (2011). Autoethnography: An overview. *Forum: Qualitative Social Research 12*(1). http://www.qualitative-research. net/index.php/fqs/article/view/1589/3095

Ellis, C., & Bochner, A. P. (2000). Autoethnography, personal narrative, reflexivity: Researcher as subject. In N. Denzin & Y. Lincoln (Eds.), *The handbook of qualitative research* (pp. 733–768). Thousand Oaks: Sage.

Fothergill, A., & Feltey, K. (2003). 'I've worked very hard and slept very little': Mothers on the tenure track in academia. *Journal of the Association for Research on Mothering, 5*(2), 7–19.

Gardner, S. K. (2013). Cumulative negativity: Reasons for women faculty departure from one research institution. *Journal of Higher Education Management, 0*(1), 148–165.

Gottschalk, L., & Mceachern, S. (2010). The frustrated career: Casual employment in higher education. *Australian Universities' Review, 52*(1), 37–50.

Grant, B. M. (2006). Writing in the company of other women: Exceeding the boundaries. *Studies in Higher Education, 31*(4), 483–495.

Grant, B., & Knowles, S. (2000). Flights of imagination: Academic women be(com)ing writers. *International Journal for Academic Development, 5*(1), 6–19.

Haraway, D. (1991). *Simians, cyborgs and women: The reinvention of nature*. New York: Routledge.

Hey, V., & Bradford, S. (2004). The return of the repressed? The gender politics of emergent forms of professionalism in education. *Journal of Education Policy, 19*(6), 691–713.

Irigaray, L. (1981). And the one does not stir without the other (H. Wenzel, Trans.). *Signs, 7*(1), 60–67.

Irigaray, L. (1985). When our lips speak together (C. Martin, Trans.). In L. Irigaray (Ed.), *This sex which is not one* (pp. 205–218). New York: Columbia University Press.

Irigaray, L. (1993a). *An ethics of sexual difference* (C. Burke & G.C. Gill, Trans.). Ithaca: Cornell University Press.

Irigaray, L. (1993b). Body against body: In relation to the mother (G. C. Gill, Trans.). In L. Irigaray (Ed.), *Sexes and genealogies* (pp. 7–22). New York: Columbia University Press.

Irigaray, L. (2000). *Democracy begins between two* (K. Anderson, Trans.). London: Athlone Press.

Irigaray, L. (2004). Animal compassion (M. G. Rose, Trans.). In: M. Calarco and P. Atterton (eds.), Animal philosophy: Essential readings in continental thought (pp 195–1201). London: Continuum.

Kimber, M. (2003). The Tenured 'core' and the tenuous 'periphery': The casualisation of academic work in Australian universities. *Journal of Higher Education Policy and Management, 25*(1), 41–50.

Klocker, N., & Drozdzewski, D. (2012). Career progress relative to opportunity: How many papers is a baby 'worth'? *Environment and Planning A, 44*, 1271–1277.

Kristeva, J. (1986). Stabat mater. In T. Moi (Ed.), *The Kristeva reader* (pp. 160–186). New York: Columbia University Press.

Laudel, G., & Glaser, J. (2008). From apprentice to colleague: The metamorphosis of early career researchers. *Higher Education, 55*(3), 387–406.

Matthews, K., Lodge, J., & Bosanquet, A. (2014). Early career academic perceptions, attitudes and professional development activities: Questioning the teaching and research gap to further academic development. *International Journal for Academic Development, 19*(2), 112–124.

May, R. et al. (2011, July 4–7) The casual approach to university teaching; Time for a re-think? In Krause, K., Buckridge, M., Grimmer, C. and Purbrick-Illek, S. (eds.) *Research and development in higher education: Reshaping higher education* (Vol. 34, pp. 188–197). Gold Coast.

Mose Brown, T., & Masi De Casanova, E. (2009). Mothers in the field: How motherhood shapes fieldwork and researcher-subject relations. *Women's Studies Quarterly, 37*(3&4), 42–57.

Probert, B. (2005). 'I just couldn't fit it in': Gender and unequal outcomes in academic careers. *Gender, Work & Organization, 12*(1), 50–72.

Raddon, A. (2002). Mothers in the academy: Positioned and positioning within discourses of the 'successful academic' and the 'good mother'. *Studies in Higher Education, 27*(4), 387–403.

Rothblum, E. (1988). Leaving the ivory tower: Factors contributing to women's voluntary resignation from academia. *Frontiers, 10*(2), 14–17.

S. (2012). Making room for motherhood in academia. http://offbeathome.com/2012/04/making-room-for-motherhood-in-academia

Schlehofer, A. (2012). Practicing what we teach? An autobiographical reflection on navigating academia as a single mother. *Journal of Community Psychology, 40*(1), 112–128.

Ward, K., & Wolf-Wendel, L. (2004). Academic motherhood: Managing complex roles in research universities. *The Review of Higher Education, 27*(2), 233–257.

Young, D. S., & Wright, E. M. (2001). Mothers making tenure. *Journal of Social Work Education, 37*(3), 555–568.

Room for Confidence: Early Career Feminists in the English Department

Helena Goodwyn and Emily Jane Hogg

In 2011, at a conference entitled, 'Women and Leadership—Closing the Gender Gap', held at Oxford Brookes University, a young woman raised her hand and asked, 'Am I allowed to be angry?' The question sent a ripple around the auditorium. Was it that this woman asked a question formed in 'the red light of emotion and not in the white light of truth' that so exercised the surrounding audience members (Woolf 1929 [2001], p. 27)? Or was it that she asked permission? According to Sara Ahmed, 'historically, the reading of feminism *as* a form of anger allows the dismissal of feminist claims, even when the anger is a reasonable response to social injustice' (Ahmed 2004, p. 177); and I often get the sense that, regarding women's place in the contemporary university, angry is the one thing I'm not allowed to be. But I am often angry.

I'm angry that only 22% of Professors and 17% of Vice-Chancellors in the United Kingdom are women and that they make up only 32% of boards of governing bodies of UK higher education institutions. I'm angry that, according to the Equality Challenge Unit, in 2013, 15% of white male academics were professors, compared to 2.8% of female BME (black and minority ethnic) academics (ECU 2013). A total of 3.3% of

H. Goodwyn (✉) • E.J. Hogg (✉)
Queen Mary, University of London, London, UK

© The Author(s) 2017
R. Thwaites, A. Pressland (eds.), *Being an Early Career Feminist Academic*, DOI 10.1057/978-1-137-54325-7_5

93

the UK population is black, compared to only 1.1% of academic staff (ECU 2013). A recent survey by the Runnymede Trust found that there are only 17 black female professors in UK universities (Runnymede Trust 2015). I'm angry that the UK academic workforce is 92.3% white (ECU 2015).

I'm angry that in April, 2015, two female researchers, writing about the gender gap in PhD-to-postdoctoral transitions, received a peer review that suggested their study needed 'one or two male biologists […] in order to serve as a possible check against interpretations that may sometimes be drifting too far away from empirical evidence into ideologically biased assumptions' (Feltman 2015). I'm angry that, also in 2015 (and the two preceding years), at the Renaissance Society of America (RSA) conference, there have been 13 plenary addresses but only one delivered by a woman, despite the fact that two of the three plenary sessions at the RSA annual meeting are named after distinguished female scholars (Howard 2015).[1]

I'm angry that studies conducted in the United States point out that women who have children are 29% less likely than women without them to reach tenure-track positions and that young women scientists leave academia in higher numbers than men because they develop a sense, during their PhDs, that the 'impediments' they'll come up against in trying to enter academia are 'disproportionate' in comparison to other career paths, and that 'the sacrifices they will have to make are great' (Rice 2012). I'm angry that men are still seen as 'ideal workers', 'able to devote all their time, energy, and weekends to research' (Kittelstrom 2010) and that women who have children whilst working for their PhD are accused of not taking their research seriously enough (Anonymous 2015).

This chapter explores the role of anger and its potential as a productive force able to develop the early career academic's confidence. It focuses in particular on the position of women in my own chosen field, English Studies. Some now say that the 'pipeline problem' in the discipline is obsolete. In the United Kingdom, in the 2008/2009 academic year, 73% of undergraduate and 71% of Master's students in English Studies were women (BPA 2011). In the same year, women made up 61% of PhD students in the subject: this is clear evidence that the leak still exists and accelerates after Master's study. One can be too alarmist here: the gender disparities in other disciplines—notably science, technology, engineering and mathematics (STEM) subjects—are far greater and a cause for significant concern. And yet, where undergraduate English is dominated by women, the further you progress in the subject, the fewer women there are. The diminishing numbers of women are indicative of experiences the statistics do not convey. In seemingly mundane, everyday ways, existing modes of exclusion are re-entrenched in the early career period in academia, and I argue that these are closely related to the conditions of the contemporary research environment.

The title of this collection is *Being an Early Career Feminist Academic in a Changing Academy* and I consider the term 'early career' to include the PhD period. Perhaps this is presumptuous. The position of the PhD student in many English departments is a liminal one; the UK academy is of two minds about how to treat the PhD student of today.[2] In research and teaching practice, as a PhD student, one is made to feel (at the most encouraging institutions) like a member of the academic community and a member of staff, but one's status as a student is ever-present. In 'The Public Sphere and Worldliness' (2015) Nigel Wood writes that the expectations for doctoral projects have significantly shifted from 'a contribution to knowledge' to that which 'might be reasonably expected from four or so years' worth of full-time study'. He adds, 'one now submits more with an eye on the clock than on any totally satisfactory sense of completion', because institutions are now monitored according to 'progression and completion statistics' (p. 55). The perception that the PhD is a time of purely concentrated research no longer fits with the model of increasing professionalization, and the term 'candidate' is much more accurate than we might have heretofore considered: the PhD student today attempts to balance her research against a plethora of other activities in a bid to be judged worthy of entrance to the academy. She organises seminar series and conferences; teaches undergraduates and sometimes Master's students; publishes; manages blogs, social media feeds and networks; presents conference papers; writes book reviews and applies for research grants. From the Master's programme to the PhD is where the acceleration towards professionalization now takes place; however, significantly, it is also where the pipeline begins its accelerated leak of women academics. Embodying a feminist politics in the classroom and in one's research practices whilst in this transitional stage is fraught with anxieties and concerns. The demands placed upon early career researchers mean that there is often a sense in which institutional expectations are high and yet belonging within the institution feels shaky and insecure. The very act of adhering to a view of the PhD student as somewhere in-between student and academic might be enough to prevent oneself from developing the necessary confidence that completing a doctorate and entry to the academy requires.

My reflections on how the conditions of the contemporary environment in the English Department might be productively critiqued through identification as a feminist early career academic will be focused here through the lens of reading and teaching Virginia Woolf's 1929 essay *A Room of One's Own*, originally delivered as a speech at Girton and Newnham colleges, Cambridge. In *A Room of One's Own*, Woolf comes to realize that anger—'an element of heat' (Woolf 1929 [2001], p. 26)—is present in all the male-authored texts she consults in her search for how to address the subject of 'women and fiction' (Woolf 1929 [2001], p. 1). This leads Woolf to the conclusion that what one might interpret as anger in the work of Professor X, Y or Z is in fact a hotly defended assertion of superiority. Because, Woolf writes—

> Life for both sexes—and I looked at them, shouldering their way along the pavement—is arduous, difficult, a perpetual struggle. It calls for gigantic courage and strength. More than anything, perhaps, creatures of illusion as we are, it calls for confidence in oneself. Without self-confidence we are as babes in the cradle. And how can we generate this imponderable quality, which is yet so invaluable, most quickly? By thinking that other people are inferior to one self (Woolf 1929 [2001], pp. 28, 29).

Woolf's argument gives no alternatives for how to generate confidence, other than the assertion of superiority over others. So how are we to generate the essential—if we choose to agree with Woolf—confidence in oneself, without encouraging the dangerous and damaging feelings of superiority outlined here? This chapter discusses the relationship between feminist anger and confidence. It considers whether identifying as a feminist in the English department, particularly as a PhD student and early career researcher, can help one to find ways to develop the 'imponderable' but 'invaluable' confidence Woolf describes, and suggests that the very act of staging feminist critique might be one way in which we can generate the confidence necessary to pursuing our academic careers.

The PhD student and the early career researcher alike share the difficult task of navigating the troubled intersection between financial self-sufficiency and self-confidence in their bids to establish themselves

as academics in the English department today. The increasing casualization of academic work is not politically neutral, but is instead productive
of particular types of research and teaching possibilities for some, while
entrenching already prevalent patterns of exclusion for others. *A Room of
One's Own* remains an important text with which to consider such issues
because Woolf's famous conclusion that 'a woman must have money and a
room of her own' if she is to write, and to think, has lost none of its material importance (Woolf 1929 [2001], p. 2).

Woolf addresses her audience in a playful, suggestive and ambiguous
way: 'I propose', she writes, 'making use of all the liberties and licenses
of a novelist, to tell you the story of the two days that preceded my coming here', with the intention of thus describing how her views came to
be formed (Woolf 1929 [2001], p. 2). Although this account is then
presented in the first person, Woolf states that '"I" is only a convenient
term for somebody who has no real being' (Woolf 1929 [2001], p. 2).
She begins, 'Here then was I (call me Mary Beton, Mary Seton, Mary
Carmichael or by any name you please—it is not a matter of any importance) sitting on the banks of a river a week or two ago in fine October
weather, lost in thought' (Woolf 1929 [2001], p. 2). Not only is a persona
adopted in *A Room of One's Own*, but the persona's fluidity and artifice are
repeatedly stressed. What we are presented with is a fictionalized 'I', and
one that is at pains to point out the fictionality of its own construction.

This chapter adopts the 'I' persona, partly to draw attention to the arti-
ficial confidence with which we construct our academic writing and also as
an experiment in co-authorship. According to Toril Moi, *Room* 'radically
undermine[s] the notion of unitary self, the central concept of Western
male humanism' through 'what we might now call a "deconstructive"
form of writing, one that engages with and thereby exposes the duplici-
tous nature of discourse' (Moi 1985, p. 7). This chapter attempts its own
form of unitary disruption through the inclusion of a number of voices
under the moniker 'I'.

This chapter also employs 'I' to signal a note of caution about its own
representational capacities. As Judith Butler argues, 'the premature insistence on a stable subject of feminism, understood as a seamless category of
women, inevitably generates multiple refusals to accept the category [...]
by conforming to a requirement of representational politics that feminism
articulate a stable subject, feminism thus opens itself to charges of gross
misrepresentation' (Butler 1990, pp. 6–7). The experiences I relate in this

chapter are not intended to be representative of 'all' women; differently socially situated women, in terms of age, race, social class and numerous other factors, inevitably have different experiences in academia. Neither do I understand these stories to be the worst nor most difficult situations women in higher education face today—in fact, their seeming mundanity is part of the point I seek to make.

Like Woolf, I consider the relationship between money and the mind as gendered, but not only gendered. The current structure of entry into academia risks re-entrenching the most harmful exclusions of British academic life—those based on race, gender, class and disability. There are no explicit rules which prohibit scholars who are black, scholars who are female, scholars with mental health conditions, scholars from ethnic minority backgrounds or scholars who went to comprehensive schools from progressing as early career academics today. However, attention to the subtle yet significant, often minor-seeming and everyday factors (or factors 'presented' as everyday, intractable, commonsensical) which function in an exclusionary and limiting way, is a necessary step towards a more inclusive and equitable academy.

How you understand the tone of this chapter informs your interpretation of its content. I began by emphasizing anger despite Woolf's suggestion that anger and bitterness impact negatively on writing. As Laura Marcus has shown, the position of anger in *A Room of One's Own* has been a key locus of debate in feminist evaluations of Woolf's text, leading critics to ask whether anger can be productive in women's writing or whether it tends, as Woolf seems at some points to suggest, to betray and undermine the writer (Marcus 2010, pp. 142–179). *A Room of One's Own* stages a critique of the distorting effects of 'anger and bitterness' on women's writing, yet it may in fact be the case that sometimes anger is necessary and appropriate to a piece of writing, and that 'anger and bitterness' might, in certain contexts, be advisable and useful literary tools.

Sara Ahmed argues that anger is crucial for feminism:

Anger [...] moves us by moving us outwards: while it creates an object, it also is not simply directed against an object, but becomes a response to the world, as such. Feminist anger involves a reading of the world, a reading of how, for example, gender hierarchy is implicated in other forms of power relations, including race, class and sexuality, or how gender norms regulate bodies and spaces (Ahmed 2004, p. 176).

Thus, while my own experiences cannot be understood to represent women's experiences in general, in enunciating the personal ways in which I have experienced academia as restricting, as angering, what I seek to do is offer a 'reading' of its broader structures and power relations.

A Room of One's Own is a set text in the first-year undergraduate module I have taught a number of times. Recently, I was trying to talk with a student about the elusive speaking voice in the essay, and the way this shapes readings of the text. The student had written an essay which referred all the way through to *A Room of One's Own* as 'a novel'. I suggested to the student that they had identified something important about it—it is not a straightforwardly polemical piece of writing, it works as much through character and the representation of inner life as through argument in the traditional sense—but to refer to the text as a novel seemed to miss something about the text's self-consciousness, or so I proposed to the student: novels, that is, do not tend to declare that they are 'making use of all the liberties and licenses of a novelist' (Woolf 1929 [2001], p. 2). I had brought along a copy of *Sexual/Textual Politics: Feminist Literary Theory* and the student and I were considering Moi's caution that 'remaining detached from the narrative strategies of *Room* is equivalent to not reading it at all' (Moi 1985, p. 3).

At that moment two men we had never met before settled their plastic trays down next to us and began a conversation about a meeting they had attended that morning. My student and I exchanged an awkward glance. Our neighbours began to eat the chicken pies on their trays and, as they did so, our sheet of paper was showered with crumbs of pastry. As we tried to discuss the persona in *A Room of One's Own*—or is it more than one persona—they loudly discussed an ongoing debate between two of their other colleagues. Turning, as is my standard practice in moments of teaching-related tension, to a kind of self-deprecating deadpan comedy, I almost-whispered, 'I know this isn't the *best* place to have an office hour'. It wasn't the best place for an office hour because it was the university canteen; however, the university canteen is often the only option for teaching associates without offices. That student left and the next one arrived, eager to discuss the implicit assumptions about class in Woolf's discussion of financial freedom. Reflecting on the inheritance from her aunt which provided her with 'five hundred pounds a year for ever' (Woolf 1929 [2001], p. 30) the speaker in Woolf's text says 'my aunt's legacy unveiled the sky to me, and substituted for the large and imposing figure of a gentleman, which Milton recommended for my perpetual adoration, a view of the open sky' (Woolf 1929 [2001], p. 32). I thought about what Henry James might have to say about the strange form of freedom such a legacy entails; my tablemates began their ice cream. If, as Woolf suggests, financial security makes an irreplaceable contribution to intellectual freedom, then the austerity dominating the current research environment in English Studies might well be having a detrimental impact on early career researchers' abilities to produce interesting work—or even to help their students to do so.

There is something embarrassing and anxiety-inducing about writing like this, about drawing attention to incidents like the office hour in a cafe. Academia is full of unwritten rules—understood by all but experienced particularly intensely by underrepresented groups—like the one that says if you complain about the rules of the game you're simply betraying your own insufficient ability to play it. Those who protest the difficulty of finding a job inevitably risk the suspicion of whoever is listening that perhaps the reason the complainer has not found a job is that they are just not talented enough, that their work is not good enough or that they are in the wrong field. To write about the in-between state of the early career academic and the financial, social and, in some cases, health costs of following this career path can sound bitter and angry; nonetheless, this essay, about everyday problems, and about *un*written rules, is a positive one, written in the hope that drawing attention to such issues furthers our understanding of the statistics provided earlier.

*

It is generally accepted today that most early career researchers will experience a 'wilderness period' of two to five years between finishing a PhD and finding a permanent job. There are exceptions, inevitably, but this has become the norm. Temporary jobs in this in-between period are scarce, highly sought-after and vary widely in terms of remuneration and allocation of research time. The conventional wisdom, another unwritten rule—passed in a whispered chain from hiring panels to anxious researchers—is that to be hired for permanent positions (and even, increasingly, for temporary lectureships), given the demands of the REF[3] which place pressures on university departments, a book under contract with a respected academic press is now a minimum requirement. Writing an academic book worth reading without time to consult archives, to read widely, to think deeply—is very difficult. However, the hiring structure in higher education (HE) employment is such that this book—the book that is becoming the prerequisite for the serious consideration of your application—has to be written before you have the job structured precisely to allow this kind of thinking and activity. This is one of the most bewildering and frustrating aspects of the early career academic's position and one that seems to rely on a now outdated view of the PhD as solely a research project. Doctoral students jump at the chance to teach, not only because it offers remuneration, but because the unwritten rulebook tells them that when it comes to that interview, the one they also need the book contract for, without teaching experience, their application will suffer.

The night before my first day of teaching I felt sick with worry and sure that I would fail in my duty, despite hours of careful planning; conversations with seasoned pedagogues, friends and colleagues; and plenty of research into classroom techniques (particularly important to my research was locating strategies to handle the dreaded and inevitable silence). Walking into the lecture theatre that first day I was immediately struck by a difference between my male and female peers. The female 'teaching associates', as we were termed, wore blazers, suit jackets, serious shirts, determined grimaces. My male counterparts wore jeans, T-shirts, affable smiles. I asked my male colleague, 'Aren't you afraid you'll be mistaken for an undergraduate?' He said he wasn't worried. Because to him it didn't matter what he wore. The moment he opened his mouth to address that room of undergraduates, his position as teacher, he felt sure, would be unquestionable. I was annoyed with myself for having agonized over my outfit and yet I knew I needed it (that is, my suit jacket); it made me feel more authoritative. Perhaps I knew 'that because I was female, I would automatically have to *prove* my worth' (Adichie 2014, p. 38).

Some recent research suggests that students give better teaching evaluation reports to male teachers than to their female counterparts (Marcotte 2014), confirming my personal experience and that of my peers. If students are systematically bringing such social prejudices into the classroom, then women are likely to find it more difficult than men to gain respect from students when they are also required to teach without the conventional resources of academic staff—without, as described above, the private offices in which to hold student consultations, plan seminars or mark work. Student feedback can be an important factor in hiring for academic jobs, and so this disparity could affect long-term job prospects. The precarious position of temporary staff within the institution might, in this way, be more detrimental to women than to men.

Where jobs are scarce, connections and networking seem to become ever more important, and early career researchers often feel particularly anxious about the place of networking in their career development. If I do not think that the position of the PhD student quite allows me to qualify as a professional on a career path, then there's no point in networking;[4] but if I believe that attending seminars and conferences (with their attendant social functions) is a form of networking open and appropriate to me as a way of making connections with others who share sympathetic research interests, then maybe I am doing a form of work that will stand me in good stead for my career prospects in years to come. Perhaps if I take on the role of postgraduate representative in a research society I will engage with other researchers, early career and otherwise, and this will feel like a form of networking within more clearly defined, even 'acceptable' parameters. Certainly the latter avoids the difficulty of 'following up' fledgling connections made at conferences, and the agony of composing an email to an established academic you admire. Maybe I do not want to engage with the idea of 'networking' at all. No one wants to be seen as a 'schmoozer'.

Julia Hobsbawm, the world's first Professor of Networking at London's Cass Business School, believes networking should be seen as a skill and not one that we should be embarrassed to discuss. Her series of programmes for Radio 4 entitled, *Networking Nation* (2014) looked at the practice of networking and attitudes towards it. Ian Jack, the *Guardian* columnist, argues, 'the idea that you have to know people to advance yourself is not a good idea' (Jack 2012); but overwhelmingly, the series of programmes presented by Hobsbawm sees networking as one of the most important 'soft' skills of the twenty-first century. The 'pub culture' of academia, which includes wine receptions, the trip to the pub after a seminar, the celebratory drink after the viva and so on, might be forms of networking some of us look forward to; however, for others, they are alienating. These informal modes of networking are often crucial for forming relationships with full-time academic staff members, relationships that can lead to teaching opportunities and invitations to participate in research activities. For those who do not drink, and for those who cannot afford to regularly spend money on alcohol—as is common during the financially insecure early career period—the drinking-centred nature of relationship-building in the academy can function as a significant barrier to the development of networks.

The attempt to meet fellow researchers and share ideas with colleagues can meet with other difficulties too. Change scenes then: here I am at a conference. Suit jacket and trousers again, but now, heels and lipstick as well. I have survived the first year of my PhD and relaxed a little, enough to feel I can demonstrate some individuality—in my room, that morning, it is individuality, not 'femininity'. The 'male gaze' (Mulvey 1975), I had presumed, did not attend academic conferences. I'd forgotten that even when conforming to the rules of traditional—and traditionally male—professional dress, a suit jacket and trousers, the female body remains an object, its distracting presence usurping any attention one might hope is being paid to one's research paper. Post-delivery I received two compliments on my appearance and one sexually aggressive insult—or was it a compliment? The National Union of Students (2013) notes that in contemporary university culture 'the concept of humour or "banter" is often used to minimize the more offensive or damaging aspects of "lad culture"'. In this case, I was so angry I never quite managed to ask in what spirit the comment was intended.

*

In the final part of this chapter, I turn to consider ways of tackling some of these issues. In particular, I suggest that the history of feminist theory and activism can be drawn into dialogue with contemporary issues in productive ways. In her 1984 book *Feminist Theory: From Margin to Center*, bell hooks discusses the difference between 'feminism as political commitment' and feminism as 'identity and lifestyle':

> We could avoid using the phrase "I am a feminist" (a linguistic structure designed to refer to some personal aspect of identity and self-definition) and could state, "I advocate feminism." [...] A phrase like "I advocate" does not imply the kind of absolutism that is suggested by "I am." It does not engage us in the either/or dualistic thinking that is the central ideological component of all systems of Domination in Western society. It implies that a choice has been made, that commitment to feminism is an act of will (hooks 1984, pp. 30–31).

In the one week a term I teach feminist theory to a room of first-year undergraduates I have sometimes asked, 'Who in this room considers themselves to be a feminist?' This is often met with a mixed response, some unease and even, on one memorable occasion, dramatic eye rolling. Those who do not raise their hands take issue with the term, complaining of its outdatedness or negative connotations. So instead of asking our students to identify as feminists, taking part in the simple act of informing our students that 'I advocate feminism' could change the atmosphere of the room, encouraging more thoughtful and engaged discussion.

Advocating feminism in the contemporary university would have broader consequences. In 2014 Chimamanda Ngozi Adichie published *We Should All Be Feminists*, based on a talk she delivered at a Technology, Entertainment and Design conference (now better known by its acronym TED) in 2012. Adichie writes anecdotally, and passionately, in this lecture that has become a highly popular text—in ways reminiscent of Woolf. She tells us, 'We should all be angry'. She reminds us, for those who say it's better now, who say that change came, and now everyone is judged equal, who say that we live in a meritocracy, 'Gender as it functions today is a grave injustice' (Adichie 2014, p. 21). 'We teach girls shame', she writes, and we teach them to 'silence themselves'. We teach them not to 'say what they truly think' (Adichie 2014, p. 33). How many times have we all been in a seminar classroom with fifteen bright young students, more than ten of whom are women, and heard only male voices respond to the seminar leader's question? How many times have we sat there ourselves in a discussion group of our peers and watched our male colleagues dominate a debate? We must encourage each other, male and female, to be more aware of ourselves in relation to each other. This could be as simple as asking others to share their opinions more often, instead of offering our own. Or, as institutions like the London School of Economics (LSE) have done, we could implement policies that insist upon equality and diversity in public lecture programmes.[5] We must remain alert to the Beadles who want to keep us off the grass and the 'deprecating, silvery, kindly' gentlemen who bar our way to the school, or the library, or the boardroom (Woolf 1929 [2001], p. 5).

In more general terms, it is, in my experience, often suggested to early career academics that they should try to be more confident, with the implicit suggestion that lack of confidence is primarily a personal flaw or fault. This seems all too reminiscent of broader contemporary cultural patterns in which, as Angela McRobbie has argued, contemporary young women are required to undertake 'self-monitoring, the setting up of personal plans and the search for individual solutions' (McRobbie 2009, pp. 59–60). However, in using this chapter to set out some incidents in my own experience that have made me angry about the position of women in academia, what I intend is to draw attention to other modes of thinking about confidence, beyond the individualised. Sara Ahmed argues that—

> feminism [...] involves a reading of the response of anger: it moves from anger into an interpretation of that which one is against, whereby associations or connections are made between the object of anger and broader

patterns or structures. Anger is creative; it works to create a language with which to respond to that which one is against, whereby 'the what' is renamed, and brought into a feminist world (Ahmed 2004, p. 176).

In naming those subtle and often unacknowledged situations and expectations which make academia a more difficult career path for women, what I seek to do is not suggest that these are the most significant challenges that women face today, or to argue that these are representative of women at large. Instead, presenting these incidents together allows links to be made between them, and, as Ahmed suggests, 'broader patterns and structures' to be identified. In particular, I suggest that there are forms of socialization and forms of institutional organization that support the development of confidence and there are others that hinder it. Feminist thought can be employed both to disentangle the social roots of the elusive quality, confidence, that some academics from underrepresented groups seem sometimes to lack. It can help us to avoid individualization, blame and shame ('Why aren't you more confident?' is seldom likely to be a helpful question, as it undermines the very self-belief it aims to establish), and it can also help to develop new forms of confidence, rooted in feminist epistemologies and ways of understanding the world. If we recognize the constructed nature of confidence, its status not simply as a property of the human individual but rather as something socially located and influenced—then feminist theory and politics has a crucial contribution to make to the formation of modes of confidence that can serve as resistance to and rebellion against current repressive institutional frameworks.

Notes

1. A group of early career scholars noted this worrying trend and wrote a statement, which was read aloud at the RSA AGM.
2. In an interview with *Times Higher Education* (2015), Simon Gaskell, Principal of Queen Mary, University of London, suggested that in the next decade universities such as Queen Mary would be likely to redefine the position of the PhD candidate from student to employee.
3. The Research Excellence Framework, or REF, is the UK's system of auditing and assessing research quality across universities. It is usually conducted every five to six years. Universities currently decide how many and which members of staff to submit to the assessment, and staff must usually submit four examples of their published work. Panels of peers (discipline specific) will then assess all the submissions

and give them a star-rating. There is also assessment of the impact of research and the research environment through written statements and examples provided by departments. The REF feeds into university rankings and into how much money a university will receive from the government and hence is highly competitive, with staff under a lot of pressure to produce and submit high-star work. The government has recently asked for a review of the REF, which is currently taking place.

4. In preparing to write this chapter I approached other early career academics, male and female, some PhD students, some who have completed their doctorates in the last two years. I asked them a series of questions about their behaviour in the classroom, teaching undergraduates, and whether they actively engaged feminist theory in their research or their pedagogical practice. They kindly agreed to add their voices to this 'I'.

5. LSE's 'Equality and Diversity in the Public Lecture Programme: Policy Statement' includes 'a requirement to ensure that chairs for lectures which are part of the public events programme are briefed to take questions (and proactively encourage questions) from a balance of those in the audience, including women and minority groups, and encourage academic departments and research centres to do the same in their own events'. http://www.lse.ac.uk/intranet/LSEServices/policies/pdfs/school/equAndDivPubLecPro.pdf

REFERENCES

Adichie, C. N. (2014). *We should all be feminists*. London: Fourth Estate.

Ahmed, S. (2004). *The cultural politics of emotion*. Edinburgh: Edinburgh University Press.

Anonymous. (2015). I'm a mother but I can still do serious research. *The Guardian*. [Online] 9 April. Available from: http://www.theguardian.com/higher-education-network/2015/apr/09/im-a-mother-but-i-can-still-do-serious-research. Accessed 30 May 2015.

British Philosophical Association. (2011). *Women in philosophy in the UK: A report by the British Philosophical Association and the Society for Women in Philosophy UK*. [Online]. Available from: http://www.bpa.ac.uk/uploads/2011/02/BPA_Report_Women_In_Philosophy.pdf. Accessed 30 May 2015.

Butler, J. (1990). *Gender trouble: Feminism and the subversion of identity*. London: Routledge.

Campaign for Science and Engineering (CaSE). (2014). *Improving diversity in STEM*. [Online]. Available from: http://sciencecampaign.org.uk/ CaSEDiversityinSTEMreport2014.pdf. Accessed 30 May 2015.

ECU. (2013). *Equality in higher education statistical report*. [Online]. Available from: http://www.ecu.ac.uk/publications/equality-in-higher-education-statistical-report-2013/. Accessed 30 May 2015.

ECU. (2015). *Academic flight: How to encourage black and minority ethnic academics to stay in UK higher education research report*. [Online]. Available from: http://www.ecu.ac.uk/wp-content/uploads/2015/03/ECU_Academic-flight-from-UK-education_RR.pdf. Accessed 30 May 2015.

Feltman, R. (2015). Sexism in science: Peer editor tells female researchers their study needs a male author. *Washington Post*. [Online] 30 April. Available from: http://www.washingtonpost.com/news/speaking-of-science/ wp/2015/04/30/sexism-in-science-peer-editor-tells-female-researchers-their-study-needs-a-male-author/. Accessed 30 May 2015.

hooks, b. (1984). *Feminist theory: From margin to center* (2nd ed., 2000). New York: South End Press.

Howard, J. (2015). To be a featured speaker at a scholarly meeting, it helps to be male. *The Chronicle of Higher Education*. [Online] 20 April. Available from: http://m.chronicle.com/article/To-Be-a-Featured-Speaker-at-a/229465/?k ey=HTknK1BjaHAQZik2ZGpJMjlTaHQ4Mh8nY3YUaHp0bl1UGA%3D %3D. Accessed 30 May 2015.

Jack, I. (2012). It's not what you know, but who – the return of an unfortunate reality. *The Guardian*. [Online] 29 June. Available from: http://www.the-guardian.com/commentisfree/2012/jun/29/julia-hobsbawm-professor-networking-elitism. Accessed 31 May 2015.

Kittelstrom, A. (2010). The academic-motherhood handicap. *The Chronicle of Higher Education*. [Online] 12 February. Available from: https://chronicle. com/article/The-Academic-Motherhood/64073/. Accessed 30 May 2015.

Marcotte, A. (2014). Best way for professors to get good student evaluations? Be male. *Slate*. [Online] 12 October. Available from: http://www.slate.com/ blogs/xx_factor/2014/12/09/gender_bias_in_student_evaluations_professors_of_online_courses_who_present.html. Accessed 30 May 2015.

Marcus, L. (2010). Woolf's feminism, feminism's Woolf. In: S. Sellers, (Ed). *The Cambridge companion to Virginia Woolf* (2nd ed.). Cambridge: Cambridge University Press.

McRobbie, A. (2009). *The aftermath of feminism: Gender, culture, and social change*. London: Sage.

Moi, T. (1985). *Sexual/textual politics: Feminist literary theory*. London: Methuen.

Mulvey, L. (2009) [1975]. *Visual and other pleasures* (2nd ed.). Hampshire: Palgrave Macmillan.

National Union of Students. (2013). *That's what she said: Women students' experiences of "lad culture" in higher education.* [Online]. Available from: http://www.nus.org.uk/Global/Campaigns/That's%20what%20she%20said%20full%20report%20Final%20web.pdf. Accessed 4 Oct 2015.

Networking Nation, No. 2 'Networking Selfie'. (2014). *BBC Radio 4.* 14 October.

Rice, C. (2012). Why women leave academia and why universities should be worried. *The Guardian.* [Online] 24 May. Available from: http://www.theguardian.com/higher-education-network/blog/2012/may/24/why-women-leave-academia. Accessed 30 May 2015.

Runnymede Trust. (2015). *Aiming higher: Race, inequality and diversity in the academy.* [Online]. Available from: http://www.runnymedetrust.org/uploads/Aiming%20Higher.pdf. Accessed 30 May 2015.

Times Higher Education. (2015). *Queen Mary University of London considers making PhD students employees.* [Online] 25 June. Available from: https://www.timeshighereducation.com/news/queen-mary-university-london-considers-making-phd-students-employees. Accessed 6 Oct 2015.

Wood, N. (2015). The public sphere and wordliness. In N. Gildea, H. Goodwyn, M. Kitching, & H. Tyson (Eds.), *English studies: The state of the discipline, past, present, and future.* Hampshire: Palgrave Macmillan.

Woolf, V. (1929) [2001]. *A room of one's own and three guineas.* London: Vintage.

"Are You One of Us, or One of Them?" An Autoethnography of a "Hybrid" Feminist Researcher Bridging Two Worlds

Sophie Alkhaled

A Feminist Is Born

I woke up feeling rather nervous. I was about to start the second grade not only in a new school but also in a completely new country. I recall putting on my new uniform and watching my sisters getting ready too. As my mother adjusted the buttons on my blue dress, she said, *"Hurry up girls, the driver will be here soon"*. I looked at her in confusion. I asked, *"What do you mean driver? Aren't you taking us to school like usual?"* My mother paused, looked troubled and replied, *"No, I am afraid I cannot take you to school anymore. But your father has hired us a wonderful driver who will look after you and make sure you get to school safely—and I will be here waiting for you when you come back home"*. I recall being perplexed by her reply rather than comforted, which clearly was her intention. *"Why can't you take us?"* I exclaimed. She replied, *"Because I am not allowed to drive in Saudi Arabia"*. I continued to protest, *"But why aren't you allowed? You drove us around all the time in the UK and Syria. I know you have a driving license. I know you can drive!"* My mother sighed, looked into my eyes and calmly replied, *"I am not allowed to drive here, because, I am a woman"*.

S. Alkhaled (✉)
Lancaster University, Lancaster, Lancashire, UK

© The Author(s) 2017
R. Thwaites, A. Pressland (eds.), *Being an Early Career Feminist Academic*, DOI 10.1057/978-1-137-54325-7_6

I was six years old and this was a profound moment in my life and the cornerstone of the feminist identity I have fostered into my early academic career. Indeed, this incident revealed to me a cold, harsh reality—that is, differences between girls and boys go beyond our biological makeup. Over my 11-year schooling in Saudi Arabia, my confusion on the subject turned into intrigue and eventually overwhelming frustration. For example, I learnt that girls did not follow the same curriculum as boys in school, as ours did not include Earth Sciences or Technical Sciences because girls could not be engineers. It was clearly stated in the mandate of the General Presidency of Girls' Education that girls' education was designed to bring her up in a proper Islamic way to perform her duty in life, which was to be an ideal and successful housewife and a good mother ready to do things which suit her nature such as teaching, nursing and medical treatment (Hamdan 2005). Women were also not allowed to vote, rent or travel without signed permission from a male guardian. I knew this was not the case in the United Kingdom, or indeed other Middle Eastern countries, and I began to appreciate how pervasive patriarchal and tribal cultural traditions influence local policies and pollute interpretations of women's human rights in the name of religion, which in this country was Islam.

Born to a Syrian father and a British mother and living between Syria, Saudi Arabia and the United Kingdom, I was brought up with a balance of both "traditional" Arab, and more "liberal" and inherently "Western" ideas of how life should be conducted. I learnt to respect and adapt to different environments and celebrate the differences each culture comprised. This was different from the life my peers led in Saudi Arabia, and I was aware of that. Every time I voiced my dismay with the inequalities outside the walls of my home, for instance, in school or to my friends and neighbours, I was reprimanded for being a "bad Muslim girl" or "rebellious". Whilst I loved Saudi Arabia and all the good it gave my family and I, I simply could not wait to move to the United Kingdom for my higher education and finally live as an equal in society. However, within a short amount of time, I realised that gender inequality was very much alive in the Western world, albeit not as overtly as in Saudi Arabia. In addition, my return to the United Kingdom less than a year after the horrific events of 9/11 in 2001 meant I witnessed aspects of "Islamphobia" and the contemporary nature of the issue of women in the Muslim world (Hamdan 2009). My feelings on the issue were somewhat paradoxical, as whilst I was aware that the Middle East was lacking in gender equality, I noticed that arguments by politicians and the media lacked cultural awareness and, on many occasions, were misleading and biased towards Western imperialism.

Furthermore, during my undergraduate and postgraduate studies, I began to uncover gaps in academic research on the Middle East, especially with regards to issues concerning women and Islam; I realised there was more room for research and understanding of women's lives in the Middle East.

After contemplating the media and academic debates, I began to realise that my bicultural position could be a valuable asset in bridging the two worlds. Growing media fascination with women in Islamic countries, the lack of academic research on the topic and my mixed feelings towards the country I once called home led me to pursue a PhD relating to women in the Middle East, with a focus on Saudi Arabia. A generous scholarship from The College of Arts and Social Science at the University of Aberdeen and the Federation for Women Graduates provided me with the opportunity to undertake research on women's entrepreneurial experiences in Saudi Arabia.

*

I was taken to my desk, on the PhD student corridor of the Business School. I was about to embark upon an incredible journey. I was away from taught courses. I was finally in a safe space, where I could research, think freely and openly discuss and contemplate delicate issues in social research. I walked into our PhD social room and heard voices, Arabic voices. My heart raced, after six years of living away from the Middle East, it felt wonderful to bring my "other half" back to life. I went in and introduced myself. I found that around 70% of the PhD students were Middle Eastern, from Egypt, Jordan, Palestine, Saudi Arabia, Kuwait and Libya. There were two of us who were women and the rest were men between the ages of 27 and 45. They were very warm and welcoming, particularly when they learnt that I was a Muslim of Syrian decent. However, our friendship began to take an uncomfortable turn when they learnt that my research went beyond "women's entrepreneurship" and was in fact examining and critiquing Muslim women's lives in the patriarchal Middle East. The men clearly felt uneasy with my research. Indeed, whilst my research was centred on a Middle Eastern country, it departed from objectivist, positivistic and quantitative methodologies in business research. Therefore, the socio-anthropological nature of my research, my debates around feminism, men, Islam, culture and my position as both an Arab and Westerner, which they believed should be an either/or binary, meant I faced hostility on a number of occasions. During one of the most heated and poignant debates, one of my colleagues firmly stated, "You have to decide, are you one of us, or one of them?" I was rendered speechless.

*

This chapter is an autoethnographic personal piece. It evolves around the abstract yet provocative question, "Are you one of us, or one of them?", which eventually and implicitly develops into the questions, "What kind of feminist am I?" and "How will this affect my academic career?" Drawing upon a feminist autoethnographic approach (Allen and Piercy 2005; Wall 2006), I illustrate the opportunities and boundaries that I faced as a "hybrid" (Abu-Lughod 2006) British/Syrian researcher during my schooling in Saudi Arabia, undergraduate/postgraduate education in the United Kingdom and postdoctoral research in Sweden. The personal narrative elucidates how I "played the game" as a feminist early career researcher in a business school, a traditionally male-dominated environment. It addresses the opportunities/challenges of practicing feminist values as a PhD student and early career researcher. Furthermore, I also address the challenges, opportunities and dangers of having to place oneself within a certain feminist category and maintain it, in and out of the classroom, and in an environment where gender is a variable on the periphery of the curriculum. I problematise being a feminist researcher in higher education who is researching "the Other" (Beauvoir 1953), in a historically male-dominated discipline. I also delve into how I aim to develop my feminist identity whilst continuing to bridge my two worlds, where the nuances of patriarchy vary explicitly and implicitly.

Before delving into the narratives, I must briefly declare my support for the notion of gender as constructed in various forms across historical, cultural and societal contexts, rather than "essentialist" or "a-historical" (Butler 2002). The welcome shift towards studies analysing what causes a certain form of construction of gender has raised awareness about loosely using categorisations such as "man", "woman", "femininity" and "masculinity", which empowered feminist research in opposing oppression (Flax 1987). I recognise that the analytical independence of sex and gender is essential for understanding the relationship between these elements and the interactional work involved in "being" a gendered person in society (West and Zimmerman 1987). However, within this narrative, my primary aim is not theoretically debating the issues around gender but to discuss how my gender, as a biological "woman", was performed and perceived (Butler 1988) across societies in the Middle East and Europe. Therefore, I find myself using the words "man" and "woman" within this narrative to illustrate the social context of "doing gender", as a relational and continuous creation of the meaning of gender through my encounters with these individuals.

An Autoethnographic Approach

Gadamer (1975) suggests that researchers should acknowledge their values and prejudices as a first step, being aware that these are embedded in their experiences of knowledge formation and also in their epistemological values. Hamdan (2009) concurs and adds that a researcher's background and personal story must be declared in order to be transparent with the reader. The introduction to this chapter sets the scene for the multifaceted nature of the formation of my feminist identity. Indeed, the realisation that men and women are "different" and that this "difference" varies across cultures, along with my frustration with gender inequality in the Middle East and the West and, furthermore, my ambition to dispel myths about women and Islam created a challenging feminist soul within myself. Therefore, taking a feminist autoethnographic approach in writing up this chapter seemed like a natural process.

Like many terms used by social scientists, the meanings and applications of "autoethnography" have evolved in a manner that makes precise definition and application difficult (Wall 2006; Ellis 2004; Anderson 2006). The term has evolved to encompass an ethnographic style of writing similar to personal narrative or autobiographical writing. Autobiographical research methods have become increasingly known as autoethnography and have been promoted, influenced and developed by a number of avid autoethnographic writers (Ellis 2004; Bochner 2000; Holt 2003). According to Wall (2006: 1)—

Autoethnography is an emerging qualitative research method that allows the author to write in a highly personalized style, drawing on his or her experience to extend understanding about a societal phenomenon. Autoethnography is grounded in postmodern philosophy and is linked to growing debate about reflexivity and voice in social research. The intent of autoethnography is to acknowledge the inextricable link between the personal and the cultural and to make room for non-traditional forms of inquiry and expression.

There is considerable latitude with respect to how autoethnography is conducted and what product results, as autoethnographers tend to vary in their emphasis on "auto-" (self), "-ethno-" (the cultural link), and "-graphy" (the application of a research process) (Wall 2006; Ellis and Bochner 2000; Reed-Danahay 1997). Indeed, some scholars follow a more evocative and emotional narrative approach (Holt 2003; Sparks 2000; Ellis 2004; Bochner 2000) whilst others argue for a more analytical autoethnographic approach (Anderson 2006) with a rigorous scientific methodology (Duncan 2004).

Evocative autoethnographers' personal narrative relies exclusively on a highly individual, evocative writing style, focusing on the ("auto-"), omitting any reference to research conventions and leaving the reader to make his or her own societal or cultural applications (Wall 2006). Evocative autoethnography requires considerable narrative and expressive skills, well-crafted prose, poetry and performance. Authoethnographers also advocate conscious positioning and reflexivity so that it is appreciated that authors write from a particular position at a specific time in their lives. In this way, they are freed from trying to write a single text in which everything is said at once to everyone (Richardson 1994, 2000a, b). The aim is to allow readers into the autoethnographer's intimate world so that they can reflect upon their lives in relation to hers/his (Sparks 2000). However, auto-ethnography is still quite vulnerable to the hegemonic pressures of more canonical, powerful discourses within mainstream methodologies and traditional epistemologies (Holt 2003). It has been criticised by scholars as being self-indulgent, individualistic and egocentric (Hufford 1995). Furthermore, the methodology of first-person narrative scholarship has been viewed as limiting human inquiry to what "I" can speak about my subject and subjectivity (Coffey 1999).

Anderson (2006) believes that the advocacy for evocative or emotional autoethnography may have eclipsed other versions of what autoethnography could be and obscures ways in which it may fit productively in other traditions of social enquiry. In his article titled, *Analytic autoethnography,* Anderson (2006) proposes five key features of analytic autoethnography that differentiate it from evocative autoethnography and place it within a traditional symbolic qualitative enquiry, whilst also making it a distinct subgenre within the broader practice of analytic ethnography. The key features are complete-member researcher status,[1] analytic reflexivity, narrative visibility of the researcher's self, dialogue with informants beyond the self and commitment to theoretical analysis. Duncan (2004) also conducted an autoethnographical study that dramatically differed from the work of evocative autoethnographers. She carried out a methodologically rigorous study focusing on the ("-graphy") process as a means to establish the quality of her autoethnography. That is, by addressing six key issues—study boundaries, instrumental utility, construct validity, external validity, reliability and scholarship—Duncan (2004) believed she was able to secure legitimacy and representation for her account and avoid criticism that other evocative autoethnographers face, therefore, placing herself "at the conservative end of the continuum of autoethnographic reporting" (2004: 8).

Feminist scholarship generally includes the experience of the researcher as part of the research process and discusses the power relations involved during this vulnerable process for both the researcher and the researched (Allen and Piercy 2005; Mauthner and Doucet 2003, 1998; Doucet and Mauthner 2008; Oakley 1981). Indeed, Allen and Piercy (2005: 156) explain that by "telling a story *on* ourselves, we risk exposure to our peers, subject ourselves to scrutiny and ridicule, and relinquish some of our sense of control over our own narratives". However, Allen and Piercy (2005), among other feminist scholars, argue that women's voices have been historically silenced in both society and scholarship, which has led women's lives to be misrepresented, distorted and repressed. Therefore, feminist scholars represent and reflect upon their experience to validate and honour their own lives and the lives of other women "in and on their own terms" and with "their own voices" (Mauthner and Doucet 2003) particularly when the status quo reflects a version of reality which often excludes women's everyday experiences (Stanley and Wise 1993).

The connection between feminism and autoethnography offering a more "fully human" method of inquiry has led Allen and Piercy to define feminist autoethnography as "the explicit reflection on one's personal experience to break outside the circle of conventional social science and confront, court, and coax that aching pain or haunting memory that one does not understand about one's own experience. It is ideally suited for investigating hidden or sensitive topics" (2005: 159). Given my personal story as a feminist early career researcher and the themes of this book, the autoethnographic form of writing seemed to fit what I was looking for in order to share my narrative. I felt that the feminist autoethnographic philosophy and methodology offered me the opportunity to provide a realistic account of my feminist academic experience, before, during and after my PhD. Therefore, for the academic purpose of writing this chapter, my "auto–ethno–graphy" will follow a more evocative style, which uses the self as the only data source (Holt 2003; Sparks 2000; Wall 2008). Whilst, as mentioned, this approach has been criticised for being too self-indulgent and narcissistic (Coffey 1999), I view my feminist autoethnography as a type of autobiographical method in the reflexive qualitative tradition where the researcher and the subject are one (Richardson 2000b).

Whilst exercising "the practice of going back and forth between inner vulnerable experience and outward social, historical, and cultural aspects of life, searching for deeper connections and understanding" (Allen and Piercy 2005: 156), I hope to capture readers' hearts with the journey upon which I am embarking—a journey which I have an emotional and undeniable connection with and which I reflexively share. However, it is important to highlight that the purpose of this chapter is not to advocate a particular style of (feminist) autoethnographic writing, as I believe that both the evocative and analytical genres can be utilised individually, variably and simultaneously depending on the topic discussed and the audience being addressed. Like Wall (2006) I began feeling uncertain regarding my knowledge and presentation as "[f]or many, especially for women being educated as researchers, voice is an acknowledgement that they have something to say" (Clandinin and Connelly 1994: 423). However, the potential power of autoethnography in highlighting the tumultuous journey of a feminist early career researcher was inspiring.

WHAT "KIND" OF FEMINIST AM I?

"You Have to Decide, Are You One of Us, or One of Them?"

My position, according to cultural anthropologists, is that of a "hybrid" or "halfie"—a person whose national or cultural identity is mixed by virtue of immigration, overseas education or parentage. It is argued that this can hold numerous advantages, as well as disadvantages (Abu-Lughod 2006). I certainly found this to be the case in my research process. After being told that I had to decide if I was essentially an "Arab friend" or a "Western enemy", I went into my supervisor's office and told her that I did not feel comfortable using feminist theories in my research. She looked astonished. She knew me well at this point. She calmly asked me why I felt this way and I explained that I was worried I would be shunned by my community, the very community I wanted to research and advance positive knowledge about. My supervisor advised me that I was not the first and would not be the last woman to face such comments. She believed I should follow the feminist path, which would help me conceptualise my research, analyse my data and highlight women's voices as authentically as possible. This was my job as a researcher. My job was not to please my peers. As I delved into the historical waves of feminism, my passion was soon reignited. I came across five main categories which still prevail today—namely, liberal feminism, radical feminism, Marxist feminism, socialist feminism and feminism in the third world (Friedman et al. 1987), which takes into account orientalism and postcolonial feminism (Mohanty 1988, 2003). As my study was based in the Muslim Middle East (Saudi Arabia), I explored the literature around third world feminism, focusing on secular feminism, Islamic feminism and Islamic female fundamentalism in the Middle East (including Iran). I found these standpoints to be the most relatable to both my research and my personal experience.

Secular feminists across the Arab region function with a dual perspective, looking outward to the West and inward to their own governments and political institutions. Departing from a political stance, they perceive that the imperialist and exploitative West represses and corrupts internal governments (Treacher 2003). More importantly, however, secular feminists call for a secular state, as they argue that the interlinking of religion (Islam), state and law precludes reform or liberation for women from patriarchal control (Mojab 2001). Secular feminists are marginalised from Arab societies for not being religious and have to fight for a public platform (Al-Ali 2000). There is a strong secular opposition, from both men and women, to Islamic movements. Muslim feminists, in contrast to secular feminists, demand women's rightful place and rights within the Islamic framework of Sharia law. Muslim feminists argue that Islam itself is not patriarchal or oppressive; on the contrary, it provides women with respect and honour. It is instead patriarchal men and the political and social systems that dominate that pollute Islamic interpretations of women's rights (Ahmed 1992; Mernissi 1991). Furthermore, whilst they argue for reclaiming the faith that provides pride and dignity to Muslim women, they argue against Western feminism, which they believe has not produced true liberation for women as women; rather, it has forced them to become more like men as they struggle to find equality at home and in the workplace. Islamic female fundamentalists are a group of women whose mission is to fight corruption and Westernisation of their society and ideology. They believe they are empowered within the safety of the classic patriarchal system, which treats them as legal minors under the guardianship of a male relative and accords them a secondary position in the household as well as in society (Yamani 1996). It has been argued that these women often resist the breakdown of the classic patriarchal system because they see no other empowering alternatives and have no ability or external support to help realise this breakdown. Therefore, their "passive resistance" is due to the appreciation that changes in the current system could threaten their short-term practical interests and lead to losing a form of protection from the very system which subordinates them (Kandiyoti 1988; Agrawal 1994).

These ideas and the scholarship that goes along with them, raise many questions for me. Given the feminist discourses surrounding Western and Islamic "otherness" (Mohanty 1988, 2003), how can I, a "hybrid" (Abu-Lughod 2006) feminist PhD researcher in a UK institution, conduct research on gender in the Middle East without assigning superiority or supremacy to Western constructions of gender? How can I represent the competing feminist discourses without exaggerating the differences? And how can I capture those aspects of the Arab region that embody patriarchy and oppression for women while simultaneously capturing their resistance, bravery and power? More importantly, what is my feminist agenda? And how can I carry this through into my academic career? The following section discusses my engagement—which continues into the present—with these questions.

A FEMINIST IS MADE...

"...At the Business School"

As discussed in the introduction, I believe a number of gender-related incidents made me into a feminist at a very young age. However, I also believe that one is born with a consciousness of gender inequality, which manifests during one's life either into eventually succumbing to the unequal status quo or developing into a feminist and activist—whether through academia or other mediums.

As the first year of my PhD came to an end, I started to develop into a more confident feminist researcher who could face criticism head on, rather than cower so that I would not upset anyone. I would hear comments on a daily basis from my PhD colleagues such as, *"Why are you researching this? Come on, you know women are kept at home because they are gems in our society, not like women in the West who are not respected. Look at me, I allow my wife to work and study. Why do you say all Arab men are the same, they are not?"* and I was told rather aggressively on another occasion by one peer (whilst waving his finger in my face), *"Make sure you say that the problems women face are from the culture, not Islam, ok? You have an obligation to do this for us. You are British, so you probably do not know this, but not all the Middle Eastern countries are the same, we have different cultures and customs, you know? So you need to read the literature on that and tell them this"*

In one breath I was an Arab woman who knew it all and was obligated to share my knowledge, and in another a British woman who did not know the difference between Islam and culture in the Middle East. I would calmly explain that I had a wonderful Arab and Muslim father who had six college/university-educated sisters and three university-educated daughters. He always encouraged our education and right to work. I would also highlight that one cannot deny that Middle Eastern countries hold some of the lowest female education, employment and entrepreneurship rates in the world. I was well aware this had nothing to do with Islam, as Islam called for gender equality in education, work and business ownership but was due to a controlling pervasive patriarchal system, which infiltrated the economic, political, social and domestic spheres. I would be nodded at in agreement, but quizzed again the next day nonetheless. Upon reflection, I find that I was subconsciously taking a Muslim feminist stance during these discussions. I believe I feared putting forward secular feminist ideas on the issue because they would be instantly debunked and I would be reprimanded for even discussing this other stance. Painful childhood memories came flooding back to me—I could not face being called a "bad Muslim girl" again.

Whilst most of these exchanges felt like a form of discussion, the most distressing confrontation I had was during the analysis stage of my thesis, as one of the male PhD students came up to me with a friend of his and said in an intimidating tone, "*This is the girl I told you about who is doing research on men and women in the Middle East...I hear you are in the analysis phase now. Listen; don't embarrass us [men]. Make sure we look good*". As uncomfortable as I felt in this situation, I glared at him and firmly stressed that I was a researcher who was following an academic process by writing up a literature review, building a theoretical framework, drawing up research questions, conducting interviews and following a scientific analysis technique; and therefore, the results were not up to me to shape, but would be theoretically grounded and academically sound. I began to worry that I was imagining these incidents and was being too "sensitive and emotional"— until I presented my research at a departmental meeting in front of the Management Studies faculty. At the end of my presentation, one of my PhD colleagues stated, "*Of course men should have priority in getting a job over women, regardless of their abilities. It is the man's job to take care of his family. Why would you want a man to not be able to provide for his family and have his kids go hungry while a woman gets the job*". Before I could answer his unfounded comment, other male colleagues jumped to my defence, explaining that that was not what I had said and he had taken my presentation out of context. It was a relief to see that it was not all in my mind.

There are two important points I must stress after sharing these narratives. Firstly, this was not just an Arab/Westerner issue, as the events described transpired at a business school, with a strong base in accounting, finance and economics, which meant that there was a general affiliation with objectivist, positivistic and quantitative methodologies in business research and that the importance of validity and generalisability of one's findings was paramount. After collecting my data in Saudi Arabia, I would hear comments from various colleagues who would state, "*What? You only have interviews with 13 women? You need questionnaires, at least 100*". I explained the nature of feminist epistemologies and methodologies, the exploratory and interpretive nature of my study, the lack of previous research to base my potential questionnaire on, the importance of interviews in hearing the women's voices rather than silencing them in recycled questionnaires and my lack of access to Saudi women participants, who were too afraid to partake in the study. However, my colleagues were never fully convinced of the study's scientific validity and contribution. Even on my viva day, I was still mocked by some who stated that they could not believe I had passed with an empirical data set of 13 interviews. Secondly, I was given support from many Arab male colleagues, who admired the discussion of delicate issues in my study and encouraged my research agenda by bringing back interesting books on women in the Middle East from their home countries when they went back for summer. Many thanked me for paving the way for their daughters' future. These moments were precious and appreciated.

"...During my Interviews"

My feminist identity was not just tested by men, but by women also. Indeed, as I entered the office of one of my interviewees, a strong and successful Saudi entrepreneur, I introduced myself in Arabic. She looked at me and said, "*Oh, you are Arab?*" I replied, "*Yes, I am, my dad is Syrian*" (until this moment, we had only communicated in English via email). She snapped, "*But your email address says your last name is Studholme; that is not an Arabic last name*". I said, "*Ah yes, my university added my husband's last name to my email address*". She scowled and then laughed as she replied, "*Wow, you are here to research us oppressed Saudi women, when your Western culture makes you take your husband's last name and lose your identity. Who is the oppressed one now? I do not understand how any woman would accept that for herself".*

My feminist researcher identity took many shapes during the interviews with these incredible women. I had briefly communicated my background and research aims with them either by telephone or email before my arrival and therefore, it was interesting to learn about the assumptions they had made about my identity. The clearest examples I can recall happened at the end of each interview when I asked them why they had agreed to participate in my study. In each interview I got one of three replies: either, *"I trusted you because you are an Arab and Muslim woman. You are one of us and won't portray us badly"*; or *"I trusted you because you are British and from a British institution and I know they instil good objective values in you to be fair and unbiased in portraying your data"*; and in one case an interviewee replied, *"Because I am also half-European and half-Arab and I believe we make the best researchers as we understand both sides".* I found these contrasting replies fascinating. I did not ask them to focus on myself, but simply to discover the reasons behind their agreement to participate. Furthermore, these women subconsciously (or arguably consciously) presumed an Islamic or secular feminist researcher identity for myself, which gave them trust and comfort to participate in a personal and sensitive study. The women, however, strongly affiliated themselves with an Islamic feminist identity. Indeed, every one of them justified her political contribution and legitimised her entrepreneurial identity by stating that the Prophet Mohamed's wives and daughters, our idols, were known to be entrepreneurs who were politically and economically engaged.

"...As an Early Career Researcher"

During and after completing my PhD I attended and presented papers at seven conferences focusing on the theme of gender in organisations, entrepreneurship, education and sociology in the United Kingdom and Europe. Whilst each conference was insightful and inspirational, I eventually found it frustrating that my abstract was read and automatically placed in an "international" themed group/stream. Indeed, by the third conference it became clear that because my title included the words "women" and "Saudi Arabia" I was added to a stream of research on women in "other" developing and third world countries, regardless of the contribution and purpose of my paper. It was fascinating hearing about gender issues in Iran, Indonesia, Tasmania, Brazil and India, but the contributions of these papers were not relevant to my research; neither was mine to theirs—and we knew this. I would look through the other streams at the conferences and realise my paper could have been better placed within other themes, even if those studies were based in the United Kingdom, United States or Canada. During the closing lecture at the last conference I attended, the organisers were boasting about the number of international abstracts they had received beyond western Europe and North America. I thanked them for this opportunity and voiced my concern that they in fact were still treating us as "the other" by placing us in themes that were implicitly deemed "international streams". It was as if researching women/gender in contexts outside of western Europe and North America was interesting but did not have significant philosophical, theoretical and methodological contributions to feminist research. Whilst our voices were provided with a platform to be heard, we remained (sub)consciously segregated from "mainstream" feminist research. In many ways this was regressive, as first-, second- and third wave feminisms have addressed these issues extensively; yet it seems that "other" forms of feminism remain regarded as secondary by some.

My biggest honour as an early career researcher took place in April 2015, as I was invited to be the first female keynote speaker at a conference at a university in Amman, Jordan. The Dean of the business school, a woman, had become aware of my research and asked me to present my research focusing on the importance of Arab women's economic and political contributions in the Middle East. The attendees were academics and non-academics from Jordan, the Middle East and North African region. My speech was the last during the final day of the conference after six academic and non-academic male speakers. As I took to the stage, it suddenly hit me—I had never presented to the very people I wanted to address for the past seven years. This made me nervous. At the end of my presentation, I was asked very interesting and constructive questions. Men gave me encouraging and overwhelmingly positive feedback. Women told me I was an inspiration and wished more Arab women would do such research. I was tremendously flattered and honoured. Of course, being within a business school environment, one male academic critiqued my findings for not being "generalisable". However, he seemed happy with my well-rehearsed feminist "justification" and explanation for my "depth rather than breadth" methodology.

After my presentation, a professor from the university pulled me to one side alone and confronted me. He harshly attacked me for being a "Western feminist", whose research was too "subjective". He stated that my work was academically weak with an imbalanced argument, as I did not discuss the negatives of women participating and being paid equally in the workplace. I kindly asked him if he could give me examples of the negatives of women equally contributing economically and politically, to which he replied, *"Well, when women work they face sexual assault and even rape, so it is safer to keep them protected in the home; why should she be subjected to this? They should not be mixing in the workplace. This is what men are like, it can't be helped"*. I did not know where to start. I realised that whilst most attendees were in agreement with me, a lot of work still needed to be done. Midway though my explanation that work and sexual assault are not directly correlated, he quickly cut me off and said, *"And why earn the same amount of money as men? As soon as a woman is highly educated and starts working and earning her own money she becomes independent. She becomes more demanding, picky and won't accept any man that asks for her hand in marriage. Then she is left a spinster. And if she is married, she neglects her home and her children... what is going to happen to the family and our society if women get equality in the workplace? The children will grow up misbehaving and be lost Muslims and useless citizens in our country."* We discussed these issues for a while and then I realised that I was not going to change his opinion in any part of this debate. I thanked him for his comments. I felt shaken up by this experience, as I never enjoy such confrontations.

As I turned to attend one of the seminar streams, a young Yemeni woman came up to me and said, *"Thank you for your presentation, it was interesting, but I don't understand, it really frustrates me, why are you fighting for us to work? You know it is the man's job to take care of his wife. She is a gem in his eye that he needs to preserve. This is what our religion says. Women like you are calling for us to work and earn money and now men are looking for brides who work so she can share the household bills. It is a big problem for us women now!"* I surmised that this woman held the Islamic fundamentalist feminist position (Yamani 1996), as she felt protected within the current classic patriarchal system (Kandiyoti 1988), which she legitimised within an Islamic framework. She seemed uneasy with the blurring of the dichotomous lines of the traditional gender roles when women participated in the workplace as men did. I explained that I believed a woman should have a fair choice and opportunity to work and take care of herself. I also explained that economically it has become almost impossible for many families to live off one income; and therefore, it made sense that women work and contribute to the household. Alas, she did not agree. She could not see how this could be empowering for women or families in society. I did not know enough about her class, education or family background, which are key factors in women's active resistance to such systems (Kandiyoti 1988), but it seemed that breaking away from the status quo was not something she could realise, regardless of her desire for it.

As I was walking down the business school corridor feeling disheartened, a young Jordanian woman with a colourful long flowing skirt and beautiful headscarf came up to me and held my hand. She looked into my eyes and said, "*Thank you Sophie. Thank you for coming from far away to tell us about your research. You have really inspired me, beyond what you can imagine. We need women like you. I am an ambitious and hardworking girl and I would like to do a PhD after I complete my master's one day. I think Arab women have so much to contribute to society. I think I can contribute a lot to my country*". My eyes filled with tears. I could not begin to describe to her how she had come at the perfect time and that I needed her in that moment just as much as she claimed she needed me.

My original perplexing question at the beginning of this chapter was, "You have to decide, are you one of us, or one of them", which I (sub) consciously evolved during the narrative of my academic journey to "What kind of feminist am I?" Amongst all the categories of feminism, I (and others) wonder, "Who am I representing?" Am I a "Western" or an "Arab" feminist? Am I a "secular" or "Islamic" feminist? Are these categories mutually exclusive? How do I fit into these categories in conferences and amongst my peers? However, these somewhat paradoxical incidents (where my hybridity was either welcomed or rejected) throughout my academic journey have made me realise that I did not need to decide what "kind" of feminist I was in order to 'be' as a feminist. My current passion and curiosity for my research subject, and the contribution to knowledge that I make, are not confined to one country or one continent or to a particular feminist approach. I am aware of the grave dangers of collectively placing women within one category without respecting the intersectional nature of women's lives (Crenshaw 1997; McCall 2005); but nonetheless, I feel that regardless of our nationality or feminist stance, many of us are fighting for the same things. We want gender equality and our human rights. We are striving for our freedom—our freedom to be educated, to work, to be paid equally, to be independent, to practice our religion, to be ambitious, to have families (or perhaps not have families) and be able to choose whether we would like to stay at home with our children or balance family life with work. We want to work in safe environments, where we are respected and commended for our efforts. We want our voices to be politically heard and represented—amongst many other wishes. Why does it matter what "kind" of feminist I am so early on in my career when I should be exploring my freedom to contemplate these notions, free from the social or academic pressure to commit to a label at this stage.

WHAT NEXT FOR THIS EARLY CAREER RESEARCHER?

Autoethnography has been an insightful tool in helping me think about my "hybrid" feminist role and in synthesising my story for this book chapter. Following a feminist autoethnography allowed me to link my personal story to the cultural, which emphasised the ever-evolving social construction of gender across cultural contexts and our constant (gender) identity negotiation process. I am aware of the vulnerability of this approach as I open myself up to criticism from both peers and non-academics, in the West and the Middle East. However, I believe that revealing my experiences as a bicultural early career researcher rather than a disembodied and disinterested third-person narrative provides a richer and more empowered illustration for the reader (Allen and Piercy 2005). Whilst at times it has been challenging, I have enjoyed focusing on the evocative "auto-" and "ethno-", being more emotional, culturally focused and evocative in my writing of this chapter. However, I have academically grounded my narrative in feminist philosophical and constructivist methodologies in the "-graphy" of my narrative. Drawing upon Richardson (2000a, b) I have consciously and reflexively departed from a particular position and specific time in my life, as an early career researcher; and hence, I do not claim that this text is intended to say "everything to everyone" but hope that it provides insights for feminist PhD students or early career researchers.

As for the answer to that binary question, "Are you one of us, or one of them?", I still do not have the answer, even after seven years as a "hybrid" British/Arab researcher. I do believe that all feminist approaches are inspiring, valid, useful, relational and heavily interconnected. Therefore, there is no rush to decide at this moment. However, the pull of holding one identity and membership in a certain feminist school of thought is still appealing; and, potentially, will become even more important to me over my career and provide a rich platform and centre from which I can develop my arguments over the course of my academic career. Time will tell.

NOTE

1. A complete-member researcher is defined as a complete member of the society being researched who has a stake in the beliefs, values and actions of other setting members. Being a member of the research group means that the autoethnographic interrogation of self and other may transform the researcher's own beliefs, actions and sense of self. The complete-member researcher must therefore be analytically reflexive in interrogating the self and writing up his/her findings (Anderson 2006). The idea of a complete-member researcher is not necessarily an approach I agree with, as evidenced by the discussion of being "in between" in this chapter.

REFERENCES

Abu-Lughod, L. (2006). Writing against culture. In E. Lewin (Ed.), *Feminist anthropology: A reader* (pp. 466–479). Malden/Oxford/Victoria: Blackwell Publishing.

Agarwal, B. (1995). *A field of one's own: Gender and land rights in South Asia* (Vol. 58). Cambridge: Cambridge University Press.

Ahmed, L. (1992). *Women and gender in Islam*. New Haven: Yale University Press.

Al-Ali, N. (2000). *Secularism, gender and the state in the Middle East: The Egyptian women's movement*. Cambridge: Cambridge University Press.

Allen, K. R., & Piercy, F. P. (2005). Feminist autoethnography. *Research Methods in Family Therapy, 2*, 155–169.

Anderson, L. (2006). Analytic autoethnography. *Journal of Contemporary Ethnography, 35*(4), 373–395.

Beauvoir, S. de. (1953). *The second sex*. London: Jonathan Cape.

Bochner, A. P. (2000). Criteria against ourselves. *Qualitative Inquiry, 6*(2), 266–272.

Butler, J. (1988). Performative acts and gender constitution: An essay in phenomenology and feminist theory. *Theatre Journal*, 519–531.

Butler, J. (2002). *Gender trouble*. New York: Routledge

Clandinin, D. J., & Connelly, F. M. (1994). Personal experience methods. In N. K. Denzin & Y. S. Lincoln (Eds.), *Handbook of qualitative research* (pp. 413–427). Thousand Oaks: Sage.

Coffey, A. (1999). *The ethnographic self: Fieldwork and the representation of identity.* London: Sage.

Crenshaw, K. (1997). Intersectionality and identity politics: Learning from violence against women of color. In *Reconstructing political theory: Feminist perspectives* (pp. 178–193). University Park: Pennsylvania State University Press.

Doucet, A., & Mauthner, N. S. (2008). Qualitative interviews and feminist research. In J. Brannen, P. A, & L. B (Eds.), *The handbook of social research.* London: Sage.

Duncan, M. (2004). Autoethnography: Critical appreciation of an emerging art. *International Journal of Qualitative Methods, 3*(4), 28–39.

Ellis, C., & Bochner, A. P. (2000). Autoethnography, personal narrative, reflexivity. In N. K. Denzin & Y. S. Lincoln (Eds.), *Handbook of qualitative research* (2nd ed., pp. 733–768). Thousand Oaks: Sage.

Ellis, C. (2004). *The ethnographic I.* Walnut Creek: AltaMira.

Flax, J. (1987). Postmodernism and gender relations in feminist theory. *Signs, 12,* 621–643.

Friedman, M., Metelerkamp, J., & Posel, R. (1987). What is feminism? And what kind of feminist am I?. *Agenda, 1*(1), 3–24.

Gadamer, H. (1975). *Truth and method* (G. Barden & J. Cumming, Trans.). New York: Seabury Press.

Hamdan, A. (2005). Women and education in Saudi Arabia: Challenges and achievements. *International Education Journal, 6*(1), 42–64.

Hamdan, A. K. (2009). Reflexivity of discomfort in insider-outsider educational research. *McGill Journal of Education/Revue des sciences de l'éducation de McGill, 44*(3), 377–404.

Holt, N. L. (2003). Representation, legitimation, and autoethnography: An autoethnographic writing story. *International Journal of Qualitative Methods, 2*(1), 18–28.

Hufford, D. (1995). The scholarly voice and the personal voice: Reflexivity in belief studies. *Western Folklore, 54,* 57–76.

Kandiyoti, D. (1988). Bargaining with patriarchy. *Gender & Society, 2*(3), 274–290.

Mauthner, N., & Doucet, A. (1998). Reflections on a voice-centred relational method. In *Feminist dilemmas in qualitative research* (pp. 119–146). London: Sage.

Mauthner, N. S., & Doucet, A. (2003). Reflexive accounts and accounts of reflexivity in qualitative data analysis. *Sociology, 37*(3), 413–431.

McCall, L. (2005). The complexity of intersectionality. *Signs, 30*(3), 1771–1800.

Mernissi, F. (1991). *Women and Islam: A historical and theological enquiry.* Oxford: Blackwell.

Mohanty, C. T. (1988). Under Western eyes: Feminist scholarship and colonial discourses. *Feminist Review, 30,* 61–88.

Mohanty, C. T. (2003). "Under Western eyes" revisited: Feminist solidarity through anticapitalist struggles. *Signs, 28*(2), 499–535.

Mojab, S. (2001). Theorizing the politics of Islamic feminism. *Feminist Review, 69,* 124–146.

Oakley, A. (1981). Interviewing women: A contradiction in terms? In H. Roberts (Ed.), *Doing feminist research* (pp. 30–61). London: Routledge and Kegan Paul.

Reed-Danahay, D. (1997). *Auto/ethnography.* New York: Berg.

Richardson, L. (1994). Writing: A method of inquiry. In N. K. Denzin & Y. S. Lincoln (Eds.), *Handbook of qualitative research* (pp. 516–529). Thousand Oaks: Sage.

Richardson, L. (2000a). New writing practices in qualitative research. *Sociology of Sport Journal, 17,* 5–20.

Richardson, L. (2000b). Writing: A method of inquiry. In N. K. Denzin & Y. S. Lincoln (Eds.), *Collecting and interpreting qualitative materials* (pp. 499–551). Thousand Oaks: Sage.

Sparkes, A. C. (2000). Autoethnography and narratives of self: Reflections on criteria in action. *Sociology of Sport Journal, 17,* 21–43.

Stanley, L., & Wise, S. (1993). *Breaking out again: Feminist ontology and epistemology* (2nd ed.). London: Routledge.

Treacher, A. (2003). Reading the other women, feminism, and Islam. *Studies in Gender and Sexuality, 4*(1), 59–71.

Wall, S. (2006). An autoethnography on learning about autoethnography. *International Journal of Qualitative Methods, 5*(2), 146–160.

Wall, S. (2008). Easier said than done: Writing an autoethnography. *International Journal of Qualitative Methods, 7*(1), 38–53.

West, C., & Zimmerman, D. H. (1987). Doing gender. *Gender & Society, 1*(2), 125–151.

Yamani, M. (1996). Some observations on women in Saudi Arabia. In M. Yamani (Ed.), *Feminism and Islam: Legal and literary perspectives* (pp. 263–282). New York: New York University Press.

PART III

Exploring Experience Through Innovative Methodologies

Exposing the "Hidden Injuries" of Feminist Early Career Researchers: An Experiential Think Piece About Maintaining Feminist Identities

Anna Tarrant and Emily Cooper

INTRODUCTION

There is increasing recognition within the academy, particularly among junior scholars, of the precariousness that early career researchers face when seeking a long-term, permanent position in academia, and the need to create spaces of support (Bazeley 2003; Gill 2009; Parreira 2015). This is underpinned by an emerging, although limited, dialogue that draws attention to what Gill (2009) has termed the "hidden injuries" of academia. In this experiential think piece, we contribute to—and extend—this conversation by reflecting on our own career histories and aspirations, and on the complexities and contradictions we face as early career feminist researchers.

In so doing, we seek to move towards a more critical and reflexive investigation of our experiences, contextualised by relevant literature. We do this as young women for whom the possibilities in advancing femi-

A. Tarrant (✉)
University of Leeds, Leeds, Yorkshire, UK

E. Cooper
University of Central Lancashire, Preston, Lancashire, UK

© The Author(s) 2017
R. Thwaites, A. Pressland (eds.), *Being an Early Career Feminist Academic*, DOI 10.1057/978-1-137-54325-7_7

131

nist research agendas in relation to men, masculinities and the pursuit of gender equality (Anna) and stigma, myths and ineffective regulatory policy surrounding sex worker communities (Emily) are a key motivation, especially within disciplines that are dominated by men. We adopt an autobiographical style to explore the tensions that arise when trying to maintain our feminist identities, especially when our practices, identities and motivations to pursue an academic career are called into question.

Key to our strategies of resilience are our regular online conversations, both public and private, which constitute our personal support network, and in which we discuss and work through the often-tricky and affective qualitative experiences of the contemporary academy. We describe this as an example of our collaborative, rather than individualised, style of working, seeking ways to progress together through support rather than competition. We hope that, in describing the strategies we adopt, we help others as they negotiate the ever-changing, fast-paced transformations of the academy, while also trying to maintain their feminist identities.

Like a number of feminist scholars before us, our writing and conversations represent a political and strategic act, bringing us together as authors and feminist researchers through a shared commitment and purpose. We recognise the method of autobiography as an additional form of empowerment. We are particularly motivated by the central tenet of North American and British feminism of the 1970s that the personal is political, which, at the time, provided opportunities for women to challenge their misrepresentation and discrimination, as well as the wider social frameworks enabling these (Valentine 1998). Influenced by postmodernist/poststructuralist thought of the 1980s and 1990s, autobiographical forms of writing became more prolific, particularly in the social sciences, as both methodological sources and as "methodologies" in themselves (Stanley 1993; Okely and Callaway 1992). While there are a number of forms of autobiography as method (Purcell 2009), "reflexive autobiography" particularly enables writers to explore individual subjectivity.

We begin our auto/biographical reflections with a brief overview of our biographies in the context of a highly masculinised academic environment. This is followed by analysis of some of the conversations we have had about the tensions we have faced and how we use technology to interrogate these experiences. We argue that this constitutes an important feminist "other" space beyond the institutional environment, where we have the opportunity to reflect on, and evaluate, these tensions and our approaches to them, both privately and publicly.

A Brief Career Biography of the Authors

We are both early career researchers currently working at British universities and have PhDs in Social Geography; a social science discipline that has traditionally valued objective science, and has long been critiqued as a masculinist discipline (Rose 1993). In the short time since we received our doctorates (Anna in 2011 and Emily in 2014), we have held multiple, short, fixed-term positions in academia (5 years and 3 years, respectively), sometimes concurrently with jobs outside of academia. We certainly are not following the individualised, male career trajectory upon which academia has traditionally been constructed: "undergraduate, PhD, perhaps a postdoc, lectureship, senior lectureship and so on" (Bagilhole and White 2013, p. 9). Such a trajectory has created tensions for us both, not least in relation to our feminist identities; on the one hand, we are critical of this trajectory and, on the other, we implicitly measure our success against it, even if we do not think we desire it. In this chapter, like Bagilhole (1993), we investigate aspects of the social and institutional environment that have contributed to these tensions and that sometimes mask our complicity when we attempt to "play the game".

Precarity and Turning Points

Employment in contemporary academia is increasingly precarious (Ivancheva 2015), which can be attributed to structural changes to universities as a result of economic recession, the rise of neoliberalism and austerity (Athelstan and Deller 2012). These processes have been accompanied by, and have arguably legitimised, extensive budget cuts and government intrusion into academic research and funding (Athelstan and Dellar 2012). Such processes directly affect the micro-politics of working in academia as a young woman, but more qualitative research about the experiences of early career researchers is warranted. We now briefly outline examples of direct challenges to our female and feminist identities as academics.

Anna

Sadly, I can recount several experiences of "cultural sexism" (Savigny 2014) in academia, involving both students and colleagues, experiences I have discussed at length with Emily online. The following extract, taken from my personal, reflective research diary, is a record of a comment that particularly challenged my identity as a woman and a feminist, and that we consider important to share here. It was made during a group conversation that had taken place with a senior female academic, involved in the Athena Swan programme:

Seminar leader: *"Why do you want your research to have impact?"*

Anna: *"Well, it's more than just about the job and the career. I really want to do something that makes a difference to people's lives."*

Senior female academic: *"I just wish to pick up on something you have said there and it's something that worries me about young, female academics, such as yourself. This idea that your career isn't important to you and that it comes second, is problematic. After all, the best way to make real impact is at professorial level, when you are more likely to attract research funding and be able to lead on research that will influence the lives of those you study".*

Alongside feeling embarrassed and distinctly not feminist, I felt like this was somewhat of a critical turning point (Holland and Thomson 2009) for me. The comments had brought to my attention the language and discourse I use, which are a manifestation of my insecure and fragile academic self (Knights and Clarke 2014), and offered an alternative. Upon critical reflection about the incident with Emily, however, it occurred to us that this senior academic was implicitly reinforcing the contradictions inherent in maintaining a feminist identity within the neoliberal academic environment. Notwithstanding the structural and institutional barriers women face in reaching senior positions in British universities, where they remain under-represented (Savigny 2014), her argument that I should explicitly acknowledge my career and desire for advancement was also implicitly advocating that I do what is necessary to achieve that; in other words that I follow the masculinist, neoliberal career trajectory in order to reach a position of power and, with it, the potential to create change. Her comment highlighted how my gendered and generational positions as a female, early career academic were potentially disadvantaging me, while she also advocated that I adopt particular practices that comply with the neoliberal and masculinist trajectory in order to achieve success.

So far, I have responded to this insight with small-scale changes to my academic practices, but changes that I consider important in maintaining a feminist identity. I recently obtained funding for an Early Career Research Fellowship, which I had been apologetic about—"I'm not sure how I got it!...Must have been luck!" In the desire to challenge this way of thinking, I took part in a research project called "Fellowship Ahoy: More than lucky?" This helped me take the time to recognise the years of hard work that went into successfully securing this funding, from networking and building relationships, to writing the bid. The tensions are still inherent, however. The philosophy of self-leadership and independence is arguably complicit with the individualised, masculine career trajectory, but recognising my success as more than just luck has been part of a process of personal growth and a challenge to the fragile and insecure subject positions that I tend to occupy. This gave me a voice and an alternative narrative that has more power to subvert than one that is fragile and insecure.

EMILY

One of the main challenges for me has been dealing with the everyday dialogues that centre on me being "the one in the temporary contract", whilst sharing similar duties with other mid- and established career academics. On several occasions, apparently "helpful chats", usually with senior male academics, that consistently referred to my being "exploited" and victimised, have proven to be complicit with the masculine patriarchal system that characterises academia. Despite hearts being in the right place and solidarity being shown, these conversations rarely held solutions (other than to leave academia) and served to reinforce the dominant, privileged position my male colleagues held, commenting on my (precarious) position while doing little to challenge it. These conversations exemplify that women's experiences in academia are still profoundly gendered and situated in institutional structures that reinforce hegemonic masculinities and the unbalanced value of women's academic contributions (Savigny 2014). My intention to fight on, supported and shared by my female colleagues like Anna, does create tension but is also a product of my need to protect my privilege as an academic woman (although not in relation to academic men) and as a feminist—desiring to achieve a position of power that will allow me to create change, that my well-meaning male colleagues are ironically trying to talk me down from.

The apologetic rhetoric Anna notes above also resonates with my own position in faculties dominated by science/environmental disciplines. The following conversation—one of my critical turning points—took place at the first internal faculty poster session I attended as a doctoral student. A senior male physics scholar looked at my poster and asked, "so…how has this got *anything* to do with the environment?" At first I wanted to walk out, but then I thought, "this is something I am going to have to get used to", and retorted, "What is your understanding of the environment? How would you define it? Just by fields and green? You live in an urban environment. That is how my project is environmental". He nodded and left.

I do consider this my first "academic win", but I was extremely uncomfortable about his condescending attitude. The out-of-place feeling it engendered intensified the precariousness that I already experienced as a part-funded, part-time, female PhD student. This also represents a tension for me. On the one hand, my defensive reaction is complicit with the competitive discourse and thus challenges my desire to dilute those practices that are characteristic of the normative trajectory. On the other, however, I consider confidently advocating for the essential role of my research to be a political feminist statement, that my research deserves a voice and is of value—both in my field, and in the more localised faculty.

There is no training available for this sort of micro-geographical struggle, but the ability to talk about these invisible barriers—and to create new spaces in order to do so—can begin to challenge the masculinised competitive trajectory and "cultural sexism" (Savigny 2014) that pervades academic environments.

FEMINIST IDENTITY AND "OTHER" SPACES

The above are examples of experiences that we discuss together by way of coping, building resilience and trying to make visible the structures that operate to influence our identities as feminist academics. They exemplify some of the injuries we have faced as early career academics and that we have sought to remedy through sharing stories and seeking mechanisms to exist—and even prosper—within the current academic mode of production (Stanley 1990). However, we are not passive agents of an oppressive system. Instead, we look to be productive about how we negotiate and manage the prevailing obstacles (Fritsch 2015) via our everyday micro-political practises. Our use of social media also provides us with feminist "other" spaces beyond our institutions through which to expose and challenge these injuries.

Friendship and Collective Coping: Talking Online

Following the feminist traditions of collaboration, support and collective working (Mountz et al. forthcoming) we see great value in supporting one another. We engage in regular conversations online. Twitter and Facebook not only enable us to include excluded and marginalised communities in our research area—especially sex workers (but also others working in academia, such as part-time, disabled, temporary contracted or unemployed academics)—in such dialogues. These extended virtual communities also widen the diversity of—and confidence in—networking opportunities, and start to challenge the notion of there being one common "good" way of progressing, "doing" academia or "being" an academic.

We also extend our private conversations by sharing our experiences more publicly, via personal blog sites, contributions to Twitter communities created via hashtags (i.e. #Acwri), peer writing groups (also in-house) and Skype. These online spaces have allowed us to air micro-struggles and to collectively share strategies and find solutions that work for the individual, thus allowing critical reflection on pressures such as the "publish or perish" imperative (Tarrant 2013).

Academic blogging is also increasingly advocated for its value in developing academic practice. In a content analysis of 100 academic blogs, Thomson and Mewburn (2013) found that academics frequently use them to write about their academic work conditions and policy contexts. Our own academic blog sites[1] provide us the space to do just this. They are driven by our feminist philosophies and are an example of how we attempt to strengthen feminist solidarity and empowerment in academia. In this sense, blogging has become an affective and emotional practice, reflective of our passion for academic life but also a key tool for maintaining a reflexive gaze on how patriarchy and capitalism operate within our working lives. A number of noteworthy blogs (e.g., The Thesis Whisperer; Academics Anonymous; From PhD to Life, The New Academic) are used in similar ways, to reflect on and discuss the experiences, challenges and opportunities faced by early career researchers trying to succeed in academia. These go beyond simply providing career advice in a pragmatic sense; they also provide a(nother) space to navigate through the emotional facets of contemporary academia and to be collectively reflexive, rather than silenced.

CONCLUSIONS

As young, female and feminist early career researchers, we have valued the opportunity in this chapter to share our gendered experiences of academia (Savigny 2014) and to outline examples of the otherwise "hidden injuries" of neoliberal academia (Gill 2009). We recognise these as products of persistent gender and generational inequalities in academia and the often implicit, but sometimes explicit, sex discrimination that affects female academics, as well as some men (Knights and Richards 2003). Indeed, it is our contention that many of these issues will remain hidden if our personal philosophies and biographies do not directly influence the ways in which we "play the game" and seek progression.

In our own feminist praxis, maintaining our feminist identities on an everyday basis has been marked by contradiction and is neither easy nor straightforward. However, we recognise that we do not have to be passive victims: we can also be agents of change and can take advantage of the possibilities offered by "other" feminist spaces beyond our institutions. We hope that, in sharing our experiences of the practices and forms of communication in which we are embedded and enmeshed on a daily basis, we become part of a growing feminist movement that challenges these gender inequalities and makes visible the structures that facilitate or create barriers to career progression for young, female and feminist early career academics.

NOTE

1. Dr Anna Tarrant, Diary of an early career academic, https://dratarrant.wordpress.com; and Dr Emily Cooper, Some of my academic musings, https://ecooper2site.wordpress.com/

REFERENCES

Athelstan, A., & Deller, R. (2012). Editorial: Theorising futures. *Graduate Journal of Social Science, 9*(2), 11–18.

Bagilhole, B. (1993). How to keep a good woman down: An investigation of the role of institutional factors in the process of discrimination against women academics. *British Journal of Sociology of Education, 14*(3), 261–274.

Bagilhole, B., & White, K. (2013). *Gender and generation in academia.* London: Palgrave Macmillan.

Bazeley, P. (2003). Defining 'early career' in research. *Higher Education*, *45*, 257–255.

Fritsch, N.-S. (2015). At the leading edge – does gender still matter? A qualitative study of prevailing obstacles and successful coping strategies in academia. *Current Sociology*, *63*(4), 547–565.

Gill, R. (2009) Breaking the silence: The hidden injuries of neo-liberal academia. In R. Flood & R. Gill (Eds.), *Secrecy and silence in the research process: Feminist reflections*. London: Routledge.

Holland, J., & Thomson, R. (2009). Gaining perspective on choice or fate: Revisiting critical moments. *European Societies*, *11*(3), 451–469.

Ivancheva, M. (2015). The age of precarity and the new challenges to the academic profession. *Studia Universitatis Babes-Bolyai-Studia Europaea*, *1*, 39–48.

Knights, D., & Clarke, C. (2014). It's a bittersweet symphony, this life: Fragile academic selves and insecure identities at work. *Organization Studies*, *35*(3), 335–357.

Knights, D., & Richards, W. (2003). Sex discrimination in UK academia. *Work, Gender & Organization*, *10*(2), 213–238.

Mountz, A. et al. For slow scholarship: A feminist politics of resistance through collective action in the Neoliberal University, *ACME: International E-Journal for Critical Geographies*. (forthcoming).

Okely, J., & Callaway, H. (1992). *Anthropology and autobiography*. Abingdon: Routledge.

Parreira, M. M. (2015). Struggling within and beyond the performative university: Articulating activism and 'work without walls'. *Women's Studies International Forum*. dOI: 10.1016

Purcell, M. (2009). Autobiography. In R. Kitchin & N. Thrift (Eds.), *International encyclopaedia of human geography* (pp. 234–239). Oxford: Elsevier.

Rose, G. (1993). *Feminism and geography: The limits of geographical knowledge*. Cambridge: Polity Press.

Savigny, H. (2014). Women, know your limits: Cultural sexism in academia. *Gender and Education*, *26*(7), 794–809.

Stanley, L. (1990). Feminist Praxis and the academic mode of production. In L. Stanley (Ed.), *Feminist Praxis: Research, theory and epistemology in feminist sociology* (pp. 3–20). London: Routledge.

Stanley, L. (1993). On auto/biography in sociology. *Sociology*, *27*(1), 41–52.

Tarrant, A. (2013). Academic writing month and the social landscape of academic practice. *The Guardian*.

Thomson, P., & Mewburn, I. (2013). Why do academics blog? An analysis of audiences, purposes and challenges. *Studies in Higher Education*, *38*(8), 1105–1119.

Valentine, G. (1998). "Sticks and stones may break my bones": A personal geography of harassment. *Antipode*, *30*(4), 305–332.

Reflecting Realities and Creating Utopias: Early Career Feminists (Un)Doing International Relations in Finland

Marjaana Jauhola and Saara Särmä

Introduction: Mission Impossible? Challenging the World Champions of Gender Equality

The above visual collage (Collage 1) depicts the lived experience of early career feminist scholars of international relations (IR) in Finland. It should make us pause. Darkness, phallic symbols, and zombie witches (from the online game 'Left for Dead') speak of the dark tones of being an academic—the grim and very masculine world of Finnish IR—in outspoken, but also in uncomfortable, ways. The images for the collage were 'crowd-sourced' from feminist IR scholars along with written reflections on what it is to do research and teach IR as an early career feminist scholar in Finland. Having read the responses, Saara used her artistic vision and worked the images into a mixed-media collage.

This piece of art conveys visually the emotionality of working in Finnish IR as a feminist scholar, and offers the viewer/reader an alternative way of engaging with these experiences as opposed to just reflecting on it

M. Jauhola (✉)
University of Helsinki, Helsinki, Finland

S. Särmä
University of Tampere, Tampere, Finland

© The Author(s) 2017
R. Thwaites, A. Pressland (eds.), *Being an Early Career Feminist Academic*, DOI 10.1057/978-1-137-54325-7_8

141

Collage 1

textually. Most of the time, in academia, the emotionality of these experiences is either missed or sidelined as unimportant. Or—which is at times even worse—they are thrown back by those in power at whomever has been brave enough to be vocal about them—labelling such experiences as problems of personality, improper and misfit behaviour, or scholarly immaturity. The myth that Finland has already achieved gender equality and the related celebration of Finland's supposedly being 'world champions' in gender equality (Julkunen 2010) is part and parcel of the wider context in which Finnish, and other Nordic, female and feminist scholars must operate and learn to cope (Husu 2001; Kantola 2005).

In this chapter, drawing from a collective memory process (see, e.g., Davies et al. 2013) with early career feminist IR scholars in Finland, we offer insights into the politics and analysis of power in the discipline of IR. The chapter unfolds in the following way: we will start by introducing the context of Finnish academic and higher education careers in general but will then paint a more specific picture of the structural inequalities that form the basis of the everyday experiences that will discussed in the later sections. We conclude the chapter by reflecting on the usefulness of combining textual and visual methodologies and where the next steps for feminist IR in Finland, and more broadly, may potentially take us.

Mind the Gender Gap: Statistics Reveal the 'Missing Women' Phenomenon

The Ministry for Education in Finland has identified a three-dimensional gender segregation in 'careers in research': (1) a vertical segregation, where the number of women decreases drastically the higher one climbs in the academic hierarchy; (2) a horizontal, persistent segregation between and within academic disciplines, especially between social sciences and humanities on the one hand and business and the natural sciences on the other; and (3) segregation in quality of employment, that is, in the gendered proportions of scholars holding permanent or temporary contracts within academia after defending their PhDs (Opetusministeriö 2006, p. 32). This is despite the fact that Finnish equality legislation (since 1987), and measures such as equality planning (since 2005), have mandated universities, and the Academy of Finland as the major governmental research funder, to draw up concrete plans for increasing gender equality within academia. According to statistics from 2010, roughly 50% of PhD students, postdoctoral, and mid-career researchers in the Finnish academy are female, and just 24% of professors. When these statistics are compared with the other Nordic countries, Finland actually seems to be doing better in all these categories (NIKK 2014).[1] However, we feel IR presents a rather different picture.

The discipline of International Relations was established in Finland in the 1960s. It is currently taught at five universities, and the number of full permanent professors in the country currently totals seven. The first feminist IR PhD thesis was defended in 2004 (Penttinen 2004), which has inspired at least one generation of feminist scholars to choose IR as their discipline either in Finland or elsewhere. As the amount of prominent feminist scholarship has increased, it has become globally acknowledged through international awards[2] and by a number of international publications (Kantola and Nousiainen 2009; Penttinen 2011; Jauhola 2015; Repo 2015; Särmä 2016; Vaittinen 2014).

Feminist IR has been (at least a small) part of IR curricula at most of the five universities since the late 1990s. Yet, maintaining a career as a feminist IR scholar is far from easy: the cut-off point of the 'gender scissors' is at the early career/postdoctoral phase. Although women have recently been hired in permanent professorships in political science, IR in Finland remains all male: all the full permanent professorships across the five universities have always been held by men, while women have held temporary senior lecturer and professor positions. One woman holds a permanent senior lecturer position (out of the seven senior lectureships that exist). A slight majority of undergraduate and graduate students and approximately half of postgraduate students are currently women.

Moreover, there is a recent generational shift in Finnish IR: the first IR professors hired in the 1960s have all recently retired, and they have been replaced by younger male professors in their 40s and 50s. This shift was directly reflected upon by several feminist scholars in our dataset—who have embarked upon their career in the past 15 years—in their responses as a turn towards anti-feminism: whereas the recently retired generation had pioneered in opening space for and actively supporting feminist work in the late 1990s and early 2000s, the new generation that now occupies the decision-making positions is closing ranks on the "malestream" and keeping feminism and feminists out. Feminists are dismissed both unofficially and officially, as will be discussed below. The contemporary context of neoliberalisation, marketization and streamlining of universities seems to be particularly harsh on those scholars who challenge the mainstream. Before moving to discuss the results of the collective memory process, we highlight here three structural factors that form the core of the problem for feminist scholars, and female scholars more generally.

First, the possibilities for females and feminists to pursue a career in IR take place in the rather peculiar structure of Finnish academia overall: there is no tenure system in place and the few permanent positions (senior lectureships and professorships) are rotated as 'musical chairs' when someone with a permanent position receives external research funding, thus opening up new temporary positions. Strategic temporary positions, such as professorships, add merit to the CVs of, in reality, mainly young men and may become useful if and when such positions are opened up later for permanent recruitment. Patriarchy is alive and well in Finnish IR, but it is masked as meritocracy. As Tara Brabazon puts it, "Patriarchy and its structures are still blocking women's progress into senior university positions, wearing the frock of meritocracy to clothe the injustice" (Brabazon 2014, p. 50).

Second, as Pietilä (2015) suggests, possible causes for the gender gap in academia may be the result of unequal treatment of men and women, which manifests both as direct/systemic and as indirect discrimination. In practice this means, for example, that merit standards are not gender-neutral, that men and women have unequal access to mentoring and social networks, and that academic excellence, and expertise in general, is constructed around gendered notions of expertise (see, e.g., Pietilä 2015, p. 7). All in all, career advancement takes place through informal and invisible processes, where the few gatekeepers, permanent professors and heads of department, play a crucial role. Most of the funding for junior academic positions comes from external funding, through research projects that are all based on short-term research contracts. Such positions are not publicly advertised, but are rather given as rewards to insiders or supervisees of professors (European University Institute 2014). Furthermore, external research funding available within Finland is extremely competitive, as less than 10% of applicants receive funding (Academy of Finland 2015).

Finally, not only do women fall short under the illusion of meritocracy (which relies on gendered notions of expertise and actively rewards young men), but women generally face different challenges to men. These include potential work–family conflicts and an inability to balance work and family life, or work and life in general. The personal costs of succeeding in an academic career are higher for women than men; for example, forming a family, which usually takes place at the early career phase, affects women more acutely than it does men. We find it important to shed light on the experiential side of these structural forms of discrimination; thus we approached fellow and former early career feminist IR scholars to reflect upon what all this means in our everyday lives. Before moving to these accounts, however, we will discuss the methodology used in our approach.

Collaging and Collecting Memories of Lived and Embodied Academic Selves

Our research methodology for this collective and reflective process was inspired by several recent and ongoing textual and visual attempts to collectively share experiences within academia. These include auto-ethnographical approaches to international relations (Inayatullah 2011; Martini and Jauhola 2014), collective biography as feminist methodology (Palmusaarinenojala 2014; Davies et al. 2013), the work of the

Bordering Actors research collective (2014)[3], collage research (Särmä 2014) and exploring collaborative methods as a critical methodology for social science (Guillaume 2015).

Collective memory work and collective biography, for example, are a set of methodologies that were developed primarily in the context of the sociology of education, drawing on the works of Frigga Haug (Haug et al. 1987). This is not a method that one should follow precisely but rather a process that provides possibilities for action (Davies et al. 2013, p. 684). Memories, recollections and, in our case, visual representations are brought into a "diffractive relation with one another" (Davies et al. 2013, p. 684). According to Guillaume, "collaboration can be a critical methodology in social sciences, namely as a critical process of knowledge production, management and valorization" (Guillaume 2015, p. 189). Moreover, "collaboration as a mode of research also implies a particular way of understanding intellectual activity and presentation of research—a dialogical mode of approaching the generation of knowledge" (Guillaume 2015, p. 192).

In our approach, we embraced the focus on the mundane and everyday experience, expecting that our intervention would allow us to "name the daily structures, stories and scenarios that undermine and minimize women in universities" (Brabazon 2014, p. 48). We also recognize that, although we have specifically targeted our questions at feminists, some of the experiences have more to do with 'being a woman' or 'man' in academia, whilst others are specific to that of 'being a feminist' and 'doing feminist work'.

We approached colleagues who had, in their works and interaction with the discipline, self-identified as feminists and contributed to the study of international relations. We approached around 20 early career and senior scholars[4] who had self-identified in a loose and wide sense as participating in the feminist IR research environment and asked them to write in response to the following questions:

1) On their experiences as early career (post-doc) feminists: what experiences, challenges and survival strategies have you met and used in the context of Finnish international relations/affairs?
2) What is your vision (realistic or utopian) of feminist international relations in Finland?

In total, we received answers from half of those we approached. The answers were read by both of us, reflected upon and then collaged together thematically. We used a mix of individual and collective collage methodology in this process (on individual collaging, see Särmä 2014). We will include all of our participant data within double quote marks, but without a reference, to make it clear which statements come from our dataset.

In addition to written texts, we also invited participants to send images that represent or relate to the themes in our questions. Images could be photos, screen captures, scraps from magazines or books, links on the internet and so on. These two sets of images were then worked into two collages (Collages 1 and 2). Collaging is a sense-making project, which aims to engage the senses beyond just our intellect (Särmä 2014; Sylvester 2009). A rationalising mode of making sense of the experiences of early career feminists in Finnish IR pushes the affective dimensions aside, yet these are equally important, if not more so, in defining one's place and possibilities in academia (see, e.g., Ahmed 2010, 2015). Visuality is a useful way of highlighting the emotional aspects of working in Finnish IR. As

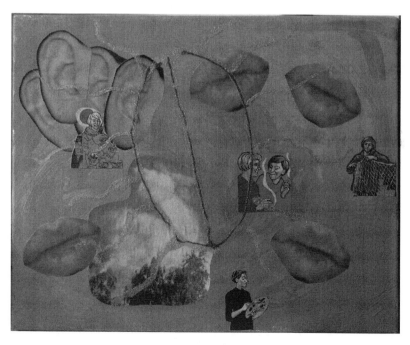

Collage 2

politics and power are present in the affective everyday encounters early career feminist scholars have with the malestream of Finnish IR, recalling and valorising emotionality textually and visually is important to us. In that sense, this chapter reports the 'past histories of contact', which relate to the particular power structures of the academic discipline of IR in Finland (see Ahmed 2004, p. 7; Irni 2013, p. 348).

Here Saara's individual artistic vision defines what the end result looks like: she chose which images to use; some of the images from the collective image set are repeated, and the sizes of the images vary. In other words, here the individual artist makes aesthetic choices using the collectively collated material. It would be possible to make the collages collectively, but for the purposes and resources available for this particular project we chose a mixed approach. We, however, acknowledge that the final writing process for this chapter follows a more canonical academic approach and reiterates subject positions of being researcher and researched. Yet the collective process will continue after this writing process is over. We will use this text as a basis for a feminist academic workshop that was organised in 2016, allowing us to use the text as material for further collaging, sharing experiences and possible activism. The rest of the chapter draws on the experiences and dreams shared with us during the spring months of 2015.

Janus-Faced Finnish IR: Living With Contradictions

In this section we focus on the questions of lived and embodied experiences of pursuing IR as a feminist scholar. We raise eight themes that each speak of and to a male-dominated, male- and masculine-normalised, academic discipline with limited possibilities offered for female and feminist scholars. All this reiterates the affective side of Collage 1.

Embodied IR and Outright Sexism

Simply to be asked the question about feminist experiences in Finnish IR brings out the affective nature of lived experience. The encounter with the question itself brings "back bad memories and experiences that one rather has wanted to forget". Furthermore, the question provokes reflections on the problematic relationship with the 'discipline'. Memories of an experience provoke feelings of shame, being sidelined and humiliated, and other unwanted feelings such as anger.

These feelings are furthermore located in the body as aches and the "taste of metal in my mouth". The feeling of being ashamed is not only internalised and targeted towards oneself, but also towards the discipline of IR, which feels violent and aggressive, but also grey and boring (Soreanu 2010; Soreanu and Hudson 2008). The feelings of being ashamed of the discipline relate to direct experience of sexual harassment and outright sexism, as this example illustrates:

> "Is the feeling of shame the result of being a young female researcher in a male-dominated department where my other (male) colleagues told me that I was hired because the head of the department wanted to have sex with me—or, when I realised that observation was true? Or was it even earlier, when as an undergraduate student I had to listen to chauvinist jokes, gendered hints and sexual harassment?"

Watching Male Colleagues Climb the Career Ladder: Subtle Sexism
Subtle sexism is also all too common. It happens with mundane gestures and comments, but also more strategically in recruitment situations and promotional situations. Male colleagues seem not to share similar experiences. Even for those who were slower to finish their PhDs, it seems to be easier for them to find salaried positions, networks and a firm 'IR identity'. It further seems that men are supported more, and are directly encouraged to apply for positions, whereas women have to struggle through websites to find out about calls for applications. Situations repeated all too often include the following: "A male doctoral student is asked about the stage of their project and offered positions and funding, even when a woman colleague at the same stage is standing right there!" Negative evaluations or indifference can at times be turned into strategic opportunities to enter the discipline/department, such as temporary part-time/hourly-based teaching positions and secretarial and administration jobs—unthreatening posts in terms of the career competition between doctoral students since they do not offer upward career advancement.

The feelings of being an outsider become magnified because Finland as a context for international relations (academia, politics and the NGO sector) is small—the overall population of Finland is just 5.5 million. This, on the one hand, makes connecting and networking relatively easy, but on the other, leads to clique formation and feelings of claustrophobia.

Indifferent Handmaidens

Even though the circles are small, feminists recollect feelings of not being taken seriously as contributors to the discipline. Reactions vary from remaining quiet and displaying neglectful indifference to aggressive and dismissive attacks. It is not uncommon to witness a male professor attacking feminists' work dismissively and maliciously in seminars. If you cannot take the attacks, it is seen as a personal weakness and scholarly immaturity—constituting embodied expressions of male dominance of IR, to which we return later in this chapter.

These hostile attacks are based on at least the following three ideas: one, that feminist engagement with international relations is not IR (Tickner 1997; Weber 1994; Zalewski 2007; Penttinen 2004, pp. 13–21); two, although 'gender' can be recognized as a 'cutting-edge' approach in IR, in reality gender is actually used as a concept in a positivist manner that has nothing to do with how feminist and gender studies scholars have been debating it for decades, (Elias 2015); three, well-meaning advice may rely on the idea that gender is 'too narrow' an approach: "Even though I have studied gender in a number of different political phenomena, internationally and nationally, producing both empirical and theoretical work, it does not count as a 'broad range'".

"Sometimes a feminist woman receives well-meaning career advice, such as, 'You should broaden your horizons, don't be doing only gender/feminism as it is so limited, if you want to get a job, you need to demonstrate that you can do a broad range of things in the field,' or 'There are jobs outside of academia, you know.' The message really being, 'Don't think we'll ever hire you'. Of course, they will commend her for all the secretarial and admin work she's done: 'Oh you are so effective, things run so much better now than when [he] was in charge'".

At times these dismissals make it to official institutional records: "The research profile of x does not represent the way in which the discipline is taught at this university. Instead, the person studies gender" (extract from a review report). While, at times, there simply are "too many applicants doing gender".

Given the opportunity to teach, feminist scholars are micro-managed—a form of controlling the feminist content of taught modules and supervision. This micro-management can still come as a surprise:

"At times, even feminists have to come to terms with the 'myth' of equality: having practiced international affairs in various expert and activist positions with like-minded colleagues, it comes as a shock to realize that integration of such perspectives to syllabus, teaching content, thesis seminars and supervision is openly and at times aggressively opposed".

Despite the fact that 'doing gender' catches the eye of committees during recruitment processes or research funding evaluations, the everyday feeling of general indifference prevails: "I don't think most of the people at my department in Finland even know what I am researching, or care". This feeling seems to get worse after having defended one's PhD, as scholars are left alone when PhD supervision is over, whereas regular PhD seminars at least provide a direct peer support network. Given the increased competition for global recognition through international university rankings, and given that state funding of Finnish universities depends on the level of documented 'internationalization' (controlled by the amount of outbound/inbound international visiting fellowships), scholarly attention is reserved for invited speakers at the expense of focusing on engaging with the work of one's own colleagues.

"I am a Feminist. I am a Dissident."

Fifteen years ago Professor Cynthia Weber recalled the reactions to her queer feminist work in IR the following way:

> "[t]hese arguments over the years have provoked two general sorts of responses—either outright hostility and dismissal or the much more frequent response of audience members joining in the conversation with their own gendered anecdotes. But the effect has often been the same—to make sex, gender, and sexuality studies a sideshow to the main event of the 'serious' theory or history. This book repackages the sideshow as the main event. It is *not* 'for the boys'. It is about them". (Weber 1999, p. xii)

This observation, we argue, is the key to understanding why the gatekeepers can be so hostile and dismissive: because it is 'about them'. Raising questions about how power, expertise and academia are gendered, racialized and sexualized is uncomfortable because its breaks the illusion of meritocracy and makes visible the inter-generational webs of relationships and gratitude)—or the lack of it—attached to 'passing down' knowledge and scholarly positions (Halberstam 2006, p. 103). We have to face the possibility that those in power in Finnish IR perhaps did not always get to where they are on pure merit.

The previous generation of (male) IR professors was regarded as having been generous to feminists and to feminist concerns, yet sometimes ignorant about feminist work:

"One of the old men of IR told me a few times, 'I don't quite get what you're trying to do here with this feminism and gender thing, but am sure it'll turn out to be great'. And I know others had similar experiences. They supported me in many ways, and when I was writing my MA thesis it was clear that I did not have to do a lot of justifying as to why I did feminist IR, because 'we already had someone who did a feminist doctoral dissertation, so it should be clear that it is a fully acceptable approach'".

These days being a dissident is more difficult, yet we keep trying. Some of us suffer from a deep dissatisfaction with IR, yet are drawn back in over and over again and want to remain. As Peter Mandaville (2011, p. 196) put it, "I hate IR, but it's where lot of my favourite people live... so I keep coming back to it". Collectively shared feelings of neglect, dismissal and outright discrimination towards feminism and feminist ideas have simultaneously meant that, since the institutionalisation of gender/feminist strands within academic associations (such as the British International Studies Association and the International Studies Association), collegial networks, meetings, workshops, conferences, and even new journals and online publication avenues (Duck of Minerva, Disorder of Things, Feminist Academic Collective) have provided important spaces—to share not only academic approaches and debates, but also affective care.

Survival Strategies: Disengagement from IR, Embracing Feminism

Alone in the pit, in the dark, in the woods.
　Seek the salvation, look, not to the light,
　but, into the eyes, of the stranger.
　To the friend, you don't know, why he's here,
　but he is, and he takes,
　and he holds and he saves. (Hast 2015)

This poem connects its verbal reflections directly with the visual (Collages 1 and 2) in an interesting, yet perhaps troublingly gendered (and indeed religious), way. How does one cope with a working environment which at times presents itself as openly hostile and mostly as subtly aggressive? Multiple strategies came up in answers we received, and here we highlight seven: giving up, turning vulnerability into a strength, use of humour, shifting focus into transnational spaces, turning discrimination into advocacy and activism, reaching out to informal caring networks and zigzagging between researcher communities.

First, some of us give up and get out altogether:

> "I gave up after ten years of trying. I could no longer take the hate towards women—that was not only addressed towards me as a person, but also towards the theoretical perspectives that I was seen to represent—critical research—although retrospectively I do not consider my thoughts at that time that critical!"

Second, some of us turn vulnerability into strength:

> "After I finished my PhD I found myself alone and isolated from the discipline and projects. I had no one to work with. I felt my value as a human being diminish in front of my eyes, but, luckily, I was able to challenge that tendency 'to be something for someone else' and transform it into embracing vulnerability: the willingness to let myself be seen".

Third, others cope through humour and laughter (Särmä 2014, pp. 40–42; Vaittinen 2015). Yet reaching such a positive stage of mind can be a major emotional process: "I had to go through a grieving and letting go process in order to cope". Letting go may mean disengagement from the formal discipline, as defined by permanent staff members through syllabus and curriculum, or the "male-dominated blah", as one respondent bluntly categorised the whole discipline.

This in practice means relocation to other disciplines, or even to another country temporarily or permanently. "I am only worried about when that will end, and if that will mean the return of all the anxieties that I am currently managing to escape. I don't want to work in Finland's politics departments and have started to apply for jobs abroad". Moving elsewhere temporarily, however, potentially hides one away from the fact that these problems do exist elsewhere too; and thus, one cannot be sure if basing oneself permanently in another national context would make things better in the longer run. Given the overall—and global—context of the neoliberal university, such experiences are being expressed simultaneously by other IR scholars, as well as also feminist scholars more generally across the globe (see, e.g., Currie et al. 2002), as this current volume shows.

Fourth, another approach, used more widely by feminist activists outside academia, is to turn the emotional and collective engagement towards
transnational spaces, such as the British International Studies Association
(Gendering IR working group) or the International Studies Association
(Feminist Theory and Gender Studies section), and increasingly, towards
various loose social media networks (email lists, Facebook groups, Twitter),
as well as feminist panels at international conferences.

Fifth, turning vulnerability and experiences of discrimination into advocacy, and retelling the history of feminist scholars of IR, are both seen as
potential coping strategies:

> "What helps me to overcome the discrimination is the thought that what
> happened to me will remain in the archives of the departmental council as
> potential research material for feminist scholars of the future; aggression is
> documented loud and clear".

Sixth, for many, finding feminist colleagues and nurturing informal support networks is the key to survival. The best parts of experiential collegial
solidarity have been colleagues' open-mindedness and non-judgementality
and the friendships that have formed. Perhaps somewhat surprisingly, collegiality and support can also come from non-academic spaces, for example, from state 'femocrats' (Yeatman 1990)—female and gender equality
bureaucrats in government ministries who often share similar experiences
of discrimination, but in the context of state administration.

Finally, at times one becomes an academic nomad, zigzagging between
communities, from one university to another—or from one department
or discipline to another—or taking up a temporary job at a research or
policy institute. This may mean, for example, commuting to another city
several hours away for a year or two. Emotionally this includes reducing
expectations to zero as regards the possibilities that the discipline of IR
can offer for a feminist scholar and not trying to take up the kind of work
that would be recognized as 'proper IR' by the powers that be. But it also
has consequences for work–life balance and management of work-related
stress at the expense of friends and family. Studies of gendered labour
markets and work–life balance in Finland suggest that men in expert and
leadership positions at work are still more likely to have a spouse and
children than women in similar positions, who are more likely to be single
with no children than their male counterparts (see, e.g., Kartovaara 2003).

Reverse Survival Strategy: Play Along

Here we describe three examples of 'playing along': toning down one's feminist agenda, being the token feminist and letting the men play along. First, some strategically choose to distance themselves from explicitly feminist approaches and to play within the rules of the malestream (or male IR [MIR,]). While adopting a feminist approach may be personally enjoyable, some want to avoid being labelled as 'too feminist':

> "Taking a feminist approach is like going through a little open gate; if you spend too much time enjoying the fresh and nourishing grass on the [feminist] side, you may be too 'heavy' to fit the narrow gate and come back to eat the (seemingly) greener grass [sources of funding, success in recruitment and forums of publication] on the [mainstream] side."

Recounted examples of going 'too far' in feminism in the responses included 'queering IR' and 'too radical' notions of gender that would question the traditional binary gender division. Here we find an interesting connection between disciplining from the outside/mainstream to self-governance and disciplining from within the feminist community, which are qualities of a 'good neoliberal citizen'. This is despite the fact that, internationally, queering the discipline and engagement with critical feminist theory are well established in feminist IR (Peterson 1999; Weber 2014).

Second, sometimes it is easy to play along, because one is accepted as the necessary token feminist to 'tick all the boxes':

> "Some IR men know that in this day and age you cannot really publish an edited volume without including a feminist chapter, so they will use you strategically".

But this playing along has an emotional downside to it:

> "because they cannot give you any substantial feedback and there is a huge pressure not to mess up because you feel like you are standing in for a whole scholarly community. So if I do bad feminist work, they'll end up thinking that all feminist work is crap".

Finally, while feminists can let male colleagues play along with feminism and enter feminist spaces, it may end up being a double-edged sword, as

feminists are not rewarded for doing feminist work. Instead, male colleagues will reward themselves for having engaged with feminism:

> "While women feminists are seen as doing overly political work, the sound-
> bites of feminism like 'personal is political' are taken up by those sympa-
> thetic to feminism to a certain extent and suddenly the arguments get heard.
> At those times it seems that appearing as a feminist ally seems to be more
> important than an actual engagement with feminist work. Once a Finnish IR
> professor actually applauded himself for having gone to listen to a feminist
> panel at a conference. Apparently they need special rewards for engaging
> with feminist work".
>
> "I guess to go to a feminist panel as an ignorant man will be uncomfort-
> able and there's some of that emotionality involved, feelings of marginaliza-
> tion and exclusions that we feminists are so well used to by now. What really
> makes privilege visible is to go to that uncomfortable space where you are
> no longer the most privileged subject who's able to define the rules of the
> game".

However, the problem remains, participants in our dataset suggest,
that most male IR scholars do not actively consult or reference feminist
work, but instead make judgements based on certain ideas they have about
feminism.

Whereas male feminists are regarded as more legitimate and, our data
suggests, have their voices taken more seriously in the discipline of IR,
female feminists are often considered to be too aggressive. Indeed, male
feminists are taken more seriously and seen as facilitators between non-
feminists (or even anti-feminists) and female feminists—on the grounds
that they are more neutral and better suited for this negotiation. Thus,
there is a gendered division in feminist scholars' experiences when it comes
to the possibility of advancing one's career and gaining the position of a
scholar who is taken seriously or a scholar who has 'made it'. These experiences clearly problematize popular claims such as that engaging men in
talking about and promoting gender equality and feminist goals will automatically lead to progress and the abolition of varying forms of misogyny
(see, e.g., #heforshe campaigns).

Re-Imagining What the Core of the Discipline Is

> "The first book I read in IR was a feminist one—I thought that was the
> mainstream!"

Entering the field 'sideways' provides perspective: being a practitioner or activist, or having a general social scientific non-IR basic education has provided important insights into seeing the boundaries of the discipline, and potentially breaking them:

> "The mainstream is detached 'from any lived reality' and [led me to] decide to 'educate oneself on gender, politics, sociology and anthropology'".

Some have experienced what it feels like when those in power in IR have supported feminism, and in fact have encouraged younger scholars to explore feminism:

> "In the early 21st century a senior male scholar provoked me to write my first article using a feminist approach. He saw that peace and development research were declining in their appeal and critique but feminist research seemed to be a powerful and promising critical movement".

> "Back at the turn of the century the biggest names of feminist IR were invited to Finland to teach courses and many feminist books were included in the curriculum. For a while there the very first book anyone reads in undergrad IR was a feminist book... So this previous generation did not shy away from feminism, even if they did not always understand all that it was about. They may have made a sexist joke every now and then, but they always knew feminism was an important part of IR".

These quotes illustrate how internalized sexism is part of the everyday practices of the scholarly community: the price of admission into IR as a feminist scholar is that one has to try to remain unmoved by, or even laugh along with, occasions of outright sexism—at least on the surface. It is entirely plausible to imagine a Finnish IR where at least one of the cores is feminist research. In fact, maybe it is not really a matter of imagination, but a material possibility: Finnish feminist IR might just need to be located in other institutional settings where the malestream is not given a place.

Do Not Romanticize the Solidarity of Female and Feminist Colleagues!
Future visions of feminist IR (FIR) included notions of harmonious cooperation:

> "What we need, and what we will get, is unity that can lead to big funding opportunities. I hope we won't judge each other."

Yet, if we now freeze the image of the female and feminist community as non-competitive and wholeheartedly supportive and inclusive for all, there is a danger of elevating feminists to super-humans:

> "Jealousy and rivalry is part of life, and FIR can hardly escape human tendencies. But so far I have felt nothing but proud of my fellow researchers, and I am sure there is a bright future for us scholars."

Associating feminists with being non-competitive and inclusive troublingly reiterates a rather gendered stereotype of women being more sensitive, caring and 'motherly', and further silences experiences of discrimination and marginalization that arise from within either feminist IR circles or more generally among Finnish women and gender/queer studies circles. It is not only the IR men in power, but women too, who work against feminism in IR:

> "Don't assume that all female scholars would agree with your feminism (in public). My other PhD supervisor (younger female professor) did not consider feminism as suitable for any 'objective' research in political science. Instead, my other supervisor (older male professor) encouraged me actively to learn more about the feminist theoretical traditions and approaches, even if I would not end up using them in my own research".
>
> "BUT, the feminist community is not necessarily an easy and welcoming community either, as various experiences of having been left out as an outsider, or questions of 'minority issues' (such as indigenous Sámi questions or studying Islam) have been ignored/marginalised".

'Add-gender-and-stir' type approaches and the study of problems related to women can be seen as legitimate in Finland's wider IR and political science community. However, explicitly feminist work is often seen as too radical. This is a twofold issue: on the one hand, feminist research is not seen as 'proper' research but as activism and politics. On the other hand, it plays into the myth that gender equality has already been achieved and that therefore, because things are apparently so positive in Finland, focusing on feminist issues is a waste of taxpayers' money, which should be allocated to research that addresses 'more serious and pressing issues'.

Envisioning Feminist Utopias for Alternative Visions of Feminist International Relations (FIR)

Collage 2 represents the ideal, collegial community of love and caring and is constructed from more uplifting images crowd-sourced from our respondents. Intervisual references are made to the Finnish author, painter and scriptwriter Tove Jansson, who became internationally famous for her Moomin characters, but whose feminist fame is based not only on the complexity of her character and career, but also on her rebellious nature and her unconventional choices in life.

The respondents reacted to our question about feminist futures in different ways: some were not able to see any positive future ahead, whereas others used the misery and negative feelings and experiences to work out a positive future. Most positive visions included working towards openness, a lack of hierarchy, and compassion. In these visions:

"More diverse and multicultural [IR] brings in the lived experiences of Finns of colour/of a nascently multicultural Finland into its work, overcoming false dichotomies of the 'outside world' vs. the 'protected inside'".

"feminist research has a strong presence in all universities in Finland, and because it is strong it is open to internal constructive criticism... recognition of multiple feminisms and the ability to work with the productive tensions within feminisms. We should take steps out of our comfort zones. Furthermore, I hope for a more radical, active, communal, philosophical approach—more hard and sensitive at the same time—feminist approaches in Finnish IR and social sciences more broadly".

Yet, some consider joining the discipline of IR as creating a dystopic future for them because "[It is] difficult to think utopias, as 'survival mode' is on".

"I want to believe alternatives are possible, but I taste metal in my mouth when I am told everything will be fine and your dreams will come true if you just go about doing what you love—should we not try to expose wrongdoings?"

"If I got a job, it would be a daily struggle against sexism, indifference and chauvinism that would burn me out and make me bitter".

"In my future vision, either there is no feminist IR in Finland, or it is in the hands of the very few persistent and angry women, barely breathing marginal activity—as it is now. Talented female and feminist researchers are capable of 'leaving on a jet plane'".

Which some of us have in fact done already—to work in academia elsewhere, or build a career in other international tasks such as humanitarian work, whence some of us have escaped to do the critical reflective work of humanitarianism instead (Martini and Jauhola 2014). Is it a spiral, if not a tunnel, without light at its end?

No Conclusions, but New Beginnings for Feminist IR in Finland?

"Feminists need to find places where they can work and be happy doing it. The fact that this study is being done probably says a lot about how hard it is to find those places".

Research quoted earlier in this chapter has shown how feminists face clear discriminatory structures, which usually materialize at the post-doctoral stage. Our aim has been to add a personal, yet collective, experiential level to this discussion. Our colleagues' diverse responses, discussed in this chapter, illuminate textually and visually how what first appears as a local experience in fact resonates with that of other contexts of International Relations and neoliberal academia more broadly.

The initial idea for this chapter emerged at the end of 2014 when we were jointly packing and emptying our offices, as the latest of our temporary contracts with the university were coming to an end and we were signing on for unemployment benefits. Instead of dealing with feelings of disappointment, desperation and anger in isolation, we wanted to draw attention to these lived experiences collectively, in order to gain and give support to each other, document these experiences and make them visible.

Moreover, we wanted to take up the challenge raised by our colleague Elina Penttinen (2013), and create a scholarly space that would be open for other kinds of emotional and affective aspects:

"In academia we have normalized a culture of separate selves struggling and competing with each other for some imagined prize of prestige or recognition that is always futurebound. Also, as long as we believe that the world of academic scholarship is about struggle, competitions and getting ahead by putting others down, that is the world we create and reinforce. There is something in academic culture that has normalized a negative critical approach to the way research is supposed to be reviewed and discussed.

This often turns into demeaning and egotistic practices that are more about building one's position by proving others wrong. There's a sense of purpose and meaning found in looking for weaknesses in other people's texts and research designs. It is truly peculiar how in the academic scholarship of IR we can spend time criticizing the world out there, and the people in power, and still maintain a position of treating each other within academia in negative, often unethical, though perhaps unconsciously so, ways. ... Conditioning into academic practice... a practice of hostility and negativity only creates more of the same". (Penttinen 2013, p. 112)

"The ethics of loving-kindness, shared joy and empathic compassion ... are not intended as a prescription of an ideal that we should reach sometime in the future. Instead, the practice of loving-kindness in the scholarly community of IR is intended as a form of inquiry, a practice in the present moment, not a goal for the future." (Penttinen 2013, p. 113)

We hope this collective writing and collaging process will live up to these new potentialities. By recognizing the diversity of our experiences of the past and the potential future, our aim has been to create a collective snapshot of the present and the recent past for feminist IR scholars in Finland. Energies that started to flow after our initial abstract-writing and correspondence with those colleagues who participated in the data collection process of this chapter have both signalled to us that this reflective collective activity is something that could provide new feminist IR beginnings. Therefore we have decided to take our feminism in/about IR into concrete academic activism such as documenting all-male panels,[5] documentary storytelling, and using this text as a basis for further collegial feminist IR discussions locally and transnationally. We embrace the change—even if the change is only momentary and minimal, and at times remains invisible.

NOTES

1. Statistics for post-docs in Finland (females 52%–males 48%), Denmark (38%–62%), Norway (48%–52%), and Sweden (43 %–57%); for mid-career positions in Finland (52%–48%), Denmark (29%–71%), Norway (37%–63%), and Sweden (48%–52%); for professors Finland (24%–76%), Denmark (15%–85%), Norway (21–79), and Sweden (20%–80%) (NIKK 2014).
2. For example, Saara Särmä's honorable mention for Best Graduate Paper by the Feminist Theory and Gender Studies Section of the

International Studies Association (2012); Tiina Vaittinen's recent honorary award for the best graduate paper in Global Health (2015).

3. Bordering Actors is a research collective of three postdoctoral female scholars who publish their research as a collective rather than as co-authored publications. This emphasizes the mutual equality of the authors. See more at http://borderingactors.org/englanti/index_e.html

4. Due to the extremely small number of IR scholars in Finland and a need to secure anonymity, we use no names, nor do we use any positions, titles, locations or specific career trajectories that would be possible to track down from individual CVs, even though some of the respondents were ready to share their experiences with their names included. For the same reason, we are not able to give the exact number or other details of those approached, nor do we want to identify—even with pseudonyms—those whose responses we use in this text.

5. http://allmalepanels.tumblr.com/

REFERENCES

Academy of Finland. (2015). *Ask and apply roadshow 2015* [Online]. Available from: http://www.aka.fi/globalassets/10rahoitus/ask--apply/124_askapply_syyshaku_2015_en.pdf. Accessed 11 Sept 2015.

Ahmed, S. (2004). *The cultural politics of emotions*. Edinburgh: Edinburgh University Press.

Ahmed, S. (2010). Feminist killjoys (and other willful subjects). *The Scholar and Feminist Online*. Issue 8.3: Summer 2010. [Online]. Available from: http://sfonline.barnard.edu/polyphonic/print_ahmed.htm. Accessed 15 Sept 2015.

Ahmed, S. (2015). *Institutional habits*. [Online] February 2, 2015. Available from: feministkilljoys.com http://feministkilljoys.com/2015/02/02/institutional-habits/. Accessed 15 Sept 2015.

Brabazon, T. (2014). 'Maybe He's just better than you': Generation X women and higher education. *Journal of Women's Entrepreneurship and Education, 2014*(3-4), 48–70.

Currie, J., Thiele, B., & Harris, P. (2002). *Gendered universities in globalized Economies: Power, careers, and sacrifices*. Oxford: Lexington Books.

Davies, B., De Schauwer, E., Claes, L., De Munck, K., Van De Putte, I., & Verstichele, M. (2013). Recognition and difference: A collective biography. *International Journal of Qualitative Studies in Education, 26*(6), 680–691.

Elias, J. (2015). *New directions and cutting-edges in IPE, IR and elsewhere*. June 9, 2015. [Online]. Available from: feministacademiccollective.com http://feministacademiccollective.com/2015/06/09/new-directions-and-cutting-edges-in-ipe-ir-and-elsewhere-2/. Accessed 11 Sept 2015.

European University Institute. (2014). *Finland, academic career structure*. 28 October 2014 [Online]. Available from: http://www.eui.eu/ProgrammesAndFellowships/AcademicCareersObservatory/AcademicCareersbyCountry/Finland.aspx. Accessed 11 May 2015.

Guillaume, X. (2015). Collaboration. In C. Aradau et al. (Eds.), *Critical security methods*. London: Routledge.

Halberstam, J. (2006). Boys will be...Bois? Or, Transgender feminism and forgetful fish. In D. Richardson, J. McLaughlin, & M. E. Casey (Eds.), *Intersections between feminist and queer theory* (pp. 97–115). New York: Palgrave Macmillan.

Hast, S. (2015). *"The Pit" (song), performed at Etmu Days cultural evening*. 22 Oct 2015 Rovaniemi.

Haug, F., et al. (1987). *Female sexualization. A collective work of memory*. London: Verso.

Husu, L. (2001). *Gender equality in Finnish academia: Contradictions and interventions* [Online]. http://csn.uni-muenster.de/women-eu/download/HusuCP01_02.pdf. Accessed 15 Sept 2015.

Inayatullah, N. (Ed.) (2011). *Autobiographical International Relations - I, IR*. London: Routledge.

Irni, S. (2013). The politics of materiality: Affective encounters in a transdisciplinary debate. *European Journal of Women's Studies, 20*(4), 347–360.

Jauhola, M. (2015). On 'Being Bored' - Street ethnography on emotions in Banda Aceh after the Tsunami and conflict. In L. Åhäll & T. Gregory (Eds.), *Emotions, politics, war* (pp. 86–99). London: Routledge.

Julkunen, R. (2010). *Sukupuolen järjestykset ja tasa-arvon paradoksit*. Tampere: Vastapaino.

Kantola, J. (2005). *Mykät, kuurot ja kadotetut: Sukupuolten välinen tasa-arvo Helsingin yliopiston valtio-opin laitoksella, Acta politica 29*. Helsinki: Yliopistopaino.

Kantola, J., & Nousiainen, K. (2009). Institutionalizing intersectionality in Europe: Introducing the theme. *International Feminist Journal of Politics, 11*(4), 459–477.

Kartovaara, L. (2003). Miesjohtajalla ura ja perhe, entä naisjohtajalla? *Hyvinvointikatsaus, 4*(2003), 2–8.

Mandaville, P. (2011). Cosmography recapitulates biography: An epilogue. In N. Inayatullah (Ed.), *Autobiographical international relations - I, IR* (pp. 196–202). London: Routledge.

Martini, E. & Jauhola, M. (2014). Journeys in Aidland: An autobiographic exploration of resistance to development aid. *Journal of Narrative Politics, 1*(1). [Online]. Available from http://journalofnarrativepolitics.com/wp-content/uploads/2014/2009/JNP-Vol-2011-Jahoula-and-Martini2011.pdf. Accessed on 23 Apr 2015.

NIKK. (2014). *Education and research*. 27 October 2014 [Online]. http://www. nikk.no/en/facts/nordic-overview/statistics-and-facts/education-and-research/. Accessed 11 Sept 2015.

Opetusministeriö (2006). *Tutkijanuratyöryhmän loppuraportti, Opetusministeriön työryhmämuistioita ja selvityksiä 2006:13*. Helsinki: Opetusministeriö.

Palmusaarinenojala, J. (2014). Kollektiivinen biografia feministisen tutkimuksen menetelmänä. *Sukupuolentutkimus, 27*(4), 42–55.

Penttinen, E. (2004). *Corporeal globalization: Narratives of subjectivity and otherness in the sexscapes of globalization*. Tampere: Tampereen yliopistopaino Oy Juvenes Print.

Penttinen, E. (2011). Heartfelt positivity as an orthogonal approach to gender, agency and political violence: Reading of the film Stormheart. In: L. Ahall & L. Shepherd (eds.), *Gender, agency and political violence* (pp. 200–215). London: Palgrave Macmillan.

Penttinen, E. (2013). *Joy and international relations: A new methodology*. London: Routledge.

Peterson, V. S. (1999). Sexing political identities/nationalism as heterosexism. *International Feminist Journal of Politics, 1*(1), 34–65.

Pietilä, M. (2015). *Tenure track and equality in the academia*. Presentation held at the symposium equality goes accessible, University of Helsinki, January 8, 2015. [Online]. Available from: researchgate.net, https://www.researchgate. net/publication/274379619_Tenure_track_and_equality_in_the_academia. Accessed 15 Sept 2015.

Repo, J. (2015). *The biopolitics of gender*. New York: Oxford University Press.

Särmä, S. (2014). *Junk feminism and nuclear wannabes: Collaging parodies of Iran and North Korea, Acta Universitatis Tamperensis 1961*. Tampere: Tampere University Press Available electronically at http://urn.fi/Urn:isBn:978-951-44-9535-9.

Särmä, S. (2016). Collaging internet parody images—An art-inspired methodology for studying visual world politics. In: Hamilton C. & Shepherd, L. J. (eds) *Understanding popular culture and world politics in the digital age*. London: Routledge.

Soreanu, R. (2010). Feminist creativities and the disciplinary imaginary of international relations. *International Political Sociology, 4*(4), 380–400.

Soreanu, R., & Hudson, D. (2008). Feminist scholarship in international relations and the politics of disciplinary emotion. *Millennium: Journal of International Studies, 37*(1), 123–151.

Sylvester, C. (2009). *Art/museums: International relations where we least expect it*. Boulder: Paradigm Publishers.

Tickner, J. A. (1997). You just don't understand: Troubled engagements between feminists and IR theorists. *International Studies Quarterly, 41*, 611–632.

Tutkijakollektiivi Bordering Actors (2014). Pääkirjoitus: Maailmanpolitiikan marginaalit - tieto, valta, kritiikki. *Kosmopolis, 44*(3–4), 3–8.

Vaittinen, T. (2014). Reading global care chains as migrant trajectories: A theoretical framework for the understanding of structural change. *Women's Studies International Forum, 47,* 191–202.

Vaittinen, T. (2015). *From the neoliberal university to cruising conferences in the Baltic.* 25 June 2015 [Online]. Available from: *feministacademiccollective. com*http://feministacademiccollective.com/2015/06/25/from-the-neoliberal-university-to-cruising-conferences-in-the-baltic/. Accessed 11 Sept 2015.

Weber, C. (1994). Good girls, little girls and bad girls. *Millennium: Journal of International Studies, 23*(2), 337–348.

Weber, C. (1999). *Faking it U.S. hegemony in a "post-phallic" era.* Minneapolis: University of Minnesota Press.

Weber, C. (2014). From queer to queer IR. *International Studies Review, 16*(4), 596–601.

Yeatman, A. (1990). *Bureaucrats, technocrats, femocrats: Essays on the contemporary Australian state.* Sydney: Allen & Unwin.

Zalewski, M. (2007). Do we understand each other yet? Troubling feminist encounters with(in) international relations. *British Journal of Politics and International Relations, 9*(2), 302–312.

PART IV

Work, Networks and Social Capital: Building the Academic Career

Challenges to Feminist Solidarity in the Era of New Public Management

Klara Regnö

Feminism(s) has (have) been a worldwide social movement of the twenti-eth century (Antrobus 2004; Baksh-Soodeen and Harcourt 2015). Great changes have taken place over the last hundred years when it comes to women's rights and place in society. Feminisms, inside and outside of aca-demia have been major forces in these changes, and the feminist move-ment has been intimately linked to the advancement of women in higher education (David 2014). Feminism in academia has empowered women (and some men) to apply critical inquiry and political understanding to methodologies of teaching, learning, researching and writing (Morley and Walsh 1995). Solidarity between women that was created through the feminist movement has been one of the basic foundations for the transfor-mation of higher education (hooks 2000).

The expansion of higher education (hereafter HE) during the end of the twentieth century entailed new opportunities for women not only as students but also as researchers and scholars, although the increase of women enrolled in HE has not been successfully transformed into more women advancing higher up the academic hierarchy (David 2014;

K. Regnö (✉)
Gothenburg University, Gothenburg, Sweden
Mälardalen University, Västerås, Sweden

R. Thwaites, A. Pressland (eds.), *Being an Early Career Feminist Academic*, DOI 10.1057/978-1-137-54325-7_9

169

European Commission 2013). Universities have never been gender-neutral meritocratic organizations: they are governed by male networks and masculine discourses, excluding, downplaying, 'othering' and sub-ordinating women (Bagilhole and Goode 2001; Morley 2013; Stanley 1997). Still, the expansionary period of global academia comprised a great vitality and richness of feminist work. Gender issues and feminist research have managed to establish themselves as legitimate elements of contemporary academia (David 2014).

Despite this there are now alarming signs that the situation is changing rapidly and that many of the victories won by earlier feminists are being contested. Over the past three decades the public sector in Sweden and elsewhere has been subjected to a series of New Public Management reforms that have attempted to fit public services into quasi-market models. In Europe, the Dutch, British and Swedish public sectors have undergone early and substantial reform, whilst other European countries have been slower to transform (Hood and Peters 2004; Ibsen et al. 2011; Forsberg Kankkunen et al. 2015).

New Public Management (hereafter NPM) is a concept that includes a broad spectrum of organizational practices. The underlying aim has been to obtain higher efficiency and effectiveness in order to get 'more value for the money'. At the heart of this are ideas of marketisation, competition and management by performance measures. This implies measurement and assessment of the organisation's performance in terms of productivity, quality and financial accountability even for small organisational units (Hood 1991; Ibsen et al. 2011; Parker 2011; Pollitt and Bouckaert 2004). In Sweden, health and social care were early to transform and HE has followed suit (Forsberg Kankkunen et al. 2015).

NPM has had a profound impact on how universities are founded and managed. HE has undergone rapid expansion since the postwar era in all parts of the world, Sweden included. Enrolments in North America and Western European universities rose by 250 per cent between 1970 and 2009 (David 2014; Eicher 1998; Fritzell 2012). State funding for education is now linked to the number of students enrolled as well as to performance measures like obtained university points and passed courses (Alexander 2000; Fritzell 2012). In addition to this, funding is also distributed in relation to the quality of educational programmes. In order to assess and ensure good value for money in academia, monitoring and control of both institutions and individuals through different performance indicators and research and education assessment exercises (RAE and EAE) have become frequent practices. Fiscal austerity is promoted by economic responsibility at low organisational levels. Each operational unit has its own budget and is responsible for the financial results. Operations are measured and assessed continuously. The impact of NPM has resulted in loss of control and autonomy for academic scholars and has been interpreted as a deprofessionalisation and proletarisation of the academic profession, running in parallel with an increased commodification of academic labour (Alexander 2000; de Groot 1997; Regnö 2013; Thomas and Davies 2002; Willmot 1995).

This chapter explores the threat NPM poses to feminist solidarity, and hence feminism in contemporary academia. NPM has created increasingly competitive environments; and the instrumentalism and marketisation of HE is reinforcing oppressive patterns in academia (Morley and Walsh 1995). Today, individualisation and competition make it difficult to sustain collaborative and inclusive feminist practices and collegiality and solidarity within and between departments.

The transformation of HE increases the divisions and inequalities between women, even those with a feminist agenda. Younger, early career academics on short-term contracts are increasingly dependent on senior academics with secure employment and have to accept poor working conditions, very heavy workloads, including a lot of teaching, in order to secure employment on a year-to-year basis. The relatively secure staff become complicit, witnessing the erosion of their colleagues' working conditions and failing to respond collectively to the decimation of a profession and to intellectual work itself (Gill 2009). It becomes increasingly difficult to remain true to a feminist agenda and the feminist principles of collective and collaborative action within the university.

This chapter explores the effects of NPM from the perspective of early career feminist scholars. NPM reforms together with heavy workloads, increased numbers of insecure short-term contracts, slow career progression, and a lack of support have augmented their stress and vulnerability. Academia has turned into a hostile environment where early career feminist scholars are required to perform at a high level of excellence and productivity in an organisational context that disempowers them materially and psychologically (Morley and Walsh 1995). There is a need for collective action to confront the deeply divisive nature of the organizational structures and practices that erode egalitarian relationships between women and feminist scholars.

Three exploratory interviews with feminist scholars were conducted during spring 2015. Efforts were made to choose informants with experience from different departments and universities. The questions focused on career history and aspirations, present working terms and conditions, relationships with colleagues, and NPM and feminism in academia. The interviews were semi-structured, lasting approximately 1.5 hours, and were recorded and subsequently transcribed and thereafter interpreted thematically using code-and-retrieve software (NVivo).

MIDDLE-AGED AND STILL 'EARLY CAREER': SHOULD I STAY OR SHOULD I GO?

The growth of temporary employment from the beginning of the 1980s is one of the most spectacular changes in Western working life in both public and private sectors, and it has become more apparent in the wake of NPM reforms (de Cuyper et al. 2008). This is, however, not applied equally in academia. The general pattern is that senior academics have full and permanent employment, while junior academics are employed in temporary positions for a relatively long time in their early careers (Lopes and Dewan 2014; Teichler et al. 2013). Women are also more often employed on short-term contracts than are men (Curtis 2011; David 2014). The employment arrangements of the scholars interviewed for this chapter are in line with this international trend. The interviewees are in their late thirties to mid-forties and have been employed in academia approximately seven to eight years since finishing their doctoral theses. During the time of the interviews they were all on fixed-term temporary employment contracts and had, but for one exception, been so since completing their theses.

The growth of temporary employment is part of the NPM regime that fosters fiscal austerity and flexibility and this has entailed a substantial shift towards job insecurity in the public sector (de Cuyper et al. 2008; Lopes and Dewan 2014). A consequence of the high frequency of short-term contracts is that the interviewed scholars have moved around a lot since they finalised their theses. They have all been employed by at least three different universities in different departments, both large and small, both within gender and feminist departments and as feminist researchers within other academic fields.

Gill (2009) discusses how precariousness has become a distinguishing feature of contemporary academic life, particularly for 'early career' scholars. Today the term 'early career' can be applied to almost the entire career of some academics given the few opportunities for secure employment that exist (Gill 2009). In Sweden the career development period preceding permanent employment has been extended; and career development generally progresses more slowly than it did ten years ago. The proportion of teachers in HE holding a career development position has shrunk considerably from 1995 to 2009. Women have a slower career progression than men and are also more frequently employed as teachers (Swedish Research Council 2015).

For many so-called early career academics it is often difficult to obtain a full-time position at one university even for a limited period of time, as the scholar needs to be funded on a departmental level and is only hired to the extent that s/he can carry out the tasks needed. Two of the scholars had also at some point held short-term jobs outside of academia in order to work full-time. All of the scholars interviewed had had at least three different employers since completing their theses. According to the Employment Protection Act in Sweden employees should be offered permanent employment after two years with the same employer. The scholars interviewed here had held contracts lasting from half a year to two years. Two had, in total, stayed for more than two years at the same employer but on different types of contracts. They describe that universities are very creative in circumventing the employment protection legislation. This creates all sorts of strange employment arrangements. The scholar in the quote below describes how she is currently employed at two different universities and funded by a third; she has research funding at the third university but cannot work there because they do not want to give her permanent employment:

Today I am employed 50 per cent on a research project at one university. However, my former university finances this research since I am not allowed to work at my former university[1]*. Then I am working 35 per cent at another university; a temporary job I am filling in for a person that is on long-term sick leave.*

The uncertain employment conditions have pernicious effects on the scholar's lives both within and outside of academia. Being middle-aged, the majority of them have children to provide for. Short-term employment makes it difficult to plan ahead, to settle and to get loans if you want to buy a house or a flat. The psychological costs of insecure working conditions can be very high for the individual. They include anxiety and stress brought about by a constant struggle for new employment contracts and research funding. The scholar in the quotation below describes this anxiety. Economic vulnerability is a material reality for her as the sole provider for children:

> *I have applied for different positions every semester, even employment outside of academia. I am always applying. It consumes a lot of time and energy, to worry. I must say that I am not the kind of person who is bitter or usually worries because it usually all falls into place in the end. But it is something about this constant anxiety that appears [towards the end of a contract]. I have to provide for a family, the economic vulnerability is a reality.*

For women with children, long working hours and commuting to different workplaces adds additional strain to a work situation that is already stressful. The gendered costs of precarious jobs in academia are starting to show in sick leave statistics. University teachers in Sweden have had a rapid increase in sick leave over recent years (an 11 per cent increase in three years). Furthermore, it is in fact one of the professions in Sweden with the highest difference in sick leave between men and women: women have periods of sick leave which are three times longer than the periods of sick leave men have (The University Teacher 2014; Swedish Social Insurance Agency 2012).

All of the scholars interviewed have tried out several different workplaces. The fact that none of them have been satisfactory has made them become increasingly tired and ambivalent as to whether they should stay in academia or not:

> *I have been very ambivalent [about academia] since completing my thesis. I believe this is a result of the fact that I have tried out several different departments. I do not feel that any of them have been satisfactory. So I still feel very ambivalent.*

One of the scholars has decided to start looking for employment outside of academia. After having worked hard for more than five years she still has no permanent employment in sight and she believes that there may be more rewarding jobs:

> *It is a struggle in so many ways, to get research funding, to work on your projects, to write, and then it feels like I have to fight for five more years to get*

[permanent employment]: Is this how it is supposed to be? I think that maybe there are other things you could do.

Even those who want to stay describe seeing other scholars, even brilliant ones, leave academia because they no longer think that it is possible for them to be the kind of scholars they want to be:

What I see is that scholars, not only in Sweden, feminists, accomplished gender scholars that have written brilliant stuff, leave academia because the working conditions and the requirement no longer comply with the things they want to do in life: like, for example, try to improve the world a bit, do decent research, disseminate research into the larger community, teach. This is no longer possible to do in a good way within academia today.

THE SEARCH FOR THE HOLY GRAIL: TO APPLY AND APPLY AND APPLY

Competition is another distinguishing feature of the NPM agenda of fiscal austerity and more value for money. Parker (2011) discusses how this line of thought is part of an underlying neoliberal ideology which values self-discipline, self-reliance and the pursuit of self-interest, since it is believed that humanity is best served by the promotion of individuality and entrepreneurship. From this perspective, he argues, everyone has the opportunity to climb the ladder of success, and failure to do so is considered primarily to be the individual's own failing to take up available opportunities. Gill (2009) points to the fact that the individualistic discourse is harmful in several ways. It turns failure into shameful records of individual shortcomings, and the reluctance to put individual failures on public display makes the individualistic discourse silencing and isolating. The response to 'failure' is to work even harder.

The career efforts of the scholars interviewed for this chapter are in line with the neoliberal agenda of individual entrepreneurship. They describe how they take on a very high level of personal responsibility for their academic careers, in terms of research applications, publication efforts and applications for vacant positions. In this sense their career struggle could be seen as a display of the neoliberal meritocratic system.

The interviewed scholars describe academic life as mostly an individualistic project that demands a lot of them, especially in terms of working hours. The response to the question of what is needed to make an academic is clear:

Money and publications. To work around the clock. I feel that is it a very individualistic project.

However, several studies of careers in academia (and elsewhere) have pointed out that the idea of an individualistic (academic) career that demands individual achievement and self-promotion is merely 'an idea' and that it stands in sharp contrast to actual career practices (Bagilhole and Goode 2001; Benshop and Van den Brink 2011; Holgersson 2013; Linghag 2009; Van den Brink 2010). Academic careers are dependent on the support of and collaboration with colleagues and superiors, and the need for sponsorship is strong. In academia career advancement demands the recognition and recommendation of colleagues typically higher up the academic hierarchy. Bagilhole and Goode (2001) discuss how men in the male-dominated academy do not have to create networks for themselves, but instead can take advantage of ready-made informal networks for information about job opportunities and recommendations from men already in the department. Career practices also include being approached, invited, recognised, included in applications and asked to participate in collaborative work and co-authorship (Bagilhole and Goode 2001; Husu 2001). Discrimination in academia can therefore be elusive and difficult to detect since it is often hidden and takes the form of 'non-events'. What happens is rather that nothing happens; the (female) scholar is not validated, read, refereed, invited or encouraged (Husu 2001).

There are, however, some descriptions by the interviewees of situations when they have been invited and acknowledged by senior colleagues. Some feel more included than others. It is interesting to note that these occasions are described as 'lucky' circumstances in the individual pursuit of a career, not normal career practices or deserved promotion and success. The scholars' notions of 'being lucky' reveal the gendered nature of career practices in academia.

I have been lucky and have obtained support from more senior scholars, both men and women. They have acknowledged my work and encouraged me in several ways. [...] They have put me forward in different arenas and have had me in mind and invited me on to projects. I have been included, and my ideas valued and taken seriously.

Competitive environments foster an elitist culture that single out 'winners' from the mediocre and award them with research grants and beneficial working employments. In an elitist culture success is equated with quality. Under the policy of building on 'excellence', institutional stratification is undertaken at universities where the 'haves' are selected from the 'have nots'. In a competitive culture where the logic builds on competition and stratification it is impossible to assign excellence to everybody. The mediocrities are needed in order to be able to single out the excellent. The number of 'winners' and 'losers', however, it can be argued, is not an expression of quality but rather the number of competitors in relation to the size of the cake (Leisyte 2006; Schoug 2002: 89 in Liinasson 2014).

In Sweden the cake has become smaller over time. Universities' dependence on external funding has increased over time. Parallel to this, the success rate at the major research funding councils has decreased, and is as low as 9 per cent at some major councils (FORTE 2014; Sundin 2014). Hence for each 'winner' there are nine 'losers' in the search for external funding. All the interviewees have applied extensively for external funding with variable results. They have all received 'some' funding after completing their theses but not much compared to the extent that they have applied. They are facing the dilemma that they have to apply for (and obtain) funding in order to be able to stay in academia. Funding and publications are prerequisites for a career. However, there is usually no time assigned for this work in short-term contracts, which turns submitting applications into an extra-curricular activity.

I think that the whole process to apply for money, and apply for more money, and apply for even more money is an exhausting task, just because the chances are so small to actually obtain any. It is exhausting to struggle and to put so much time and effort into doing this. In my case it has been rewarding but it is hard to acquire research funding.

The dependency of external funding in combination with short-term contracts put the researchers in an extremely vulnerable situation. Even for the most experienced researcher it is almost impossible to constantly have external funding with a success rate of 9 per cent. One of the scholars was employed in a department where the head of department said that all early career scholars would be 'out by next year' if they did not have external funding, regardless of whether they were funded in other ways.

The constant process of applying for funds is extremely time-consuming; and in most cases this time is wasted given the fierce competition and low success rates. The interviewee below describes how constant insecurity has impacted negatively on her ability to write and be creative:

> *It is many months that have been wasted by writing applications and by worrying [about the future]. In a way this actually blocks the whole ability to think and write.*

The quotation shows that stress and anxiety associated with insecure working conditions and extensive application efforts have very pernicious effects for the scholar. Time to be creative and to write is needed at early career stages in order to make a name for oneself: but instead time is usually stretched and precarious.

THE QUEST FOR EXCELLENCE: TO PUBLISH OR PERISH

The fact that universities nowadays are competing in a global market where education is a global commodity is also affecting the working conditions of early career scholars. The global competition has streamlined the demand for universities' outcomes and products. There are signs of increasing convergence of organisational structures, research and teaching schemes (Parker 2011). Universities' higher management officers are increasingly focusing on their institution's placement in rankings. A distinguished position in the ranking serves as the arbiter of high academic standards and excellence and is a forceful tool in attracting students and research funding (Erkkilä 2013; Münch 2014; Parker 2011). These ranking practices entail frequent audits of researchers, departments and educational programmes, including teaching, learning and research assessments such as the RAE and EAE, as mentioned above (Parker 2011; Thomas and Davies 2002).

The interviewees describe how power is forcefully wielded in academia through these assessments, rankings and publication targets. They are powerful steering tools as well as time-consuming administrative practices that put extra burden on those bearing an already heavy workload. To supply information for different assessment exercises can be very demotivating, especially when scholars feel that the audit is poorly designed and misses the point of academia. The scholar below describes how she has put a lot of effort into an exercise that she felt was a complete waste of time:

> *Those mindless assessments! The last one we conducted was a sham. Even the experts had a hard time conducting it in a satisfactory manner. It is a complete disaster that we spent such an incredible amount of time on something that was so poorly designed. It was completely meaningless.*

Competition is now apparent in every aspect of academic life, and is especially pronounced when the university releases bibliometric rankings. The same assessment tool is used for everyone regardless of academic discipline. The scholar below describes how this ranking is seemingly transparent but in reality very difficult to comprehend and plays an important role as a steering mechanism. In the list that is sent out to all staff, the high performers are effectively singled out from the less so in a very visible way:

> *The bibliometric ranking is used very explicitly at my university. It is sent out to all employees so you can check what ranking you have got as a result of this complicated calculation that I do not understand. Some people are highlighted in the document, if they are top 10 or top 25 per cent [in the ranking]. [...] I assume that the ranking is a result of the bibliometric calculation. We are told that they are going to use this as a means to distribute funding internally at the university. It seems so transparent, it is displayed to everyone, but at the same time it is completely incomprehensible. No one seems to understand how it is calculated and what counts. Most things you do, do not seem to count. Not the things I have done anyway. I was recently employed at the university and the things I have published prior to this is not included in the ranking either [...] I always find 0 next to my name. I am no big shot. It is really competitive in that sense. Your place at the bottom is extremely visible.*

The same scholar highlights that different disciplines also have different publication strategies. So even if the assessment system is the same for everyone it is not power neutral. The design favours certain modes and traditions of publication. The scholar describes how feminist researchers doing qualitative research in the field of social sciences and humanities are not favoured in these systems.

> *Natural science and technical areas of research are going to get much more money in this [publication governed] model for distribution of funding.*

Their publication strategies are completely different from the ones applied in the humanities and social sciences. In their field an academic paper can consist of only 3,000 words, fairly short papers. While in the social sciences and the humanities they are expected to be much longer, 8,000–10,000 words. So the conditions differ totally. But we are assessed in the same way, although they can write a number of papers during the time it takes me to eventually write one.

The competition also fosters a system where everyone feels that they have to perform at their best all the time to meet the high requirements for career advancement and permanent employment. Publications and other qualifications are accumulated and there is this constant anxiety that if you do not keep up with the pace you fall behind in your career. The interviewees describe being expected to publish at a steady, high rate. The problem is that this does not comply with the actual research process in empirical research. You do not publish constantly. Usually it takes a year or two to gather and analyse the empirical material. The interviewee below describes it as a kind of 'ketchup effect', where the publications come at the end of the project:

With research it is often a kind of ketchup effect. You gather empirical material and then a year or two later you publish.

The demand for extreme productivity takes place at the expense of other activities. Activism is an important part of the feminist agenda for all the interviewees. They want to contribute to social movements aiming at changing the world in the direction of greater equalities. The heavy workload, however, makes it difficult for scholars to take on anything but what is directly required of them. The scholar in the quotation below says that for periods of time she has not had time nor energy to engage in activist work, although this is very important to her, both personally and professionally:

I am an activist as well and I think that this is beneficial to my research too. It gives me new ideas. [...] But for periods of time I have refrained from activism although I do not wish to. It is because I had no energy left.

The narrow focus on publications also downplays and makes other contributions feminist scholars make to academic life and society invisible, like, for example, external contacts and collaborations, public lecturing, and contribution to the development of the community:

> *There are many worthwhile contributions that are not paid attention to: collaborations and external contacts you have, if you contribute to community development, public lecturing and knowledge diffusion for example. All these things are suddenly invisible.*

Scholars also highlighted another associated problem with the sole focus on journal publication: it tends to limit and confine research to an elitist practice relevant only to a few. Through journal publication academic research becomes accessible almost only to university peers. When the distance between academic feminism and social movement in society increases, this can be interpreted as a de-radicalisation of feminist knowledge (David 2014; hooks 2000). As feminists, the interviewed scholars find it frustrating that modes of publications that reach a wider audience outside of academia do not 'count' towards their career advancement:

> *Textbooks, for example, do not count when you list your publications, you have to publish papers in academic journals. [...] This research, however, only reaches quite a limited audience since papers only are available through university libraries and you may have to be an enrolled student or employee to access these journals. There is a very limited distribution. It is a small world. Even though it can be very international, it is very confined at the same time.*

Parker (2011) discusses how the new trends of accountability in HE can be seen rather as a redirection of accountability, where the focus has shifted from a broad scope of accountability to community and society, to a narrow financial accountability. The scholars find the commodification of academic writing where the form of publication is valued, rather than the content and outreach, very de-motivating. They wish to reach out to wider audiences and contribute to a social, egalitarian movement:

> *I see no point in writing just to obtain higher scores [in the ranking]. I feel that the whole point of doing research is lost then. I believe that this is one of the things that is dysfunctional [in academia]. I think that something is wrong with the research community and universities when I get more credit from publishing an inferior paper in a highly ranked journal than a paper that reaches out and that people actually read.*

Sometimes the results of such a strong focus on publication can be surprising; even teaching can occasionally get excluded from the definition of academic work:

A head of department once told me—it was during a heavy teaching period— that teaching is not our core business. I find this rather interesting because I would have thought that teaching is part of the core business at a university. It was so very apparent that teaching is not valued.

Statements like the one above are painful to scholars trying to survive in academia on short-term teaching contracts. Narrow definitions of academic work make much work appear superfluous or turns it into an extra-curricular activity. It has become increasingly difficult for scholars to engage in activities that used to be part of collegial responsibility, such as reviewing articles and grant proposals (Gill 2009). When the job becomes estranged from the aspects that make it worthwhile, scholars can feel increasingly alienated in academia; this was certainly true for the interviewed scholars. To create a feeling of meaningfulness and satisfaction becomes yet another individual responsibility for the scholar:

The dissatisfaction that I feel, I believe, stems from that fact that I really do work a lot, but the things I do, do not count for real. Then the challenge is to create this feeling of meaningfulness for myself. The system does not help me to feel satisfied with what I do. It is rather the case that the only things that count are just the things I do not have time assigned for in my contract but am supposed to do in my spare time.

The scholars interviewed describe how intellectual labour has been increasingly fragmented, and commodified (de Groot 1997; Dominelli and Hoogvelt 1996; Willmott 1995). This is in line with the overall trend within NPM where top-down management has become the dominant decision-making mode in a similar way to scientific management and Taylorism (Dominelli and Hoogvelt 1996; Parker 2011; Taylor 1911). Assessments, rankings and publication targets work as disciplinary regimes that undermine the autonomy and authority of academic scholars and disqualify their professional judgement of scientific quality. Power has been redistributed from professional groups to top management, where professional groups have lost authority while the demand for transparency and control has increased their administrative burden.

Very often little or no administrative support is on hand for researchers; this has increased the number of 'illegitimate' tasks, defined as mainly administrative non-research and education-related tasks (Björk et al. 2013; Parker 2011).

This shift in power distribution in academia is visible through the lack of support in combination with the high level of personal responsibility that early career scholars are expected to take on. This loss of control over the content and quantity of work puts the scholars in a position where they have to deal with the reality of being over-burdened with work, and at the same time deal with feelings of inferiority caused by the notion that they are doing too little or the wrong things. The scholar below describes how mentally and physically exhausting this is:

All of life is suddenly permeated by the sensation of never ever being on time, always being deficient in some way, being late and not able to meet deadlines, not having published enough, working at night to correct exams and encourage students. It is such an incredibly huge investment in work with very little payoff. You turn out being rather tired and bitter.

Extensive Teaching and Proletarisation of Early Career Academics

The rapid expansion of academia in Europe (and elsewhere) has transformed HE from elite to mass education. In most European countries, Sweden included, student numbers have increased more than tenfold between 1955 and 1994 (Eicher 1998). This rapid expansion has continued: between 1990 and 2010 the number of students in Sweden more than doubled. Funding, however, has not increased to the same extent. There have mainly been reductions in funding in order to offset anticipated productivity increases. This means that resources per student have decreased in real terms (Fritzell 2012). The mass enrolment in university has fundamentally changed working conditions for university teachers. Teachers work long hours in order to cope with large student groups; administrative demands and follow-up and control of teaching efforts have also increased (Parker 2011).

All the interviewed scholars point to the fact that the time assigned for teaching does not nearly reflect the actual workload. Time is assigned in a standardised mode and can be changed in order to meet budgetary constraints. It is the standardised models, not the time it actually takes to teach, that determines how much time the scholars get for teaching, as this interviewee outlines:

I am supposed to teach 20 per cent and work 80 per cent on my research project. The problem is that 20 per cent teaching does not take 20 per cent of my working time, but instead much more, because it is not fully financed and this is linked to funding assigned to each student. I am given too few hours to conduct the task. The percentage only serves as a symbol and a guide to the economist that pays my salary. It has been calculated in a formula that does not cohere with reality. One year you can get 100 hours for one course. Next year when the university's economy is better, you are assigned 200 hours to do exactly the same course.

The pressure from an increasing workload has created a system of sub-contracting academic labour (Hey 2001). Short-term contracts used to be mainly limited to research positions and tied to specific research projects. Today, however, short-term employment to a large extent also characterises teaching posts at the lower end of the pay scale (Gill 2009; Lopes and Dewan 2014).

The expansion of higher education has created a more diverse student and scholarly body but without ending old social-inequality patterns based on gender, class and ethnicity/race higher up in the organization (David 2014; de Groot 1997). In Sweden, as in the rest of Europe, the percentage of women decreases at higher levels in academia. (European Commission 2013, Swedish National Agency for Higher Education 2011). Women constitute 65 per cent of the enrolled students, 51 per cent of the PhDs and only 24 per cent of the full professors (Statistics Sweden 2014; Swedish National Agency for Higher Education 2011). Women tend to teach, while men tend to do research (David 2014; Swedish Research Council 2015). Teaching becomes equivalent to 'housework' in academia. Women in academia are found in less prestigious positions with poor career prospects.

Early career scholars (largely women) without permanent employment are placed on the periphery and move from department to department in order to secure new employment. More established scholars with permanent positions have greater opportunities to ease their workload by hiring teaching services from junior scholars. Scholars who do not have research funding find themselves in weak bargaining positions. One of the scholars describes how she at times has worked more than 100 per cent full time because she feared losing her employment if she turned down one offer or tried to renegotiate the terms of her employment:

> *It was totally crazy to work more than 100 per cent at two different workplaces but I felt that I had to prove myself to be so immensely capable so that they would want me to stay [laughter]. Get a foot in the door, make an impression. I think this has characterised much of my academic career: to always want to show how good, capable and available I am in order to secure a new job. If you do not have research funding, it is fixed-term contracts as a teacher that you can get. Then you need to show that you are incredibly competent all the time and say yes to an awful lot of things.*

She reflects upon the fact that this may not be beneficial for her long-term advancement but believes that it is difficult to say no since this can negatively affect future possibilities for employment. She points to a dilemma for early career scholars without external funding: on the one hand, in order to secure employment they have to say yes to extensive teaching offers; on the other hand, in order to secure permanent employment they are expected to publish, which is very hard to do when they are overburdened with teaching:

> *I see that I prioritised the wrong things. I should have said no to quite a lot of things. At the same time, I know that this could have affected the possibility of continuing to be employed. That is what makes it so difficult. If you only have temporary employment and do not know how many percentages [of full time employment/ FTE equivalent] you have next semester, if you are not accommodating enough, your percentage could be reduced and then the [university] ends up not needing your services. It's not so easy to renegotiate your working conditions.*

To sustain a high rate of publication is almost impossible if you are on a teaching contract. And for scholars who try, it comes at a high individual price, as the interviewee in the quotation below describes:

> *Even if you are only employed as a university teacher where you may have 10 per cent research in your employment, you are still expected to publish a bunch of papers during those years when you are almost exclusively teaching. To me it is a great mystery how this can be carried out if you do not want to work all the time. I have tried that too but I stopped doing that because I feel that I want to have a good life too.*

Individualisation of Organisational Structures

Despite the profound impact of NPM in academia, its effects are seldom discussed as the results of structural features of contemporary academia. Instead they are treated as individual experiences and problems (Gill 2009). For example, the heavy workload is not regarded as an organisational concern. On the contrary, it is seen as a personal problem for each scholar that can best be addressed individually. Complaints are also silenced in the daily interactions between feminist scholars, undermining the possibilities for collective action (Gill 2009).

One of the scholars interviewed describes how one of her colleagues turned to the head of department to discuss her work situation that she was finding unbearable, and not compatible with having children. The poor working conditions did not result in collective collegial action; instead she was told by her senior colleague that the only way to stay in academia was to learn to cope with the situation:

> *In this profession you cannot plan your work. If you want to work in academia you have to able to handle working late nights and weekends.*

Moreover, senior scholars tell their younger colleagues to 'lower their ambition'. This may, however, be difficult for many reasons (should the scholars even wish to follow this dubious advice!). First of all, as the interviewee in the quotation below concludes, the job may not be worthwhile if you lower your ambitions too much:

> *Here [in my department] they say that you have to lower your ambitions. But I feel that I want to do a good job. I may as well not teach at all if I am supposed to lower my ambition and only teach out of habit. Then it is better that I do not teach at all.*

Secondly, a poor performance can also have negative consequences for the individual scholar. Since each examined student brings money to the department, it is important to maintain the quality at a level that enables students to complete their courses and assignments on time. Failing students usually also entails extra work, more supervision or additional exams to correct. Furthermore, negative feedback on course evaluations can also impede future possibilities of obtaining employment:

> *If people do not finish on time this usually affects me negatively. Then this person needs to do an extra assignment and the department does not receive fund-*

ing. In addition it does not look good if I supervise a lot of students and no one finishes their work on time. [...] Moreover, if you do a very poor job and get very negative feedback, it does not look good either.

Apart from the individual distress associated with temporary employment, it also has a negative impact on the quality of the education provided by the department in which the early career academic works (Lopes and Dewan 2014). Work once rewarded with permanent employment as a lecturer is redesigned as temporary employment. When teaching staff change frequently it becomes difficult to ensure continuity and quality over time. Moreover, temporarily employed scholars are expected to participate in and are evaluated and assessed on developmental work, although it may not be part of their job description. When they engage in such work the efforts are foiled when their employment is terminated:

We worked quite a lot on pedagogical development with all the teachers in my department. This work collapsed when two of us could not stay.

CHALLENGES TO FEMINIST SOLIDARITY

This chapter shows how the organisational practices associated with NPM become coercive forces that have a profound impact on the lives of early career academics. The scholars describe the gendered costs, such as anxiety and stress, associated with the increase of temporary employment in academia. Women have slower career progression than men and all the interviewed scholars have been on short-term contracts for a long time in their careers. Being middle-aged with families and children to provide for and with no permanent employment in sight they describe life in academia as a struggle requiring huge investments and offering very little payoff. As a result of this they have become increasingly ambivalent about whether they should stay in academia.

Moreover, they feel that there is no room for them to be the kind of feminist scholars they want to be in contemporary academia. The orientation towards revenue generation and cost minimisation, where economy ranks higher than all other activities, forces academics to work in a more isolated mode (Parker 2011). When scholars can only obtain 'revenues' via either underfinanced teaching or external research funding, other activities such as meetings, seminars, informal collegial conversations, meetings with students and developmental work are not financed, and given the heavy workloads, very difficult to take on. The imposition of measurements of productivity and quality has decreased the collegial face-to-face encounters (David 2014). As a result of this, work in academia has become quite a lonely task. The feminist practices of sharing, collaboration and mutual support that the scholars treasure are thus undermined in this environment. Even in socially satisfying work environments the interviewees do not really feel that they have time to engage in each other's work:

> *Now I work in a feminist environment, which is multi-disciplinary and the people are nice. Still the work situation is very much like in all the other departments where I have been employed. For example, I teach a course; no one ever asks me how I am doing. It appears to be my own little project, although teaching is a central activity at the university. We never have any staff meetings. We never discuss the content. No one asks. No one cares, as long as there is no major catastrophe.*

Moreover, feminist practices and publication traditions are not valued or validated. Practices, such as public lecturing, community activities and change projects are not measured in current assessment systems. This puts a heavy burden on feminist scholars who want to sustain feminist practices and remain in academia to do both: both engage in feminist politics and publish in the 'right' journals. This gives scholars the ambiguous experience of working extremely long hours and at the same time having the feeling of not doing enough and of being inferior. They report that the current system rewards academics that focus primarily on their own careers and publications and do not engage in collective activities. One of the scholars gives this bleak description of the career path of successful feminist scholars:

> *They produce these papers in the right journals. They do not care if the content is too similar. They become associate professor rather quickly, just in a few years. They do not engage in a lot of collective activities.*

As feminists they find it hard subscribing to an agenda where publications in the 'right' journals with inferior material ranks higher than high-quality research that reaches out to a wider audience. They feel that this is challenging the whole idea of a feminist project aimed toward greater equalities.

Competition is very pronounced in every aspect of the interviewees' scholarly lives. It accounts for an increase in oppressive, inequitable, competitive, individualist, self-serving practices in academia, even amongst and between feminist scholars (David 2014). Competition stands as the opposite to a feminist emancipatory and egalitarian agenda. It foments inequalities, since the underlying idea is to single out the 'haves' from the 'have nots'. The requirements for extreme publication rates also foster inequality between scholars, since a high publication rate usually calls for a sole focus on research and writing. This increases the divisions between different categories of staff in departments: those with and without permanent employment; those who teach and those who do research.

Feminists who take on accessible management positions in neoliberal academia become hostage to the system and act out the brutal practices of increasing inequalities. They are caught in the tension of having to change the rules to subvert the system on which they are dependent (David 2014; Morley 2013). The interviewees describe how senior colleagues have difficulties in sticking to their solidarity agenda in the competitive academic environment.

> *It is very hard to stay in academia, even as a full professor. It is rather tough battles between professors over PhDs and research agendas, a lot of university politics. It may not be an easy task to exercise solidarity. It is always competition between what is best for the individual and for the collective.*

In this competitive atmosphere where everyone is overloaded with work, fighting for their own survival, it becomes difficult to maintain collegial generosity. Competition between academics both within and between generations has heightened (David 2014). The scholars speak about uncomfortable tensions and even detachment between the ideals of feminism and actual working practices in academia:

> *My impression is that feminist strategies are quite decoupled from work life in academia. The things people write about are not carried out in practice. I think the hierarchal system prevails. Feminist strategies like sisterhood or the promotion of feminist research are not apparent. I see more competition between feminists than collaborative sisterhood. The tone of voice is not always that respectful. I sometimes lack the acknowledgment of the fact that there are different types of research. The focus is rather, like in academia, on competition on creating your own academic platform.*

Senior colleagues, most of them also overburdened with work, are trying to keep their heads above water. One way of doing so is to subcontract teaching labour. This, however, makes them complicit in the exploitation and reproduction of poor working conditions for their colleagues. As long as women are using their privilege to dominate other women, feminist solidarity cannot be fully realised (hooks 2000).

This chapter wishes to draw attention to the fact that there is an urgent need to acknowledge and address the increasing inequalities within academia and to discuss what this does to us as feminists and to our feminisms. One of the questions that needs to be raised is whether it is possible to use universities as platforms for egalitarian movements when the conditions we as feminists are working under are profoundly unequal, sometimes even within the same department. hooks (2000) concludes that sisterhood and acts of solidarity are made possible across boundaries of race and class because individual women are willing to divest their power to dominate and exploit subordinated groups.

The challenge, therefore, is how we shall begin to resist. Feminist academics today must reclaim collaborative, feminist solidarity. One of the interviewed scholars stresses that the way forward lies in the pursuit of a feminist, intersectional solidarity agenda:

We have to advance as a collective. We help each other, challenge and protest together.

Together we can find ways to challenge competition and individualism in order to create more inclusive and egalitarian universities.

Acknowledgements The author thanks the interviewed scholars for their generous records of life in academia, Dordi Westerlund for valuable comments on the draft versions, and the editors Dr. Amy Pressland and Dr. Rachel Thwaites for supportive and constructive comments and suggestions throughout the process—true feminist practices!

NOTE

1. The Employment Protection Act in Sweden states that, when an employee has worked for two years at a university she should be offered permanent employment. Since this scholar's former university was not willing to offer her permanent employment her contract was not renewed. Instead, her former university is transferring her research funding to another university.

REFERENCES

Alexander, F. K. (2000). The changing face of accountability: Monitoring and assessing institutional performance in higher education. *The Journal of Higher Education, 2*(4), 411–431.

Antrobus, P. (2004). *The global women's movement: Origins, issues and strategies.* London: Zed.

Bagilhole, B., & Goode, J. (2001). The contradiction of the myth of individual merit, and the reality of a patriarchal support system in academic careers. A feminist investigation. *European Journal of Women's Studies, 8*(2), 161–180.

Baksh-Soodeen, R., & Harcourt, W. (Eds.) (2015). *The Oxford handbook of transnational feminist movements.* New York, NY: Oxford University Press.

Benshop, Y., & Van den Brink, M. (2011). Gender practices in the construction of academic excellence: Sheep with five legs. *Organization, 19*(4), 507–524.

Björk, L., Bejerot, E., Jacobshagen, N., & Härenstam, A. (2013). I shouldn't have to do this: Illegitimate tasks as a stressor in relation to organizational control and resource deficits. *Work & Stress, 27*(3), 262–277.

Curtis, J. W. (2011). Persistent inequity: Gender and academic employment. Prepared for *"New Voices in Pay Equity". An Event for Equal Pay Day, April 11, 2011. American Association of University Professors.* [Online] Available from: http://www.aaup.org/NR/rdonlyres/08E023AB-E6D8-4DBD-99A0-24E5EB73A760/0/persistent_inequity.pdf. Accessed 07 Jan 2016.

David, M. E. (2014). *Feminism, gender and universities: Politics, passion and pedagogies.* Farnham: Ashgate.

de Cuyper, N., De Jong, J., Isaksson, K., Rigotti, T., & Schalk, R. (2008). Literature review of theory and research on the psychological impact of temporary employment: Towards a conceptual model. *International Journal of Management Reviews, 10*(1), 25–51.

de Groot, J. (1997). After the ivory tower: Gender, commodification and the 'academic'. *Feminist Review,* Spring 1997 *55,* 130–142.

Dominelli, L., & Hoogvelt, A. (1996). Globalization, contract government and the taylorization of intellectual labour in academia. *Studies in Political Economy, 49*(Spring). 71–100.

Eicher, J.-C. (1998). The cost and financing of higher education in Europe. *European Journal of Education, 33*(1), 31–39.

Erkkilä, T. (2013). *Global university rankings: Challenges for European higher education.* Basingstoke: Palgrave Macmillan.

European Commission. (2013). *She figures 2012. Gender in research and innovation. Statistics and indicators.* Brussels: European Commission. [Online] Available from: http://ec.europa.eu/research/science-society/document_library/pdf_06/she-figures-2012_en.pdf. Accessed 07 Jan 2016.

Forsberg Kankkunen, T., Bejerot, E., Björk, L., & Härenstam, A. (2015). *New public management i kommunal praktik. En studie om chefers möjlighet att* hantera styrning inom verksamheterna Vatten, Gymnasium, och Äldreomsorg. ISM-rapport 15. [New Public Management in the Public Sector. A study of managers' ability to deal with managerial control in the operations Water, High School, and Elderly Care. ISM Report 15]. Göteborg: Institutet för stressmedicin. [Online] Available from: http://www.vgregion.se/upload/Regionkanslierna/ISM%20Institutet%20för%20stressmedicin/Publikationer/ISM-rapporter/ISM-rapport%2015%20ver%204_webversion.pdf. Accessed 07 Jan 2016.

FORTE. (2014). *Fortes årsredovisning 2014.* [Swedish Research Council for Health, Working Life and Welfare, Annual Report 2014] [Online] Available from: http://forte.se/wp-content/uploads/2015/10/fortes-arsredovisning-2014.pdf. Accessed 07 Jan 2016.

Fritzell, A. (2012). *SULF:s skriftserie. Fortsatt utbyggnad—Fortsatt urholkning.* [Swedish Association of University Teachers. Continued Expansion—Continued Erosion] Stockholm: Sveriges universitetslärarförbund. [Online] Available from: http://www.sulf.se/Documents/Pdfer/Press%20opinion/Skrifter/sulfskrift_xxxx_urholkningwebb.pdf. Accessed 07 Jan 2016.

Gill, R. (2009). Breaking the silence: The hidden injuries of neo liberal academia. In R. Flood & R. Gill (Eds.), *Secrecy and silence in the research process: Feminists reflections.* London: Routledge.

Hey, V. (2001). The construction of academic time: Sub/contracting academic labour in research. *Journal of Education Policy, 16*(1), 67–84.

Holgersson, C. (2013). Recruiting managing directors: Doing homosociality. *Gender, Work & Organization, 20*(4), 454–466.

Hood, C. (1991). A public management for all seasons? *Public Administration, 69*(1), 3–19.

Hood, C., & Peters, G. (2004). The middle ageing of new public management: Into the age of paradox? *Journal of Public Administration Research and Theory, 14*(3), 267–282.

hooks, b. (2000). *Feminism is for everybody. Passionate politics.* Cambridge, MA: South End Press.

Husu, L. (2001). *Sexism, support and survival in academia: Academic women and hidden discrimination in Finland.* Helsinki: Helsingfors universitet.

Ibsen, C. L., Larsen, T. P., Madsen, J. S., & Due, J. (2011). Challenging Scandinavian employment relations: The effects of new public management reforms. *The International Journal of Human Resource Management, 22*(11), 2295–2310.

Leisyte, L. (2006). *The effects of New Public Management on research practices in English and Dutch universities.* Presented at the Second International Colloquium on Research and Higher Education Policy. UNESCO Headquarters, Paris 29 November–1st December 2006. [Online] Available from: http://unesdoc.unesco.org/images/0015/001530/153097e.pdf. Accessed 07 Jan 2016.

Liinasson, M. (2014). Maktens skiftningar. En utforskning av ojämlikhetsregimer i akademin. [Shifts of Power. An exploration of inequality regimes in academia.]. *Tidskrift för genusvetenskap*, 35(1), 73–97.

Linghag, S. (2009). Från medarbetare till chef: Kön och makt i chefsförsörjning och karriär [From Employee to Manager: Gender and Power in Management Succession and Career]. Stockholm: Kungliga Tekniska högskolan.

Lopes, A., & Dewan, I. (2014). Precarious pedagogies? The impact of casual and zero-hour contracts in Higher Education. *Journal of Feminist Scholarship*, 7(8), 28–42.

Morley, L. (2013). The rules of the game: Women and the leaderist turn in higher education. *Gender and Education*, 25(1), 116–131.

Morley, L., & Walsh, V. (1995). Introduction. Feminist academics: Creative agents for change. In Morley, L. & Walsh, V. (Eds.), *Feminist academics. Creative agents for change*. London/Bristol: Taylor & Frances.

Münch, R. (2014). *Academic capitalism: Universities in the global struggle for excellence*. New York and Abingdon: Routledge.

Parker, L. (2011). University corporatisation: Driving definition. *Critical Perspectives on Accounting*, 22(4), 434–450.

Pollitt, C., & Bouckaert, G. (2004). *Public management reform: a comparative analysis. New public management, governance, and the neo-Weberian state*. Oxford: Oxford University Press.

Regnö, K. (2013). *Det osynliggjorda ledarskapet: kvinnliga chefer i majoritet*. [Invisible management: Women managers in majority]. Stockholm: Kungliga Tekniska högskolan.

Schoug, F. (2002). Vetenskapssamhället som konkurrenssystem. Doktorander, doktorer och feministiska perspektiv [Science as a competitive system. Graduate students, PhDs and feminist perspectives]. *RIG – Kulturhistorisk tidskrift*, 85(2), 73–94.

Stanley, L. (1997). *Knowing feminisms: On academic borders, territories and tribes*. London: Sage.

Sundin, A. (2014). *PM Underlag till kartläggning av HS-området*. [Documentation of statistics for the Humanities and Social sciences.] [Online] Available from: http://www.vr.se/download/18.3d1748ef1494efled285d011/141441757195O/PM+Underlag+kartläggning+HS-området.pdf. Accessed 07 Jan 2016.

Statistics Sweden. (2014). *Women and men in Sweden. Facts and figures*. Örebro: Statistics Sweden. [Online] Available from: http://www.scb.se/Statistik/_Publikationer/LE0201_2013B14_BR_X10BR1401ENG.pdf. Accessed 08 Jan 2016.

Swedish National Agency for Higher Education [Högskoleverket]. (2011). *Forskarkarriär för både kvinnor och män? – Statistisk uppföljning och kunskapsöversikt. Rapport 2011:6 R*. [Research Career for Both Women and Men?—

Statistical Overview and Research Review. Report 2011:6 R]. Stockholm: Högskoleverket. [Online] Available from: http://www.ukambetet.se/downlo ad/18.1ff6bf9c146adf4b496743/1404208759184/1106R+Forskarkarriär+f ör+både+kvinnor+och+män++statistisk+uppföljning+och+kunskapsöversikt. pdf. Accessed 07 Jan 2016.

Swedish Research Council [Vetenskapsrådet]. (2015). *Forskningens Framtid. Karriärstruktur och karriärvägar i högskolan.* [The Future of Research. Career Structure and Career Paths in Higher Education] Stockholm: Vetenskapsrådet. [Online]. Available from: https://publikationer.vr.se/produkt/forskningens-framtid-karriarstruktur-och-karriarvagar-i-hogskolan/. Accessed 07 Jan 2016.

Swedish Social Insurance Agency [Försäkringskassan]. (2012). *Socialförsäkringsrapport 2012:14. Sjukskrivningar i olika yrken under 2000-talet. Antalet ersatta sjukskrivningsdagar per anställd.* [Social Insurance Report 2012:14. Sick days with compensations for different professions in the 2000s]. Stockholm: Försäkringskassan.

Taylor, F. W. (1911). *The principles of scientific management.* New York: Harper & Brothers.

Teichler, U., Arimoto, A., & Cummings, W. K. (2013). *The changing academic profession: Major findings of a comparative survey.* Dordrecht: Springer.

The Univeristy Teacher [Univeristetsläraren]. (2014). Kvinnliga universitetslärare oftare långtidssjukskrivna. [Women university teachers more often on long term sick leave]. *The University Teacher no 11-14.* [Online] Available from: http://www.sulf.se/Universitetslararen/Arkiv/2014/Nummer-11/ Kvinnliga-universitetslarare-oftare-langtidssjukskrivna/. Accessed 07 Jan 2016.

Thomas, R., & Davies, A. (2002). Gender and new public management: Reconstituting academic subjectivities. *Gender Work & Organization, 9*(4), 372–392.

Van den Brink, M. (2010). *Behind the scenes of science: Gender practices in the recruitment and selection of professors in the Netherlands.* Amsterdam: Pallas Publications.

Willmot, H. (1995). Managing the academics: Commodification and control in the development of university education in the UK. *Human relations, 48*(9), 993–1027.

Inequality in Academia: The Way Social Connections Work

Irina Gewinner

INTRODUCTION

Scholarly discussions on inequality and discrimination in academia often address two of the most common types: gender inequality/discrimination (Forster 2001; Husu 2005; Husu and Koskinen 2010) and—closely connected to it—wage inequality/discrimination (Bellas 1994; Knights and Richards 2003). Evidence of persistent gender inequality in academia—concerning career advancement and wage gaps—has been gathered in different countries, implying the existence of inequality regardless of socio-economic orientation or form of government (Tam 1997; Fogelberg et al. 1999; Majcher 2002; Metcalfe and Afanassieva 2005). These discussions frequently maintain that academia per se still functions according to the old classical—Humboldtian—model[1]: it demands a full commitment of one's effort and time, thus being more suitable for men than for women (e.g., Bagilhole 2007). One of the features of the Humboldtian model is the division between public and private life, where women must concentrate on the latter, accepting social demands to be primary (if not primarily) childcare providers and home-keepers (e.g., Pfau-Effinger 2006).

I. Gewinner (✉)
University of Hanover, Hanover, Germany

© The Author(s) 2017
R. Thwaites, A. Pressland (eds.), *Being an Early Career Feminist Academic*, DOI 10.1057/978-1-137-54325-7_10

195

In the case of socialist Russia post-1917 Revolution, which established a social order different from capitalism, the ruling party offered women formal equality with men, a claim recorded in the Soviet Constitution 1936 (Ajvazova 1998). Officially, women were granted equal rights and guaranteed full participation in the labour force on the same footing with men, including in academia. This allowed the governing Communist party not only to "build communism", but also to abandon the need for developing any social policies necessary to address gender inequality. In reality, women in universities were often hired to teach and carry out administrative work with little responsibility, thus enabling men to focus on research and publishing (Smolentseva 2003). This does not differ much from the organisation in academia in countries with a capitalist tradition, and although women could access the mid-level of academic hierarchy (for example, head of department) during the Soviet period, their chances of career advancement remained relatively low (Dezhina 2003). Social gender inequality remained unaddressed and problems which it carries for women surfaced in the post-Soviet Russia after the breakup of the USSR.

What makes the modern Russian case so noteworthy? According to "official" discourse, inequality between men and women in academia no longer exists (Grinenko 2014; Gurjanov 2015). In reality, women often get stuck somewhere in the middle of the professional hierarchy working as instructors and lecturers, thus reproducing similar patterns of inequality we know from Western societies. Inequality between women and men in academia is often explained by individual factors (social background, human capital, marital status, children, etc.). Studies imply that, besides skills and productivity, which are very important for career advancement (e.g., Cole and Zuckerman 1984), women tend to choose less competitive occupational fields and accordingly a priori are excluded from the top-ranking positions in academia (Dua 2007). Moreover, research shows similar patterns of division of labour inside academia in Western Europe and in Russia—universities expect women to accept responsibilities in teaching, while men concentrate on research and publishing (Bagilhole 2007; Winslow 2010).

Another concept explains inequality in academia at the institutional level. It argues that women have to overcome more obstacles on their way to the top-ranking positions in academia than their male counterparts. Scholars call it the "glass-ceiling" effect (Morley 1994; David and Woodward 1998; Majcher 2002; Mählck 2003; Acker 2009). While exhibiting features of (subtle) institutional gender discrimination in academia similar to those found in capitalist societies, the Russian case stands out as a special one since it exemplifies an even more deeply rooted mechanism of inequality: women in academia consider gender disparities a natural (and even acceptable) state of affairs (Dezhina 2003; Goguzeva 2009; Ostapenko 2014).

So far, a significant amount of research on gender inequality in academia has focused on micro- and macro-levels of explanation of the disparities between men and women, and Russia shows similar patterns of gender inequality to Western countries (Sillaste 2001; Goguzeva 2009). This challenges the alleged peculiarities ascribed to socialism and suggests different explanations of gender inequality in academia. Alternative approaches—for example, stereotype perspective, social networks involvement, path dependency, etc.—have often been neglected by scholars. In this paper I attempt to highlight factors that impact gender inequality in modern-day Russian academia—namely, participation in scientific events as a means of access to social networks and a source of occupational advancement. By doing so, I aim to shed light on internal processes of career advancement and patterns of interaction within academia that may contribute to inequality between men and women.

Two crucial circumstances should be designated here. Firstly, whereas a great body of studies addresses promotions and results of gendered career advancement by investigating professorship status and differences between male and female professors (Baus 1994; Engler 2000) in a retrospective way, far less is known about the very beginnings and early career trajectories in academia. Indeed, by using a prospective methodology, I aim to show how female academics at an early stage of their professional careers perceive their career advancement in the frame of social-networks involvement. Thus, the main focus of this study is Russian PhD students and women in their early academic careers (i.e., post-docs)—those who have decided to stay in academia after completing graduate studies. Specifically, I wish to investigate where and how inequality begins, and I will attempt to do so by answering several questions: Do early career female academics participate in scientific events like conferences, workshops, and so on? Do they always have access to such events or are they selected by gatekeepers? Are there any indications of a correlation between involvement in social networks and career success? In other words, are early career female academics excluded from scientific networks?

Secondly, most documented studies so far have concentrated on inequality in academia in Western societies (Germany, the United States, the United Kingdom, among others), while our knowledge of post-socialist cases is far more scarce and unsystematic. Yet, it is of great importance to understand whether processes leading to inequality could also be generalized for post-socialist countries and whether inequality in academia is being reproduced there in similar ways. Some notable exceptions offered research findings on Poland (Majcher 2007; Siemieńska 2007); Croatia (Pološki and Petković 2004) and Bulgaria (Stenova 2009, as summarized by Garvis 2014), thus providing examples of opportunities early career women academics have in these countries and their experience with inequality. This chapter aims to expand our knowledge of Russian academia.

THE RUSSIAN SETTING

The organization of the qualification stage in an academic career in Russia slightly differs from the European model. Whereas PhD candidates in Western Europe are provided with more academic freedom and their work is subject to self-management, their Russian counterparts are enrolled into full-time university doctoral/post-doc teaching programs with obligatory participation in lectures and seminar work, or into a long-distance-learning PhD course. Moreover, these programs require two mandatory exams during post-graduate studies, held in front of a council of senior researchers that decides whether a candidate proceeds or repeats the exams. Doctoral candidates choose a supervisor that guides them through the qualification phase—a condition applied for by young academics everywhere. Unlike Western European post-graduates, Russian PhD candidates are rarely employed by the institution they seek to obtain a degree from; they are more likely to work outside the university in the commercial or public sector in order to finance their career advancement (Rosstat 2016). Nevertheless, full-time Russian PhD candidates and post-docs benefit from state bursaries (41 Euros/month for the PhD stage and 68 Euros/month for the post-doc stage in 2015).

Since the Soviet period, the Russian model of academia has combined teaching and research "under one roof". The management of academia wished to keep together teaching and research activities of scholars in order to avoid leaks of knowledge and its transfer to other universities, making research at teaching institutions virtually impossible, as teaching was unofficially considered the primary task at universities (Smolentseva 2003). For strictly scientific purposes, the state created research institutes of applied science that ran an exclusively academic track and were subordinate to the Academy of Sciences (Smolentseva 2003). Representing the post-Socialist legacy, both universities and purely academic research institutes under the Academy of Sciences were allowed to grant doctorates to young academics in Russia.

During the postwar Soviet period (1960–80s), a scientific career was regarded as highly prestigious and desirable among young people (Cherednichenko and Shubkin 1985). Researchers enjoyed high social status and were to a certain extent privileged due to additional vacation days, childcare services, among other perks. Established scientific schools—especially accountable to the Academy of Sciences—incorporated research and teaching simultaneously and ensured a direct interaction between mentors and young researchers, thus attracting gifted early career academics. From the institutional perspective, scientific schools served as a mechanism of career development and integration into the scientific community, providing a supportive mentoring environment for young researchers. Informal connections within and between scientific institutes especially contributed to the pluralism of the scientific elite and spurred knowledge production and its exchange (Lubrano 1993). Social networks within scientific schools maintained continuity of generations and retained the accumulation of knowledge, especially at purely academic research institutes under the Academy of Sciences. During the post-Soviet period, these schools deteriorated primarily due to a lack of financial resources and a serious brain drain among the early career academics (Ushkalov and Malakha 2001). Since the assertion of intellectual property rights, the mechanism of academic career development has deteriorated significantly, for existing social networks no longer ensured empowerment of young academics. A structural approach can partially explain the destruction of continuity of academic traditions by accentuating the unprecedented loss of appeal of an academic career in general (Goguzeva 2009; Sivak and Yudkevich 2013). Additionally, a micro-sociological perspective sheds light on factors of success considered secondary—namely, age, motivation, academic experience and productivity/efficiency of early career academics. As these determinants of career advancement are usually more relevant and rewarding for males, they can partly explain career growth of young academics, often reflecting the Matthew effect of institutions or mentors they are working for: "popular" mentors with outstanding reputations attract gifted early career academics, and their synergistic output gets more credit than that of other young researchers working with less eminent scholars

Table 1   Dynamics of academic degree awards in Russian academia as a percentage of the total number of researchers (1990–2013)

Year	1990	1994	1998	2000	2005	2010	2013
PhD	12.8	18.5	20.5	19.7	19.4	21.2	21.9
Tenured professorship	1.6	3.5	4.9	5.1	5.9	7.2	7.4

Source: The author's own calculations based on Rosstat (Russian statistical yearbook) 2014

(Merton 1988). Indeed, the number of early career academics receiving scientific degrees has increased significantly since 1990 (Table 1), also under conditions of considerable decline in the quality of scientific work (Smolentseva 2003).

However, individual efforts alone can hardly result in the successful career development of early career academics, given the insurmountable isolation from the scientific community nationally and internationally. Specifically, Russian early career academics anticipating an academic career, are constrained by obsolete equipment, outdated Russian-language library resources and limited or non-existent access to international scientific journals (Balabanov et al. 2003; Ascheulova and Dushina 2012). Under such circumstances, the crucial role in career advancement of early career academics is played by their mentors and the contacts they possess. However, for financial reasons mentors often take on an overload of teaching duties at several institutions simultaneously and sometimes are not integrated into the international scientific community themselves, a peculiarity counterproductive to the advancement of young researchers. For such reasons, access to broader social networks within the (international) community becomes of paramount importance for early career academics to establish a scientific career. This can be achieved through participation in scholarly events (conferences, workshops) and mobilisation of social capital (Bourdieu 2011).

This situation seems to be most difficult for early career female academics in Russia since men are considered by society to be better at networking and publishing. Apart from the widespread patriarchal views (conforming to the Humboldtian model of academia) supported by both men and women within Russian academia (e.g. survey results by Vinokurova 2009; Kashina 2005), a lack of women's social capital is one of the hurdles early career female academics face: "if a woman applies for financial support for her research, she must be 1.5 times more productive than men and initially present solid scientific results in order to be taken seriously" (Ershova 2014, p. 90). This fact implies that women—especially early career women academics—are not likely to be taken seriously by the scientific community or academia management, whereas their male counterparts enjoy professional and financial support. As Smolentseva argues, "promotions do occur but the process does not encourage the external mobility of academic staff, and sometimes the outcome has little to do with individual effort" (Smolentseva 2003, p. 405). It means that the administration makes the decision regarding appointment having already chosen one candidate, thus making faculties dependent on the university management, not to mention frequent "inbreeding", or in other words continuation of working at the same institution where one had studied (Smolentseva 2003). Indeed, as Fig. 1 reveals, more men than women reach higher positions: a doctorate degree is crucial for career advancement, thus making career advancement complicated for women without a PhD or a tenure professorship. As one can see, the proportion of men in the highest positions in academia (president or rector) decreased very slightly throughout the 15-year observation period. At the level of faculty and chair management, men dominate as well—although with a tendency to change. Strikingly, the proportion of (young) men and women at assis-

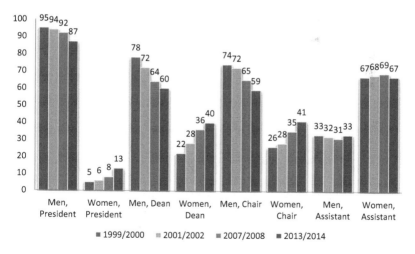

Fig. 1 Teaching and scientific staff and management in Russian academia, in % (*Source:* Rosstat (Russian statistical yearbook) 2002, 2007, 2012, 2014, own calculations)

tant positions has remained constant during the last 15 years. Whereas starting early career positions are open for both, men constitute only one third of the lower staff level in Russian academia.

So far, Russian academia resembles the structures of academia in other western countries—the majority of women are relegated to positions of ordinary "performers" playing a primary role in the educational process and a subordinate one in scientific work.

Can social networks explain the inequality gap between men and women in early career?

As outlined above, Russian academia has much in common with gendered patterns of career development in other countries and incorporates a deeply rooted gender asymmetry: whereas men enjoy rapid career advancements, women frequently get stuck at the lowest positions of academia and are not as likely to get promoted (Sedliak 1990; Matiushina 2007; Ablazhey 2010). Interestingly, in Matiushina's study (2007) the overwhelming majority of women (78%) explained this fact by discussing the time investment and the opportunities their male counterparts have: "men have more successful careers because they have more time and opportunities than women".

What opportunities are meant here? As shown above, social capital and networks are crucial in explaining why women do not find themselves on a more equal footing with men in academia, which is especially important for those at the early stages of their career. Scientific productivity, or performance, is tightly connected to the access to and involvement in social networks inside and outside academia. Indeed, social networks are pervasive and in many cases provide a significant means for improving performance. First suggested by Granovetter (1995), all job-related contacts may be divided into so-called "strong and weak ties". As Granovetter points out, at least one third of all job changes occur via contacts—family or social ones; strong ties are family-oriented, destined to support an individual and to provide one with direct help rather than simply information. Strong ties exist in order to build a stable network of close contacts and to exclude extrinsic ones. On the other hand, weak ties are supposed to deliver information and—according to the market and competition principal—to provide the best qualified people with the most suitable jobs. "Weak ties" may be of paramount importance for career advancement in academia and elsewhere since they are more important for career improvement than familiar strong ties.

As already mentioned, the majority of Russian PhD candidates are not employed at the institutions they will receive their doctorates from. However, they are enrolled in teaching programs at these universities, which puts them in a precarious position. On one hand, PhD seekers have a stronger affiliation to the institution they are taught at. On the other hand, from the point of view of career advancement, doctoral candidates are not regarded as equals with the established scholars, and are assigned a subordinate position as students. This leads to a lack of recognition and failure to acquire the "habitus" that is especially important for acceptance in the local scientific community (Bourdieu 2011). In this regard, "weak ties" are advantageous for early career academics because they boost their chances for recognition and promotion, primarily by mentors and peers. However, this can be problematic for the reasons described above: either the peers are in the same situation as students, or the mentors are too busy or do not work on an international level. It must be remembered that participation in scientific events for the purpose of presenting research and exchange of experiences is regarded as a source of social capital. Indeed, conferences, workshops and project meetings provide not only opportunities to present academic research, but also the best chance for establishing informal contacts that may be crucial for further career development within academia. Drawing upon theoretical considerations pertinent to weak ties and "habitus", I put forth a hypothesis that those early career academics who aspire to an academic career are more likely to seek participation in scholarly events, whereas those who are unsure of their career aspirations are less likely to resort to such practices. I will test these hypotheses below.

Lin (2001), developing Granovetter's idea in his resources theory, argues that contacts represent a type of social capital: weak contacts, such as acquaintances, provide access to better social capital as an instrumental measure, since powerful acquaintances can provide better positions, connections and income for highly qualified individuals. Both types of contacts are of extraordinary importance mainly for young academics who would like to advance their careers. Early career academics must not only integrate into the university they came from, but they also must find a path into the (inter)national scientific community they want to be recognized in, which is much more complicated. Hence, a requirement in order to establish a solid foundation for an academic reputation leading to early career advancement should be either an internationally recognized scientist who is a mentor as a strong tie and/or a network of weak ties (Krais 2000; Zimmer et al. 2007). My next, related hypothesis states that

(conferences, workshops, etc.) trying to link perspectives of both actors—applicants and gatekeepers. As hypothesised above, doctoral candidates with a strong orientation towards an academic career would tend to attempt to join a scientific community beyond their local institution. For that reason, I asked my respondents, first, why they were seeking to obtain a PhD and, second, what type of a career they anticipated. Of the final sample of 49 early career females contacted, most women were aged 23–30, a typical age for Russian doctoral students and those with a PhD. The majority of women were already married or in a partnership (60%), and this was also representative of the average age of marriage in Russia; about 24% of them had children. A minority of respondents reported they strove for an academic career or to stay in academia to ensure family subsistence because their partners worked elsewhere. One-third of early career females sought to obtain a PhD in order to get better career opportunities outside of academia, and another third were driven situationally, being undecided career-wise at the moment of this study. As to the fields of study they had chosen, these were relatively similar to the European distribution: women in this study did research in humanities, social and natural sciences.

Due to their restricted information sources and limited ability to speak English, a large proportion of early career female academics in Russia are likely to participate in domestic/national conferences. Overall, women at the early stage of their academic careers are more likely to travel to conferences compared to their male counterparts, which can be clearly seen in case of the so-called new European constellation. However, apart from uncertainty about their proficiency in communicating in English, which often appears as an obstacle, young academics do not enjoy generous funding to cover travel expenses. Travelling abroad means spending one's own resources. Therefore, early career women are generally less mobile internationally and circulate within the established structure of or local scientific events they already know. This finding on the generally limited mobility of Russian academics corresponds to recent Russian scholarly discussions: they explain the formation of local academic monopolies due to immobility (Sokolov 2012).

An interesting peculiarity lies in the fact that only a few early career female academics pursue participation in scholarly events: most women apply virtually involuntarily, that is, only at the insistence of their mentors. It seems that early career academics prefer to carry out their first career steps in academia with minimal effort, without "wasting time" on international conferences and other scholarly events. They believe that these do not bring them benefits in terms of career advancement—a result rather pertinent to those undecided about their future career. Additionally, in Russia, special incentives for publishing in a foreign language or participating in scholarly events abroad hardly exist. In an effort to try to change this situation mentors attempt to model the academic behaviour of their protégées by "forcing" them to participate in appropriate events.

An exception is presented by a small group of those who deliberately attempt to establish an international academic career, which confirms my first hypothesis. These early career women more often come from the European part of Russia: Moscow (for instance, Higher School of Economics) or St. Petersburg (European University in St. Petersburg). These institutions enjoy a positive international reputation and try to attract established scholars from other countries in order to guarantee a solid education for their students. Being internationally-oriented, such universities explicitly support not only (empirical) research by those in the early career stage, but also participation in relevant scientific events and building academic networks in their respective fields of study.

My second assumption was based on the expectation that early career female academics with a strong mentor are more likely to be included in scientific events due to the deliberate or indirect support of their mentor. In this study, I sought to discover whether this exclusion from an international conference due to a lack of a mentor is actual or perceived. From applicants' perspective, I investigate the frequency of exclusions as compared to admissions and the way applicants experience communication with conference organizers. On the organizers' side, I elucidate the driving forces and mechanisms of exclusion/communication the gatekeepers' practise.

The rate of admission to conferences was higher in cases where an applicant was forced to apply by a mentor, even without any reference or referral. On the contrary, the rate of rejection was higher when an applicant was proactive and sought to participate on the basis of her or his own efforts (possibly because the mentor was not interested or recognized). This finding confirms my second hypothesis: some respondents reported a nearly 100% rate of acceptance when applying on a mentor's recommendation and only a 50% acceptance rate when applying on their own initiative. Moreover, abstracts rejected for conferences within Russia were accepted for oral presentations abroad—a fact that does not necessarily prove discrimination but at least illustrates an ambiguity in the decision-making process in Russia. Additionally, women reported that their male counterparts were unlikely to seek conference participation on their own, applying only on their mentor's recommendation. These facts imply the existence of solid professional networks of senior scholars who are interested in educating and promoting "decent" male successors, thus forcing women to face an unequal contest (created by male networks) on their own.

According to my sample, abstracts for papers from multiple authors were more likely to be accepted for conferences, provided men were named as co-authors: 20% of respondents mentioned this circumstance in their answers. Additionally, annual conferences tend to be more open towards new participants—a feature more inherent in conferences organized by so-called progressive organizers: while previous contributors have a good chance to present again, newcomers are also welcome. The organizers often use this as a way to promote the fact that the conference received a large number applicants from the academic community of scholars.

Unfortunately, the transparency in decision-making of conference organizers leaves a lot to be desired: in my study, I could find little contact information about appropriate persons who select participants or draw up conference programs. The reasons for rejection are usually not explained: upon request one may at best receive a meagre answer like, *"The number of applications far exceeded the number of slots and decisions were made on first-come-first-served basis"*— a response indicating the primacy of everything but quality. A deeper analysis reveals that decisions about acceptance or rejection are strongly influenced by the application procedure itself (paper title without an abstract) as well as by recognition/affiliation of the applicant, both sides of a single coin: the level of identification in the scientific community, either of an applicant "herself" or of her mentor. Interestingly, my subsequent examination of available conference programs from the humanities revealed that some presentations hardly matched the conference topic and could easily have been replaced by others that were rejected.

All in all, there is a distinction between the so-called old Soviet and new European universities and the way they treat early career academics—and this distinction is reflected in other findings. The "old Soviet" system represents the rigid communication and work relationship that existed between mentor and protégé in the 1970s. According to this model, the mentor plays the role of a parent, giving advice and taking care of his or her students. It is up to the mentor to decide whom to promote—and it occurs often on the basis of the mentor's personal experiences, frequently going hand in hand with patriarchal views on work and abilities of protégées based on their gender. Thus, male early career academics were and continue to be preferred over females. Indeed, early career female academics from the regional universities described their relationship to a mentor as a father-daughter one, with fewer prospects for development and career advancement. This protective, paternalistic relationship often included so-called "explanatory conversations" described by Pushkareva (2007): young female academics are encouraged behind the scenes to "concede" shortly before their final stage of PhD. During this "discussion", it was suggested to the female PhD candidates that they fail and/or trade academic work for anything else to clear the path for their male counterparts—future professors and managers of academia (Pushkareva 2007). Indeed, in about 20% of the cases, my question on satisfaction with the mentor resulted in reports about how reluctant same-gender mentors to advance women in academia, thus reflecting the widespread view of the naturalness of gender inequality in the academic circles.

In contrast, in the so-called new European constellation, work between mentors and early career academics highlighted such arrangements where the former guided the latter according to strictly professional standards, thus trying to minimize personal attitudes that could influence work prospects of the young academics. Early career female academics from these universities reported better work experience and higher satisfaction with their mentors regarding participation in scientific events. They explicitly pointed to their successful conference participation achieved through their own efforts without a referral by a powerful mentor.

Against this background, my initial findings indicate that Russian academic communities build informal networks that are likely to select conference applicants on an insider–outsider basis. A possible explanation for this could be that senior members of networks either search for young talents at conferences—which is less likely, since senior members seem to keep their distance from young participants throughout conferences—or they already act as mentors for "their own" protégées. Hence, assumptions about the formation of "scientists' mafias"—especially prevalent among the ageing personnel of Russian academia—can be confirmed, thus unveiling a disadvantage for early career female academics pursuing professional advancement.

CONCLUSION

I have argued here that early career female academics are more likely to be excluded from scientific networks and from participation in scholarly events like conferences or workshops. According to the thesis put forth by Granovetter (1995), weak ties should provide the best-qualified individuals with the best positions, which, as academia is expected to be a meritocracy, should be an indisputable fact. Contrary to expectations, the strong ties between young academics and their mentors are frequently those that promise career advancement, especially at the early career stages in academia. This finding does not contradict the assumption that weak ties work after the scholar achieves recognition in the community. So far, the hypothesis that the weaker the contact (peers or other scholars), the more likely the access to better social capital (participation in academic events) has proven to be largely untrue for Russian academia, with the minor exception of the so-called new European constellation of work between mentor and early career academics. The early career academics in my sample also made it clear that when trying to successfully access conferences and social networks, personal motivation and a clear plan for an academic career went hand-in-hand with good mentoring, thus representing the social and the relational cooperation between the mentor and the young academic.

Contrary to expectations, discrimination against early career female academics in the form of rejecting their conference submissions was not perceived to be real by participants in my study, as it is so subtle. An application's success is more likely when a mentor refers or applies together with his/her protégée—a gesture which senior members of academia are willing to make for both sexes but which does not prevent them from preferentially promoting a male protégée later on. Thus, it appears that hierarchical structures of Russian academia remain misogynist with little sign of improvement.

These findings have certain policy relevance: in Soviet times, the so-called "women's issue" was heralded as having been solved (Ajvazova 1998) and women were proclaimed to be treated equally, thus making it unnecessary to support them as a separate group. This did not represent the social reality, however, and widespread sexist attitudes remained unchanged for decades to follow. This "women's issue" continues to be widely ignored in post-Soviet times, despite the fact that all the evidence does not support this old claim regarding equality. As demonstrated by this study, Russian early career female academics often experience even worse discrimination than their peers do in Europe—a topic which needs to be studied and discussed more broadly.

NOTE

1. The Humboldtian model goes back to the times of the German scholar Alexander von Humboldt: he proclaimed science suitable for men due to their ability to invest full time in it and to dedicate themselves completely to their work in Academia. Women, on the contrary, are much more constrained and—according to Humboldt—are supposed to support men so that they can fully concentrate on science.

REFERENCES

Ablazhey, A. M. (2010). Generations in science: The case of an empirical analysis. *Sotsiologiya nauki i tekhnologii, 2*, 47–56 (in Russian).

Acker, J. (2009). From glass ceiling to inequality regimes. *Sociologie du Travail, 51*(2), 199–217.

Ajvazova, S. G. (1998). *Russian women in the labyrinth of equality (Essays on political theory and history)*. Moscow: RIK Rusanova (in Russian).

Allakhverdian, A.G. & Agamova, N.S. (2000a). *Discrimination of professional rights of scientists as a factor of "brain drain"*. Available from: http://russcience.euro.ru/papers/all-ag.htm. Accessed 5 June 2015. (in Russian).

Allakhverdian, A. G., & Agamova, N. S. (2000b). Russian women in science and higher education: Historical and scientific aspects. *Voprosy istorii estestvoznaniaya i tekhniki, 1*, 141–153 (in Russian).

Ascheulova, N. A., & Dushina, S. A. (2012). Academic career of a young scientist in Russia. *Innovatsii, 7*(165), 60–68 (in Russian).

Bagilhole, B. (2007). Challenging women in the male academy: Think about draining the swamp. In *Challenges and negotiations for women in higher education* (pp. 21–32). Dordrecht: Springer.

Balabanov, S. S., Bednyj, B. I., Kozlov, E. V., & Maksimov, G. A. (2003). Multidimensional typology of doctoral students. *Sotsiologicheskij zhurnal, 3*, 71–85 (in Russian).

Baus, M. (1994). *Professorinnen an deutschen Universitäten. Analyse des Berufserfolgs*. Heidelberg: Asanger.

Bellas, M. L. (1994). Comparable worth in academia: The effects on faculty salaries of the sex composition and labor-market conditions of academic disciplines. *American Sociological Review, 59*(6), 807–821.

Berezina, A. V., & Vitiukhovskaia, Y. A. (2014). Image of woman as a teacher in mass-media and in Russian society. *Chelovek v mire kultury, 1,* 3–9 (in Russian).

Bogdanova, I. F. (2004). Women in science: Yesterday, today, tomorrow. *Sotsiologicheskie issledovaniya, 1,* 103–112 (in Russian).

Bourdieu, P. (2011). The forms of capital. *Cultural theory: An anthology,* 81–93.

Cherednichenko, G. A. & Shubkin, V. N. (1985). *Young people come into life: Sociological studies of choice of profession and employment issues.* Mysl'. (in Russian).

Chikalova, I. (2006). Women in contemporary Belarus science. In *Woman. Society. Education: Proceedings of 8th international interdisciplinary conference, Minsk, 16–17th December 2005* (pp. 27–38). Minsk: Zhenskij institut "Envila" (in Russian).

Cole, J. R., & Zuckerman, H. (1984). The productivity puzzle: Persistence and change in patterns of publication of men and women scientists. *Advances in Motivation and Achievement, 2,* 217–258.

David, M., & Woodward, D. (1998). *Negotiating the glass ceiling: Careers of senior women in the academic world.* London: Falmer Press.

Dezhina, I. G. (2003). Effect of grant funding on the situation of women in the Russian science. *Sotsiologicheskij zhurnal, 4,* 86–100 (in Russian).

Dua, P. (2007). Feminist mentoring and female graduate student success: Challenging gender inequality in higher education. *Sociology Compass, 1*(2), 594–612.

Engler, S. (2000). Zum Selbstverständnis von Professoren und der illusio des wissenschaftlichen Feldes. In B. Krais (Ed.), *Wissenschaftskultur und Geschlechterordnung. Über die verborgenen Mechanismen männlicher Dominanz in der akademischen Welt* (pp. 121–151). Frankfurt/New York: Campus.

Ershova, N. (2014). Problems of Russian women in scientific activity. *Vestnik RGTeU, 6*(86), 84–92 (in Russian).

Felber, C., & Baume, B. (1997). Karrierenchancen, aufhaltsamer oder aushaltsamer Abstieg. Wissenschaftlerinnen aus Ost und West im Interview. In H. Macha & M. Klinkhammer (Eds.), *Die andere Wissenschaft: Stimmen der Frauen an Hochschule.* Bielefeld: Kleine.

Filippov, V. (2013, September 16). A scientist has to do science. *Rossijskaia gazeta.* Available from: http://www.rg.ru/2013/09/16/ran.html. Accessed 5 June 2015.

Fogelberg, P., Hearn, J., Husu, L., & Mankkinnen, T. (1999). *Hard work in the academy: Research and interventions on gender inequalities in higher education.* Helsinki University Press, POB 4 (Vuorikatu 3), FIN-00014 University of Helsinki.

Forster, N. (2001). A case study of women academics' views on equal opportunities, career prospects and work-family conflicts in a UK university. *Career Development International, 6*(1), 28–38.

Garvis, S. (2014). Are you old enough tobe in academia? You don't have grey hair. Constructions of women in academia. In N. Lemon & S. Garvis (Eds.), *Being "in and out": Providing voice to early career women in academia* (pp. 19–30). Rotterdam/Boston/Taipei: Sense Publishers.

Goguzeva, T. S. (2009). Gender analysis of contemporary traditions in the system of higher education. Available from: http://edit.muh.ru/content/mag/ trudy/01_2009/10.pdf. Accessed 07 Apr 2016. (in Russian).

Granovetter, M. (1995). *Getting a job. A study of contacts and careers* (2nd ed.). Chicago and London: The University of Chicago Press.

Grinenko, S. V. (2014). Gender asymmetry in education. *Sovremennye nauchnye issledovaniya i innovatsii. 12.* Available from: http://web.snauka.ru/ issues/2014/12/41818. Accessed 9 Mar 2016. (in Russian).

Gurjanov, P. A. (2015). Gender asymmetry in education in Russia. *Gumanitarnye nauchnye issledovaniya. 7.* Available from: http://human.snauka. ru/2015/07/11881. Accessed 29 Mar 2016. (in Russian).

Hadani, M., Coombes, S., Das, D., & Jalajas, D. (2012). Finding a good job: Academic network centrality and early occupational outcomes in management academia. *Journal of Organizational Behavior, 33*(5), 723–739.

Husu, L. (2005). Women's work-related and family-related discrimination and support in academia. In M.T. Segal & V. Demos (Eds.), *Gender realities: Local and global* (Advances in gender research, Vol. 9) Bingley: Emerald Group Publishing Limited.

Husu, L., & Koskinen, P. (2010). Gendering excellence in technological research: A comparative European perspective. *Journal of Technology and Management Innovations, 5*(1), 127–139.

Kashina, M. (2005). Female career and professional self-fulfillment in academia: Predefined script. Available from: http://ssrn.com/abstract=2525089. Accessed 5 June 2015. (in Russian).

Knights, D., & Richards, W. (2003). Sex discrimination in UK academia. *Gender, Work & Organization, 10*(2), 213–238.

Krais, B. (2000). Das soziale Feld Wissenschaft und die Geschlechterverhältnisse. Theoretische Sondierungen. In B. Krais (Ed.), *Wissenschaftskultur und Geschlechterordnung. Über die verborgenen Mechanismen männlicher Dominanz in der akademischen Welt* (pp. 31–54). Frankfurt/New York: Campus.

Lin, N. (2001). *Social capital: A theory of structure and action.* London and New York: Cambridge University Press.

Lubrano, L. (1993). The hidden structure of Soviet science. *Science, Technology & Human Values, 18*(2), 147–175.

Mählck, P. (2003). *Mapping gender in academic workplaces: Ways of reproducing gender inequality within the discourse of equality.* Doctoral thesis at the Department of Sociology, No 33 SE- 901 87. Akademiska avhandlingar vid Sociologiska institutionen: Umeå universitet. 200 p.

Majcher, A. (2002). Gender inequality in German academia and strategies for change. *German Policy Studies, 2*(3), 35.

Majcher, A. (2007). Seeking the guilty: Academics between career and family in Poland and Germany. In R. Siemienska & A. Zimmer (Eds.), *Gendered career trajectories in academia in cross-national perspective* (pp. 298–321). Warsaw: Wydawnictwo Naukowe Scholar.

Matiushina, Y. (2007). Gener-centered approach in personnel managment in Academia. *Kadrovik. Kadrovyj menedzhment, 1*, 70–74 (in Russian).

Merton, R. K. (1988). The Matthew effect in science, II: Cumulative advantage and the symbolism of intellectual property. *Isis*, 606–623.

Metcalfe, B., & Afanassieva, M. (2005). The woman question? Gender and management in the Russian Federation. *Women in Management Review, 20*(6), 429–445.

Mirskaia, E. Z., & Martynova, E. A. (1993). Women in science. *Vestnik Rossijskoj akademii nauk, 63*(8), 693–700 (in Russian).

Morley, L. (1994). Glass ceiling or iron cage: Women in UK academia. *Gender, Work & Organization, 1*(4), 194–204.

Novikova, T. (2008). Personnel outflow from the Russian science: Win or loss? *Sotsiologicheskie issledovaniya, 9*, 93–101 (in Russian).

Ostapenko, A. B. (2014). Gender asymmetry of status-role distribution in educational system in Russia and the US (comparative analysis). Available from: http://scjournal.ru/articles/issn_1997-292X_2014_9-2_27.pdf. Accessed 9 Mar 2016. (in Russian).

Pfau-Effinger, B. (2006). Wandel der kulturellen Konstruktion des 'Universitäts-Professors' und Karrierechancen von Frauen. In Vorstand des Deutschen Hochschullehrerinnenbundes e.V. (DHB) (Ed.). *Strukturwandel an deutschen Universitäten—Vorteil(e) für Frauen?* Berlin.

Pološki, N. & Petković, Z. (2004). Women's career opportunities in higher education institutions in Croatia: Empirical evidence. Galetić, L. (ed.) *2nd International Conference "An enterprise odyssey: Building competitive advantage": Proceedings* (pp. 1433–1446). Zagreb: Graduate School of Economics and Business: Mikrorad.

Pushkareva, N. L. (2007). Ethnography of contemporary Russian science: gender aspect. In E. R. Iarskaia-Smirnova & P. V. Romanov (Eds.), *Social transformations of professionalism: Views from outside, views from inside* (pp. 111–133) (in Russian). Moskva: Variant.

Sedliak, U. (1990). Czech women in science. *Sotsiologicheskie issledovaniya, 3*, 69–71 (in Russian).

Siemieńska, R. (2007). The puzzle of gender research productivity in Polish universities. In R. Siemieńska & A. Zimmer (Eds.), *Gendered career trajectories in academia in cross-national perspective* (pp. 241–266). Warsaw: Wydawnictwo Naukowe SCHOLAR.

Sillaste, G. (2001). Gender asymmetry in education and science: Sociologist glance. *Vysshee obrazovanie v Rossii, 2,* 96–106 (in Russian).

Sivak, E. V., & Yudkevich, M. M. (2013). Academic profession in a comparative perspective: 1992–2012. *Forsajt, 7*(3), 38–47 (in Russian).

Smolentseva, A. (2003). Challenges to the Russian academic profession. *Higher education, 45*(4), 391–424.

Sokolov, M. (2012). On the process of sociological (de)civilization. *Sotsiologicheskie issledovaniya, 8,* 21–30 (in Russian).

Strekalova, N. (2002). Gender asymmetry in academia: problems and solutions. *Vysshee obrazovanie v Rossii, 5,* 62–64 (in Russian).

Tam, T. (1997). Sex segregation and occupational gender inequality in the United States: Devaluation or specialized training? *American Journal of Sociology, 102*(6), 1652–1692.

The Russian statistical yearbook: Statistical digest. (2014). Moskva: Rosstat.

Thelwall, M., & Kayvan, K. (2014). Academia.edu: Social network or academic network? *Journal of the Association for Information Science and Technology, 65*(4), 721–731.

Ushkalov, I. G., & Malakha, I. A. (2001). The "brain drain" as a global phenomenon and its characteristics in Russia. *Russian Social Science Review, 42*(5), 79–95.

Vinokurova, N. (2009). Women in science and education: Gender equality, gender inequality. *MCE, 1,* 299–311 (in Russian).

Winslow, S. (2010). Gender inequality and time allocations among academic faculty. *Gender & Society, 24*(6), 769–793.

Women and men of Russia. (2002). Moskva: Rosstat.

Women and men of Russia. (2007). Moskva: Rosstat.

Women and men of Russia. (2012). Moskva: Rosstat.

Women and men of Russia. (2014). Moskva: Rosstat.

Women and men of Russia. (2016). Moskva: Rosstat.

Zhukova, N. (2012). The problem of brain drain estimated by professional community in 1991–2000. *Vestnik TvGU, seriya "Istoriya", 4,* 130–139 (in Russian).

Zimmer, A., Krimmer, H., & Stallmann, F. (2007). Women at German universities. In R. Siemieńska & A. Zimmer (Eds.), *Gendered career trajectories in academia in cross-national perspective* (pp. 209–240). Warsaw: Wydawnictwo Naukowe SCHOLAR.

Feminist Work in Academia and Beyond

Órla Meadhbh Murray, Muireann Crowley, and Lena Wånggren

Being a feminist is hard work. It is exhausting to constantly find one's person and beliefs at odds with the structures and organisation of the social world. The white supremacist capitalist patriarchy (hooks 2000, p. 4) in which we live constantly asks us to justify our experiences, our beliefs, and ourselves, alongside just getting by. This chapter springs out of many discussions, workshops, and rants,[1] not only in academic environments but in cafes, friends' homes, and in emails. Coming together to try to make sense of our own and our colleagues' experiences as early-career feminist academics in a marketised university, we seek to unite the experiential and the theoretical in our everyday lives and struggles, negotiating hierarchies within the place of privilege that is the university.[2] Overworked, passionate, casualised, angry, between jobs, scared, doing unpaid work, joyful, and exhausted, we try to explore exactly what counts as feminist 'work' in academia.

Universities continue to be 'white, male institutions of privilege and reproduction' (Heidi Mirza quoted in Williams 2013) with inherent structural processes of discrimination and exclusion. The marketisation of higher education in the United Kingdom and beyond has reinforced and intensified these institutional hierarchies, and inequalities have deepened.

Ó.M. Murray • M. Crowley • L. Wånggren (✉)
University of Edinburgh, Edinburgh, UK

© The Author(s) 2017
R. Thwaites, A. Pressland (eds.), *Being an Early Career Feminist Academic*, DOI 10.1057/978-1-137-54325-7_11

215

In recent decades, students and staff have suffered from increased tuition fees, funding cuts, increased workloads and a focus on 'measurable' productivity, degradation of pay and working conditions, casualisation and job insecurity, and neoliberal managerial techniques (Gill 2010; Brown and Carasso 2013).

Employment on the basis of insecure fixed-term and hourly contracts is now commonplace among early-career academics. As Ana Lopes and Indra Dewan report, the emotional impact of job insecurity and exploitation entails stress, decreasing self-confidence, and negative thoughts of the future—with some of their respondents mentioning 'being close to 'breaking point''' (Lopes and Dewan 2015, p. 34; see also Reevy and Deason 2014). Hourly-paid staff work many hours without pay and are often without basic facilities such as an office space, access to printing and other resources, or training. The University of Edinburgh, where we work, had the highest number of staff on hourly contracts (23 per cent) in the United Kingdom, as revealed in a 2013 investigation, with the Humanities and Social Sciences employing almost half (47 per cent) of their staff on hourly contracts (Morgan 2013). In addition to causing insecurity, anxiety, and financial difficulties among casualised staff, this precarious situation also causes substantive problems in creating an inclusive education that is accessible for all at every level—not just for elite white men.

Reflecting on our experiences as casualised and early-career feminist academics in a neoliberal university, we want to explore the negotiation of feminist aims within these institutional boundaries. We realise that our experiences are not all-encompassing or universal, but particular, and as white feminists at a research-intensive Russell Group university we move in a particularly privileged academic sphere. We take as a given that feminist research is a form of feminist activism within academia, but wish to go beyond this and frame issues such as casualisation, workload, and preconceptions around the academic 'lifestyle', so prevalent in our current workplaces, as feminist issues. Importantly, by highlighting the specific difficulties faced by early-career feminist academics, we by no means want to suggest that more senior or permanent staff have fewer struggles—but merely point out that they are at times slightly different ones. While permanent staff tackle increasing workloads, stress, or performativity measurements, early-career academics face teaching without resources or without much autonomy, worrying about future employment, and trying to stay afloat while working various jobs to pay the rent. The marketised university harms us all, students and staff at all levels, and many of the problems that early-career and senior academics face overlap and intersect, especially experiences of racism, sexism, and other forms of oppression.

In exploring everyday struggles in academia as feminist issues we hope to highlight the invisible work that gets done but not acknowledged within the workplace. As Henry Giroux argues, in order to build a possible politics of resistance, we must pay attention to 'the ways in which institutional and symbolic power are tangled up with everyday experience', while linking individual responsibility with a 'progressive sense of social agency' (Giroux 2003, p. 100). Such thinking can be applied to the everyday practices and challenges of working in and through academia. By asking who organises the post-seminar wine reception, whose shoulders we cry on, who challenges everyday discriminatory comments, and whether or not this is considered work, we want to highlight the gendered, racialised, and classed hierarchies of academia, and their institutional reproduction. To do this we will use an expanded notion of work to highlight all that we and others do as early-career feminist academics that is not recognised by the institution, alongside the everyday work that is necessary to survive as historically oppressed or marginalised people in the neoliberal university space.

BEYOND 9 TO 5: AN EXPANDED DEFINITION OF WORK

As human beings we must do everyday life tasks (getting dressed, cleaning, cooking), alongside supporting ourselves and dependants through paid employment and/or negotiation of the welfare state and other means of support, and the emotional, social and particular work of caring for others if we have children or other caring responsibilities. The ever-expanding list of activities people engage in can be exhausting. If one is further marginalised by society there are even more complex and exhausting activities to add to these daily tasks: the ongoing exertion necessary in managing a chronic illness, negotiating an ableist world as a disabled person, dealing with street harassment, coming out, challenging racism or cis-sexism, putting up with hurtful remarks and ignorant comments, or trying to explain to others why what they said or did was upsetting. Many of these activities are also forms of activism: putting up with and trying to change the organisation of society that oppresses us, then trying to connect with other people and develop networks of support and resistance and organising campaigns, joining unions, voting, petitioning, marching, striking... the list goes on. All of this is work. Yet often these activities are not considered to be work, or to be 'proper' work. In a patriarchal capitalist economy these tasks are not valued as work sufficient to be remunerated or appreciated as 'contributing' to society, as they do not explicitly generate profit or production but function rather as *re*productive labour (Davis 1981; Federici 2012).

Feminist conceptualisations of work expand the definition of work to include the invisible work often done by women, and often hidden in the private sphere of the home and family. The 'double day' (Hartsock 1983) and the 'triple shift' (Duncombe and Marsden 1995) acknowledged that many women entering the workforce were not just working paid jobs but also doing household labour, including housework and childcare, alongside emotional work (for example, caring for others who are ill, disabled, upset, in crisis, or just the everyday work of recognising and empathising with the moods of others). Other feminist theorists, such as Maria Mies (1986) and Silvia Federici (2008, 2012), provide clearer explication of the gendered, racialised, and classed nature of the division of labour under capitalism and the unpaid and unseen labour of women upon whose backs wage exploitation occurs and social relations are reproduced.

In this chapter, we will be using Dorothy Smith's (2005) conceptualisation of work widened as a framework that acknowledges a huge array of activities that are often not thought of as work: unpaid, emotional and social labour, including 'anything done by people that takes time and effort, that they mean to do, that is done under definite conditions and with whatever means and tools, and that they may have to think about. It means much more than what is done on the job' (Smith 2005, p. 152). Marjorie L. DeVault and Liza McCoy (2006) identify three main strands within this notion of work: paid or unpaid jobs, everyday life work, and activist work, as outlined in the examples above. While this definition may seem vague and abstract, it is intentionally so in order to provide a broad concept for us to embellish with our everyday experiences. Experience-based knowledge production is crucial in highlighting that which has been made invisible, so as to bring to light the work that is often unappreciated and unpaid but requires time, effort, and means.

By centring experience-based knowledge, particularly that of women, at the heart of a feminist understanding of society, Smith's conception of work (1987, 1994, 2005) has highlighted the unappreciated, invisible work of women done in the academy and other knowledge-producing institutions to ensure that certain white Western male elites could become knowledge producers throughout history. In the Cartesian tradition, believing that one's mind could produce theory and ideas dislocated and free from social location and the messy world of the body, these elite men produced 'objective' knowledge while their material needs were taken care of by their wives, secretaries, cleaners, assistants, and other underlings. These feminised jobs were and are done by working-class men and women, people of colour, and people from the global South (some of these identities often overlapping and intersecting). Oppressed peoples' experience-based understanding of all these undervalued and underpaid roles alongside the invisible work that falls in between official categories of 'wife' and 'assistant' are vital in destabilising narrow notions of work and in challenging the historic exclusion of other voices from the 'objective' framework of academia.

Through Smith's expanded notion of 'work', which includes the invisible emotional and social labour that is essential to the running of the university, yet is often unpaid and underappreciated, we will provide a feminist critique of the neoliberal university. This feminist definition of 'work' makes possible a revealing of hidden hierarchies and unrecognised work: we see that work carried out by groups—women, people of colour, disabled people, casualised staff, postgraduate students—that are often silenced through the hierarchical structures of the university is essential yet often unacknowledged or not valued as 'proper' academic work.

LOCATING FEMINIST WORK IN EVERYDAY THEORY AND PRACTICE

What does it mean to work as a feminist academic; as a feminist in academia? Smith's expanded notion of 'work' forces us as feminists to consider how, and to what degree, the work we do alongside and around our feminist research enacts the feminist principles our research espouses. As feminist academics in the Humanities and Social Sciences, it may be taken for granted that our research will attempt to address, challenge, destabilise, unpick, and/or resist the manifold manifestations of both individual acts and institutional patterns of sexism, racism, homophobia and transphobia, and ableism in culture and society, as our research aims to be both the product and the practice of an intersectional feminism (Crenshaw 1989, 1991). But how do we act out our feminism in other everyday activities; how do we express our resistance to the totalising impositions of the neoliberal university? What does feminist work look like in the quotidian transactions and interactions of higher education?

By viewing our feminist work in academia and beyond as much more than paid labour, we can highlight the hidden intersecting hierarchies in academia, which further opens up discussions regarding the divide between theory and practice, academia and activism: if feminist work involves various types of activities, how do we clearly separate them—and should we? As Simone de Beauvoir has pointed out, 'In truth, there is no divorce between philosophy and life' (2004, p. 217). Feminism is by its nature both theoretical and practical, requiring personal as well as para-academic (Wardrop and Withers 2014) or extra-academic work. Importantly, feminist theory is not inherently emancipatory or revolutionary—as bell hooks notes, it 'fulfills this function only when we ask that it do so and direct our theorizing towards this end' (hooks 1994, p. 61). In UK marketised universities, feminism and feminist theory might become commodities that only the privileged can afford. As Shaunga Tagore expresses in her slam poem,'Your ideal graduate student is / someone who doesn't have to experience community organizing / because you've already assigned them five chapters to read about it' (Tagore 2009, p. 39). When a Master's course in Gender Studies costs several thousand pounds and requires full-time attention by students often working part-time or with caring responsibilities, academic feminism falls short. But, hooks asserts, such processes of commodification can be disrupted and subverted when 'as feminist activists we affirm our commitment to a politicized revolutionary feminist movement that has as its central agenda the transformation of society' (1994, p. 71). In a neoliberal university system this impetus to bind together theory and practice, philosophy and life, becomes even more crucial.

Expanding 'work' to encompass the unpaid emotional and social labour carried out by many individuals within the university serves not only to provide a feminist critique of the neoliberal university, but also to remind us as feminists of our responsibility to recognise various acts and activities outside of paid labour as forms of feminist work. This may seem self-evident, but remains worth restating to underline the continuity between feminist theory and practice: feminist academic work does not end with the successful publication of an article in a prestigious journal (which will be read only by a few, probably academics) or with the delivery of a conference presentation (which will be heard by only a few, probably academics). The push to publish and produce other 'outputs' is increasing in the current climate of accountability. Indeed, exercises like the Research Excellence Framework (REF), where institutions have their research assessed and rated in a painstaking and admin-heavy process, has presented us with the managerial notion of 'impact'; academics are now pressured to justify the 'impact' that their research has had.[3] A job that one of us applied for required the applicant to describe the impact their research has had not only on society but also on 'the economy', a rather odd criterion for a position in the Humanities and Social Sciences.[4] The limits of this kind of exercise do not allow for more complex explanations regarding the role of education in society. This short-term notion of 'impact' is a reductive way of looking at how people interact and learn, ignoring the dialectic and ongoing nature of the teaching and learning process. Who knows what long-term effects a text or a workshop might have—in ten years, in twenty years? Who knows the 'impact' a piece of research, a course, an academic might have on peoples' lives?

Such exercises might be subverted and used for feminist ends: for example, this very chapter involves us making visible and challenging neoliberal structures in the academy, while also furthering our publishing records to help us progress within this system. Similarly, Susan Wright (2015) explains how under the new Danish academic publishing classification system the counting of blog articles and other media 'created the hilarious situation of [an academic] earning a point every time he criticised his dean in the press' (Wright 2015, p. 319). However, such strategic engagement with these pressures cannot be the sole means of doing feminist work, as not all feminist work can be translated into 'REF-able' 'outputs' and the continuation of this competitive ranking system for publications merely encourages academics to continue increasing their 'output' in order to compete for prestige and funding against each other to the detriment of writing quality and personal well-being, creating a 'toxic' (Gill 2010) environment of competition and individualisation. As feminists working in academia, we want to look beyond the accountability measures, going beyond the institution's demand of us to 'play the game', using the privileged positions we are in to make our work matter both within and beyond the university—we cannot be feminists on paper alone.

Due to increasing workloads and unpaid labour within the academy, the idea of taking on more feminist work in addition to our research might seem 'too much'. Indeed, trying to meet the ever-increasing demands put upon us is not only ineffective (or rather impossible) but dangerous, as it reinforces an individualised adaptation rather than collective resistance to these changes (Pereira 2015; Gill and Donaghue 2015). However, the everyday nature of much of this work involves a different way of doing things, rather than just 'doing more'. Silvia Federici (2008) discusses the everyday nature of resistance to capitalism through building alliances, solidarity, and collectivities, warning that '[w]e have to ensure that we do not only confront capital at the time of the demonstration, but that we confront it collectively at every moment of our lives'. This can take the form of events, reading groups, and other networks 'within' the university, and organising events and building alliances 'outside of' the university in order to bring people together to exchange experiences and ideas and build networks of solidarity. Similarly it might involve connecting feminists in academia to other campaigns and projects outside of the university in order to better intertwine our practice with theory and root our privileged knowledge-making positions in broader grass-roots organising.[5] Some of this work is much more situated in our everyday academic tasks and interpersonal interactions in the workplace: the challenging of specific explicit instances of sexism, racism, homophobia and transphobia, or ableism occurring in our workspaces. Other everyday situated feminist work may consist in joining a trade union and supporting student and other staff actions and campaigns such as the SOAS Justice for Cleaners Campaign.[6]

There are also much more subtle processes of exclusion amidst the murky hierarchies of academic prestige. Val Gillies and Helen Lucey point out that the 'everyday process of negotiating institutional power relations, despite its central role in building and sustaining an academic career' is relatively under-examined in studies of higher education (Gillies and Lucey 2007, p. 1). Highlighting the specific challenges faced by PhD students who have not followed the 'conventional' path into academia, and who may also have family and work commitments that preclude the possibility of making use of opportunities to build networks with their peers and fellow scholars, Gillies and Lucey underline the importance of interactions that take place in the 'extra-academic' spaces of the university. These are the unstructured, relatively unregulated spaces within the university, such as the post-seminar wine reception, the postgraduate induction meeting, the discipline-specific reading group, or the unexpected encounters in the hallways of university buildings. In these spaces, the traditional hierarchical relationship between staff and students, and amongst the students themselves, may not be governed by expectations of classroom etiquette, but nevertheless tends to fall into the structure that replicates the university's hierarchy.

However, we believe that feminists can effect change through everyday work in academia by mobilising their academic and social capital to confront formal and informal hierarchies within the university and begin to challenge these hierarchies. Doing so may mean creating new extra-academic spaces that are specifically targeted at inclusion, communication, and collaboration, or addressing these hierarchies through activities such as teaching or trade union organising. In thinking beyond the marketised university, we pay attention to the symbolic power of local spaces of discussion, debate, and collaboration rather than the creation of larger 'impact' projects that speak to 'stakeholders' rather than to citizens.

'How Did You Find Out About the Job?'

'After the Seminar, Over Wine'

Perhaps the most easily identified extra-academic space is the drinks reception that bookends many academic events—seminars, lectures, conferences, launches, exhibitions—where lecturers, postdoctoral researchers or tutors, and PhD, Master's, and sometimes undergraduate degree students rub shoulders in close quarters. In such informal spaces, it is expected that students should feel comfortable approaching staff, or that, likewise, staff or more senior doctoral researchers will take the opportunity to welcome younger and more junior students into the fold by introducing them to colleagues. However, in our experience, this is frequently not the case. As Jo Freeman observes, '[a]ny group of people of whatever nature that comes together for any length of time will inevitably structure itself in some fashion … [and] it will be formed regardless of the abilities, personalities, or intentions of the people involved' (2013, p. 232).[7] In academia, these structures tend to mirror existing inequalities, and so serve to perpetuate them. Staff and students tend to socialise in these scenarios with their peer and friendship groups, naturally gravitating towards those in similar positions. At any such event, you may observe small cliques engaged in conversation, with a few unattached individuals hovering at the edges of groups or on the periphery of the space itself. Although there is nothing inherently blameworthy in such interactions, their invariability is problematic. As Heidi Mirza states in a 2013 *Guardian* article, 'Higher education is about peer review and has a fundamentally nepotistic way of operating. It's about networking and people support people they know who are like themselves, who they feel will mirror their own areas of interest' (quoted in Williams 2013). As Mirza points out, this nepotism is predisposed to reproduce the university as a site of white, male, and class privilege, and actively marginalises people of colour in particular. These processes, as Freeman suggests, do not reflect individuals' intentions as much as their compliance with the path of least resistance.

As postgraduate students and early-career academics progress through academia, they gradually accrue academic and social capital, which in turn facilitates their interaction with more senior colleagues, and, in cynical terms, their career progression. Although it can be easily claimed that the onus is upon individuals to muster up the courage to build personal and professional relationships that will support their career, this is easier for those who are already received and perceived as 'belonging' to higher education in the first instance—that is to say, often white, often male persons already in privileged positions. Indeed, the institutional processes of exclusion and marginalisation in higher education actively shut out certain members, leaving individuals from historically oppressed groups of people being 'presumed incompetent' (Gutiérrez y Muhs et al. 2012), often causing a so-called 'impostor syndrome': the feeling that one does not belong, that one is not worthy to inhabit the academic space, believing that everyone else in the room is more qualified.

The onus therefore is rather on individuals 'not to pull up the ladder behind them', as one colleague phrased it, but rather for feminist academics of all genders to undertake, where possible, the emotional and intellectual work of including those who have yet to find their footing. This work is especially important for people in positions of privilege, whether that be white or male privilege, or in terms of job security, as their position is already acknowledged and more secure in the university hierarchy. This means approaching the person standing on the edges of the gathering, asking questions of the quietest person in the group, and facilitating introductions between newcomers and your own colleagues. It means seeking out those who are newly arrived to the institution and connecting them with others who may share their research interests if not your own. It means advertising opportunities, whether paid or unpaid, rather than simply handing them to friends or students. It also means considering people as individuals with full and complicated lives, rather than purely as researchers who disgorge information about their subject on demand, and asking, 'How are you?' rather than only iterations of 'How's work?'

As early-career feminist academics, the longer we spend in the university the more we accrue the academic and social capital that allows us to move more confidently through these extra-academic spaces; we must then mobilise that capital not just on the behalf of, but rather with and to leave space for, others. Some of us move more easily than others; as white women in spaces of institutional whiteness (Phiri 2015), we know that mobilising such capital might be easier for us than for those negotiating not only complex gendered but also racialised barriers or other microaggressions and processes of exclusion. The aim is not to impose ourselves or our friendship on others, or to silence other peoples' voices while making our own louder, but to repeatedly enact a gesture of welcome that facilitates others' inclusion in the friendship networks that are so integral to success within academia, while also respecting and valuing difference. This repeated act of welcoming is feminist work; it is both a political and ethical activity in which we affirm our responsibility to challenge the invisible hierarchies that characterise extra-academic spaces. It can be tiring work, in which we create moments of discomfort when we deviate from the path of least resistance to instead undertake the emotional and intellectual labour of meeting others on their terms. It is the everyday work of our feminist activism.

But there is an inherent risk to this hopeful but occasionally exhausting practice of emotional work or labour. We feel this when we experience what Arlie Hochschild (1983) describes as 'the *pinch between* a real but disapproved feeling on the one hand and an idealized one, on the other' (pp. x, xi); when to reach out, speak up, or step back requires an effort that diminishes our personal resources. Indeed, some researchers have argued that '[a]ppeals to the dispositional aspects of the emotional labourer do not ... reduce the risk of exploitation but rather shift it to that of voluntary exploitation' (Constanti and Gibbs 2004, p. 248). Such a view seems to preclude the possibility of emotional work being purposeful or constructive to any degree. However, it does highlight the problematic nature of feminists' emotional labour. Furthermore, within the context of higher education, the often-gendered division of labour may mean that early career female academics are vulnerable to expectations of providing this form of labour for both their colleagues and their students (Bellas 1999; Koster 2011; Leathwood and Read 2008; Morley 1998; Tunguz 2014). Intersecting with this expectation is the reality of intensified workloads in United Kingdom further and higher education, as well as organisational pressures to meet performance targets with regards to student satisfaction that place staff, particularly casualised staff, under increased pressure to display 'appropriate behaviours and emotions', which may be defined in terms of 'niceness', toward their students (Ogbonna and Harris 2004; Tunguz 2014). Female academics of colour may also find that their white colleagues are allowed to 'duck diversity' and the accompanying emotional labour in their teaching (Schueths et al. 2013).

To put it succinctly, the risk is that 'issues of oppression and difference can be contained and dealt with via the emotional labour of feminist academics, leaving the rest of the academy untouched' (Morley, p. 26). Nevertheless, we would posit that acknowledging and naming the quotidian acts of our feminist praxis 'as work' might provide a starting point to consider the inequalities so prevalent in higher education, so that feminists of all genders can work and organise to address them both locally and systematically.

Un(der)appreciated and Un(der)paid: Teaching and Organising Events

In addition to work in extra-academic spaces, one of the main ways in which we may do feminist work in the university is through teaching: that aspect of our work that offers 'the space for change, invention, spontaneous shifts' (hooks 1994, p. 11). This is where one gets to question students' perceptions and preconceptions, and also one's own. Many of us remember having a teacher who inspired us, challenged us, and made us read all those fantastic texts which enabled us to see the world differently. The classroom in this way becomes a central space in which to continue our feminist work. However, a marketised higher education system which values profit over critique threatens not only the existence of seemingly 'unproductive' fields such as Gender Studies or the Humanities,[8] and of our work as feminist researchers, but also our teaching. Within a neoliberal framework focusing on the profitability of education, and with demands for ever-increasing productivity, time-consuming feminist pedagogies marked by problem-based learning and a critique of established knowledge (Crabtree et al. 2009) might be overlooked in favour of less complex perspectives.

Teaching is often underappreciated and underpaid, with student feedback increasingly being used as a marker of value. The Edinburgh University Students' Union (EUSA) has been running the 'Teaching Awards' since 2009, in which students nominate staff for awards such as Best Postgraduate Tutor or Best Lecturer. The aim is to recognise good teaching and to encourage the university to do so too, which is much appreciated by staff, some of whom now actively want to get nominated. However, student evaluation of teaching is not always benevolent, and student satisfaction should not be used as a proxy for quality, particularly when taken in isolation. In the National Student Survey,[9] student satisfaction is (supposedly) measured but it has become a way of punishing and micromanaging staff, forcing institutions to posit education as a commodity to be evaluated in a customer service model. Instead of changing workload models to allow more paid time for teaching, staff are asked to simply 'time manage' better and do more work in less time. In addition, as Michael Messner (2000) has noted, female teachers and teachers of colour tend to be more critically evaluated by students than their male white counterparts. Student satisfaction surveys and evaluations could thus prove particularly bad for women or members of other historically oppressed groups, who may be subject to the biases of students who might judge them more harshly, basing feedback on gender performance or appearance (Bates 2015; Garden 2015).

Furthermore, stress and intense workloads mean less time for proper preparation and time given to students. Similarly, the job insecurity and casualisation prevalent among early-career academics leave educators without basic resources such as office space or printing facilities, training, or paid time to meet students. Casualisation of academic staff means cheap labour for the universities, who keep tutors, course organisers, and lecturers on short fixed-term (four or nine months, to cover a semester or two of teaching) or even hourly contracts— most often teaching-only contracts which offer no career development or progression opportunities and no paid annual leave. Colleagues (with many years of postdoctoral work behind them) at our own university have organised full courses, teaching postgraduate as well as undergraduate courses, on hourly contracts paid at the rate of a PhD tutor. One of us recently organised and taught an undergraduate course in a different part of the university than the one in which we normally work, a course which involved 30 hours in the classroom, face-to-face with students, not counting the administrative and preparation work. A request to be paid for the full number of hours worked (after the initial offer of six hours' pay) was met with surprise and resistance. In the last few years various UK universities have advertised not only unpaid postdoctoral research fellowships, but also even unpaid teaching fellowships (see, e.g., Mendelsohn 2013), some of which were withdrawn after pressure from media and from trade unions.

Unpaid work does not only concern teaching. As described in the previous section, in a large research-intensive institution such as the University of Edinburgh, many of us organise events outside our official remit as student or tutor or researcher. As we do this to meet like-minded fellows and to take part in the wider research community, we would rarely consider asking to be paid for such work. An increasingly important act of resistance against the devaluing of our labour and the erosion of the basic principle of paying workers for their work involves merely asking to be paid. The culture of working for free has become so entrenched that even when reflecting on and researching these topics, as we are, there is still embarrassment or a reluctance to ask to be paid for the hours worked. Full-time permanent staff are expected to work unpaid, too, on top of taking on extreme and unmanageable workloads, and casualised and early career staff are expected to work for free as well. For instance, when submitting an application for funding to run an event, it often seems 'inappropriate' to factor in wages for the organisers, despite the extensive work done behind the scenes to put on such an event. Rather the 'payment' is another item for the CV, the joy of vocational work, and the appreciation of more senior and secure colleagues who may one day respond with research assistant positions, tutoring opportunities, or even crucial informal recommendations for jobs.

In working long hours for free, we are encouraging a race to the bottom of our own worsening working conditions. Considering the ever-increasing demands on feminist academics to work unpaid, and to give up more and more of ourselves, we recognise that an absolutely crucial part of doing feminist work in academia—for feminists of all genders—is organising in our workplaces. We have spent too many hours marking essays unpaid because of our care and sense of and duty for our students, have had too many instances of being 'presumed incompetent', and have spent too much energy worrying about not being able to pay the rent to not see the necessity of working within trade unions and elsewhere collectively to try to right these unjust working conditions and hierarchies. After all, women and feminists have long organised through trade unions as a way of fighting against gendered and other injustices (Boston 2015). Even small victories, such as reformulating workload models, or negotiating for slightly better job security, can make an enormous difference for teachers as well as for students.

CONCLUSION

Since we gained entry into this exclusive space, we, as feminist academics in the United Kingdom, have necessarily worked in, against, and beyond the white, male institution of privilege that is the university. However, feminist work is often exhausting, and there are limits to what we can do while maintaining our health and any semblance of a 'work–life balance'. Writing this chapter, and working in a marketised university system, we face a problematic question: while we highlight the importance of doing feminist work—much of which is unpaid—in classrooms and extra-academic spaces, can we simultaneously protest against reproducing the patterns in which women and/or people of colour do unappreciated and unpaid work? These two strategies have to come together: we have to somehow do both, while also taking care of ourselves. Feminist work in our classrooms and extra-academic spaces might offer possibilities for countering market-driven models of education, but when faced with increasing workloads and job insecurity, we find it becomes harder for our forms of feminist work to fit in alongside our paid (and unpaid) work. In our contemporary neoliberal universities we cannot, as Maria do Mar Pereira notes, simply 'work harder, manage our time better' (2012, p. 133). Instead, we must make realistic adjustments to our working conditions, while simultaneously collectively fighting for better conditions; we need to 'both *be realistic and demand the* (allegedly) *impossible*' (Pereira 2012, p. 134). If we fall ill from overwork or stress, no one will be there to question hurtful remarks in the classroom or organise collegial events. As Audre Lorde notes, 'Caring for myself is not self-indulgence, it's self-preservation and that is an act of political warfare' (1988, p. 131). Taking care of yourself and others is also a political act; it is feminist work.

This emphasis on the revolutionary nature of care of ourselves and each other—a 'feminist ethics of care' (Mountz et al. 2015)—became evident when one of us co-organised a writing retreat for PhD students, in which there was a dual emphasis on writing and well-being, stemming from the ongoing informal discussions about mental health and the lack of work–life balance. It also emerged from our anxieties around writing, which is often a solitary and unclear process. The focus was on creating a supportive 'retreat' environment in which we could openly and honestly discuss our writing concerns, share tips and methods, and build a better writing and research community. When planning the schedule we decided to include walks, meditation, communal meals, discussion groups, free time, and drinks in the evening, so as to be able to share experiences and have regular breaks. In the current individualised and stressful marketised university, taking breaks, weekends, and holidays becomes a revolutionary act, particularly if you talk about it and encourage others to do the same, organising collectively.

In writing this chapter, we hope to emphasise the everyday feminist activist work that we can do within the academic sphere to destabilise the neoliberal university, and perhaps by extension alleviate the guilt that we sometimes feel about not doing enough. We want to highlight that many everyday acts, whether writing journal articles or marching on the streets, are feminist work and thus revolutionary acts of resistance. Through identifying spaces where invisible feminist work—the unpaid, emotional, and social labour—is done and underappreciated, carried out by those marginalised in academia, feminists can find opportunities to resist and agitate for change. Part of this change comes through identifying this invisible work, making it visible, acknowledging it as 'real' work, and thus rendering it 'countable' in the unending quantification of activities in higher education. This ensures that hourly-paid staff get paid for more of their work and that, for fixed-term and permanent staff, such work can be counted in workload models and contribute to decisions around promotion. However, such exposing of invisible work must also be combined with other feminist work, specifically collective and collegial work in extra-academic spaces, teaching, collaborations, and trade union organising. Through these activities we may hope to challenge the putative dichotomies of theory and practice, academia and activism, and agitate for change in higher education and beyond.

NOTES

1. On the editors' request we include a note on the use of the word 'rant' in this context. Feminist and other movements have long organised in part by sharing experiences of injustice, be it in consciousness-raising groups or through highlighting marginalised voices by other means (see, e.g., Ahmed 2004). We are aware of the negative (patriarchal) connotations of the word and use it consciously, appreciating the political potential of sharing experiences in order to promote action. As Maria do Mar Pereira (2015) notes, one should not underestimate the power of academic 'small talk' in disrupting harmful academic cultures.
2. We use the term 'early career researchers' to include postgraduate students, who are increasingly shouldering the burden of organising within their departments—whether it be setting up seminar series, tutoring other students, or writing journal articles—to begin climbing the greasy pole of professional advancement in academia. The

invisible work is beginning earlier and earlier, with some undergraduate students beginning to plan academic careers and expanding their CV through extracurricular commitments in order to stay 'competitive', particularly with a view to securing scarce scholarships for postgraduate study. We also wish to challenge the hierarchy between students and staff: students are workers too, and considering their activities as work, particularly the often extensive political organising, helps uncover more feminist work occurring within the neoliberal university.

3. For an extended critique of the Research Excellence Framework, see Derek Sayer (2015) *Rank Hypocrisies: The Insults of the Ref*, London: Sage Swifts.

4. Then again, the higher education portfolio is now housed under the UK government's 'Department for Business, Innovation & Skills' (BIS) which, according to its website, 'is the department for economic growth' (2015). While higher education is devolved to the Northern Irish Assembly, Scottish Government, and Welsh Government, the UK government's emphasis on the economy still impacts universities and colleges in the devolved nations, particularly through UK-wide funding bodies such as the Economic and Social Research Council, which receives much of its funding through BIS (ESRC, 2015).

5. If one is doing a research project on gender theory, one can organise a film screening on International Women's Day or a Reclaim the Night march, or if working on postcolonial or antiracist theory, one might organise workshops during Black History Month or participate in ongoing antiracist campaigning. If one is working on queer theory, if time and energy allows, why not get involved with local LGBTQI+ campaigns?

6. For more information see: http://soasunion.org/campaigns/priority/j4c/ and https://www.facebook.com/SOAS-Justice-For-Cleaners-487787121252241/timeline/.

7. We would like to thank Eva Giraud for allowing us to read a draft of her chapter, 'Feminist Praxis, Critical Theory, and Informal Hierarchies' (2015) prior to its publication in *Journal of Feminist Scholarship7* (8). Her use of Jo Freeman's 'The Tyranny of Structurelessness' has informed our understanding of how hidden hierarchies develop within academic communities.

8. For example, Nira Yuval-Davis (2011) discusses the closure of the Gender and Ethnic Studies centre after 'restructuring' at the University of Greenwich, which prompted her move to the University of East London. She highlights that the process of structuring and closing centres/departments is happening across UK universities, particularly Social Sciences and Humanities departments.

9. The National Student Survey (NSS) is an annual UK-wide undergraduate final-year student satisfaction survey. The survey collects student satisfaction ratings in university league tables, and the results are put on the Unistats comparison website aimed at those deciding on a university course. It is run by Ipsos Mori on behalf of the Higher Education Funding Council for England (HEFCE), with universities and student unions often encouraging students to fill it in due to the increasing importance of the results. With the announcement of the Teaching Excellence Framework, the NSS is likely to become even more important, as it may become one of the measures used to rate teaching 'excellence'.

REFERENCES

Ahmed, S. (2004). *The cultural politics of emotion.* Edinburgh: Edinburgh University Press.

Bates, L. (2015, February 13). Female academics face huge sexist bias. *The Guardian.* Available from: http://www.theguardian.com/lifeandstyle/womens-blog/2015/feb/13/female-academics-huge-sexist-bias-students. Accessed 25 May 2015.

Bellas, M. L. (1999). Emotional labor in academia: The case of professors. *Annals of the American Academy of Political and Social Science. 561*(Jan), 96–110.

Boston, S. (2015). *Women workers and the trade unions* (2nd revised ed.). London: Lawrence & Wishart.

Brown, R., & Carasso, H. (2013). *Everything for sale? The marketisation of UK higher education.* London: Society for Research into Higher Education.

Constanti, P., & Gibbs, P. (2004). Higher education teachers and emotional labour. *International Journal of Educational Management, 18*(4), 243–249.

Crabtree, R. D., Sapp, D. A., & Licona, A. C. (Eds.) (2009). *Feminist pedagogy: Looking back to move forward.* Baltimore: The John Hopkins University Press.

Crenshaw, K. W. (1989). Demarginalizing the intersection of race and sex: A black feminist critique of antidiscrimination doctrine, feminist theory, and antiracist Politics. *University of Chicago Legal Forum, 139*, 138–167.

Crenshaw, K. W. (1991). Mapping the margins: Intersectionality, identity politics, and violence against women of color. *Stanford Law Review, 43*(6), 1241–1299.

Davis, A. (1981). *Women, race and class*. London: The Women's Press.

Department for Business, Innovation & Skills.. (2015). *GOV.UK*. Available from: https://www.gov.uk/government/organisations/department-for-business-innovation-skills. Accessed 20 Aug 2015.

de Beauvoir, S. (2004). Existentialism and popular wisdom (Marybeth Timmermann,Trans.). In: Simons, M. A. (ed). *Simone de Beauvoir: Philosophical writings* (pp. 203–220). Urbana & Chicago: University of Illinois Press.

DeVault, M. L., & McCoy, L. (2006). Institutional ethnography: Using interviews to investigate ruling relations. In D. E. Smith (Ed.), *Institutional ethnography as practice* (pp. 15–44). Oxford: Rowman & Littlefield Publishers.

Duncombe, J., & Marsden, D. (1995). 'Workaholics' and 'whingeing women': Theorising intimacy and emotion work—the last frontier of gender inequality? *The Sociological Review, 43*(1), 150–169.

Economic and Social Research Council (ESRC).. (2015). *What we do*. Available from: http://www.esrc.ac.uk/about-esrc/what-we-do/index.aspx. Accessed 21 Aug 2015.

Federici, S. (2008). Precarious labor: A feminist viewpoint, In: Team Colors Collective (ed). (2008) *In the middle of a Whirlwind: 2008 convention protests, movement and movements*. New York: The Journal of Aesthetics and Protest. Available at: https://inthemiddleofthewhirlwind.wordpress.com/precarious-labor-a-feminist-viewpoint/

Federici, S. (2012). *Revolution at point zero: Housework, reproduction, and feminist struggle*. Oakland, California: PM Press.

Freeman, J. (2013). The tyranny of structurelessness. *WSQ: Women's Studies Quarterly, 41*(3/4), 231–246.

Forrester, G. (2005). All in a day's work: Primary teachers 'performing' and 'caring'. *Gender and Education, 17*, 271–287.

Garden, A. (2015, April 21). Students, don't rate me on my appearance but on my teaching. *The Guardian*. Available from: http://www.theguardian.com/higher-education-network/2015/apr/21/students-dont-rate-me-on-my-appearance-but-on-my-teaching. Accessed 20 Aug 2015.

Gill, R. (2010). Breaking the silence: The hidden injuries of the neoliberal university. In R. Ryan-Flood & R. Gill (Eds.), *Secrecy and silence in the research process: Feminist reflections* (pp. 228–244). London: Routledge.

Gill, R., & Donaghue, N. (2015). Resilience, apps and reluctant individualism: Technologies of self in the neoliberal academy. *Women's Studies International Forum*. doi:10.1016/j.wsif.2015.06.016.

Gillies, V., & Lucey, H. (Eds.) (2007). *Power, knowledge and the academy: The institutional is political*. Basingstoke: Palgrave Macmillan.

Giroux, H. (2003). Utopian thinking under the sign of neoliberalism: Towards a critical pedagogy of educated hope. *Democracy & Nature, 9*(1), 91–105.

Gutiérrez y Muhs, G., et al. (Eds.) (2012). *Presumed incompetent: The intersections of race and class for women in academia.* Logan: Utah State University Press.

Hartsock, N. (1983). *Money, sex and power: Toward a feminist historical materialism.* New York: Northeastern University Press.

Hochschild, A. (1983). *The managed heart: The commercialization of human feeling* (2nd ed.). Berkeley: University of California Press.

hooks, b. (1994). *Teaching to transgress: Education as the practice of freedom.* London: Routledge.

hooks, b. (2000). *Feminism is for everyone: Passionate politics.* Cambridge, MA: South End Press.

Koster, S. (2011). The self-managed heart: teaching gender and doing emotional labour in a higher education institution. *Pedagogy, Culture & Society, 19*(1), 61–77.

Leathwood, C., & Read, B. (2008). *Gender and the changing face of higher education.* Maidenhead: Open University Press.

Lopes, A. & Dewan, I. (2015). Precarious pedagogies? The impact of casual and zero hour contracts in Higher Education. *Journal of Feminist Scholarship. 7*(8), 28–42. Available from: http://www.jfsonline.org. Accessed 29 May 2015.

Lorde, A. (1988). *A burst of light: Essays.* Ithaca: Firebrand Books.

Mendelsohn, T. (2013, October 21). Teaching is not its own reward: Durham University in unpaid jobs row. *The Independent.* . Available from: http://www.independent.co.uk/student/news/teaching-is-not-its-own-reward-durham-university-in-unpaid-jobs-row-8894458.html. Accessed 21 Aug 2015.

Messner, M. A. (2000). White guy habitus in the classroom: Challenging the reproduction of privilege. *Men and Masculinities, 2*(4), 457–469.

Mies, M. (1986). *Patriarchy and accumulation.* London: Zed Books.

Morgan, J. (2013, September 5). UCU homes in on widespread use of zero-hours deals. *Times Higher Education.* Available from: http://www.timeshighereducation.co.uk/news/ucu-homes-in-on-widespread-use-of-zero-hours-deals/2007035.article. Accessed 25 Mar 2015.

Mountz, A., Bonds, A., Mansfield, B., et al. (2015, forthcoming). For slow scholarship: A feminist politics of resistance through collective action in the neoliberal university. *An International E-Journal for Critical Geographies.*

Morley, L. (1998). All you need is love: Feminist pedagogy for empowerment and emotional labour in the academy. *International Journal of Inclusive Education, 2*(1), 15–27.

Ogbonna, E., & Harris, L. C. (2004). Work intensification and emotional labour among UK university lecturers: An exploratory study. *Organization Studies, 25*(7), 1185–1203.

Pereira, M. M. (2012). Uncomfortable classrooms: Rethinking the role of student discomfort in feminist teaching. *European Journal of Women's Studies, 19*(1), 128–135.

Pereira, M. M. (2015). Struggling within and beyond the Performative University: Articulating activism and work in an 'academia without walls'. *Women's Studies International Forum.* doi: 10.1016/j.wsif.2015.06.008.

Phiri, A. (2015). Critical spaces: Processes of Othering in British institutions of higher education. *Journal of Feminist Scholarship. 7*(8), 13–27. Available from: http://www.jfsonline.org. Accessed 29 May 2015.

Reevy, G., & Deason, G. (2014). Predictors of depression, stress, and anxiety among non-tenure track faculty. *Frontiers in Psychology, 5*(701), 1–17.

Schueths, A. M., Gladney, T., Crawford, D. M., Bass, K. L., & Moore, H. A. (2013). Passionate pedagogy and emotional labor: Students' responses to learning diversity from diverse instructors. *International Journal of Qualitative Studies in Education, 26*(10), 1259–1276.

Smith, D. E. (1987). *The everyday world as problematic: A feminist sociology.* Toronto: University of Toronto Press.

Smith, D. E. (1994). A Berkeley Education. In K. P. Meadow Orlans & R. A. Wallace (Eds.), *Gender and the academic experience* (pp. 45–56). Lincoln: University of Nebraska.

Smith, D. E. (2005). *Institutional ethnography: A sociology for people.* Oxford: AltaMira Press.

Smith, P. (1992). *The emotional labour of nursing.* Basingstoke, UK: Macmillan Education.

Tagore, S. (2009). A slam on feminism in academia. In J. Yee (Ed.), *Feminism for real: Deconstructing the academic industrial complex of feminism* (pp. 37–41). Ottawa: The Canadian Centre for Policy Alternatives.

Tunguz, S. (2014). In the eye of the beholder: Emotional labor in academia varies with tenure and gender. *Studies in Higher Education,* 1–18. . Available from: http://www.tandfonline.com/loi/cshe20. Accessed 26 Aug 2015.

Wardrop, A., & Withers, D. (Eds.) (2014). *The para-academic handbook: A toolkit for making-learning-creating-acting.* Bristol: HammerOn Press.

Williams, R. (2013, January 28). The university professor is always white. *The Guardian.* Available from: http://www.theguardian.com/education/2013/jan/28/women-bme-professors-academia. Accessed 25 Mar 2015.

Wright, S. (2015). Knowledge that counts: Points systems and the governance of Danish universities. In A. I. Griffiths & D. E. Smith (Eds.), *Under new public management: Institutional ethnographies of changing front-line work.* Toronto: University of Toronto Press.

Yuval-Davis, N. (2011). *The politics of belonging: Intersectional contestations.* London: SAGE Publications.

PART V

Envisaging Feminist Futures

On Becoming "Bad Subjects": Teaching to Transgress in Neoliberal Education

Katherine Natanel

In October 2013, I began the first of two years as a Senior Teaching Fellow at SOAS, University of London. Buoyed by the prospect of temporarily leaving research to focus on teaching, I had spent part of the preceding summer reading works on critical and feminist pedagogy. I was particularly inspired by work on education as a "practice of freedom" as developed by Paulo Freire (1996 [1970], 1998) and bell hooks (1994), whose experience as scholars and educators promised new ways of constructing knowledge and community. Holding fast to the conviction that I might "teach to transgress" (hooks 1994) within feminist classrooms, I was surprised to quickly encounter the logics of neoliberalism within and without these critical spaces. Previously, I had imagined feminist politics to act as a kind of safeguard against the intrusion of capitalist ideology into the classroom. Protecting learners and instructors alike from atomisation, competition and the logics of individual gain, feminism would build solidarity and militate against inequality, generating safe spaces of inclusion and exploration.

Yet almost immediately I encountered neoliberalism through the combination of circumstantial and structural factors, which together

K. Natanel (✉)
SOAS, London, UK

© The Author(s) 2017
R. Thwaites, A. Pressland (eds.), *Being an Early Career Feminist Academic*, DOI 10.1057/978-1-137-54325-7_12

239

shaped my feminist classrooms. At the same time as I accepted a fixed-term fractional position, I was also elected to the school's branch of the University and Colleges Union (UCU) as the first ever fractional staff representative. Throughout the year and a half of my tenure, this position would consistently keep at the fore of my consciousness the concerns, struggles and varying plights of my colleagues employed in precarious conditions similar to my own. During the course of the 2013–14 academic year, UCU campaigned heavily and mobilised extensively in response to the offer of a one per cent pay rise (Shaw 2013; Press Association 2014; UCU 2015), which fell far short of meeting the 13 per cent loss in pay experienced since 2008 by many working in the higher education sector.[1] This call to collective action produced strikes, rallies and teach-ins that electrified the atmosphere at our school, stimulating discussion and creativity among participants as well as support within the student body.[2]

However, while the actions of academic staff were largely understood and encouraged by SOAS students, a number of offhand comments made during office hours and in hallways alerted me to a sense of dissatisfaction felt by some. "How long will you keep rescheduling classes? I am *paying* for this, you know?" one particularly aggrieved young woman asked somewhat rhetorically upon the announcement of further strike action. With the steep rises in tuition fees imposed by many universities in autumn 2012 (Sedgi and Shepherd 2012), for some students education had become a transaction, a form of knowledge "banking" apart from the system outlined and contested by Freire (1996 [1970]), which will be discussed below. This new transactional approach to education has been effectively entrenched through the recent announcement of a Teaching Excellence Framework (Ratcliffe 2015) and the oversight of universities by the Competition and Markets Authority (Morgan 2015)—though both ostensibly aim to strengthen teaching in higher education, these government-led initiatives position students as consumers whose assessment of the classroom experience will impact university funding and leave academics vulnerable to legal action.

As these lived experiences of precarity and shifting student expectations indicate, market logics and uncomfortable choices increasingly frame the classrooms of many early career academics who seek to establish themselves as scholars and educators in the United Kingdom. Based on three years of experience as a Graduate Teaching Assistant (GTA) and two years as a Senior Teaching Fellow, this chapter examines the challenges facing feminist early career scholars who "teach to transgress" (hooks 1994) in the context of neoliberalism. While the precarity of fractional and part-time contracts affects emerging academics across disciplines, the prospect of years spent patching together employment in higher education yields particular tensions for feminist scholars. Faced with the seeming hypocrisy of (politically) teaching to transgress while (personally) obeying the limits of an exploitative system, this account sheds light on how feminist educators bargain or negotiate with power, balancing professional development with personal and political costs.

The chapter first details conditions of the rising precarity produced through the increasing commodification and casualisation of education in the United Kingdom, focusing on the experiences of early career academics often positioned on the "front line" of the classroom. I then consider the tensions specific to feminist classrooms and pedagogical practices, reflecting on five years of providing Gender Studies tuition at SOAS, University of London. Here, I discuss what it means to teach students of Gender Studies to identify power, understand structure, locate agency and practice resistance, while remaining subject to—and reproducing—the logics of neoliberalism. However, rather than positing a zero-sum game in which early career academics either accede to the demands of the neoliberal market or part ways with higher education, the third section of the chapter suggests that those of us who bargain with power might understand ourselves to be "bad subjects" (Althusser 1971)—incompletely interpellated into the system and poised to disrupt. The challenge facing feminist bad subjects is how to become agents of the very transgression we teach, actively contesting neoliberal logics as we carve out new spaces within academia.

Neoliberal Precarity

As recent academic articles and media accounts highlight, higher education has increasingly become a site of isolation and disenchantment for scholars who survive the rigours of doctoral study and find themselves entering a flooded job market. This saturation has produced—and thus far maintains—exploitative conditions that threaten to entrap early career scholars in insecure, low-paid and highly demanding positions, many on the "front lines" of the classroom.

Within higher education, the conditions and prospects confronting doctoral students and immediately post-doctoral scholars reflect the growing commodification and casualisation of academia. Promising low-paid and highly demanding positions as Graduate Teaching Assistants and (recently graduated) Teaching Fellows, many UK universities advertise fractional part-time positions as a means of supplying the labour needed to meet the demands of student enrolment at a relatively low budgetary cost (Gill 2009: 233). Squeezed by the pressure of meeting Research Excellence Framework (REF) standards (Radice 2013: 413; Barkawi 2013; Jump 2013)[3] and the realities of sector-wide cuts imposed in conditions of economic austerity (Barkawi 2013), universities increasingly view recent graduates as a particular kind of resource—highly knowledgeable, eager to establish a career and fresh to an extremely competitive job market (Calkin 2013; Grove 2014). Together, these circumstances leave early career scholars vulnerable to exploitation, vying against each other in order to gain the experience as educators and researchers that will enable employment in seemingly elusive permanent full-time positions.

While competition is not new to academia—indeed, many scholars understand and experience this practice as driving the precision of our work and the development of our profession—the conditions faced by early career academics certainly are. For many newly post-doctoral scholars, the period of low-paid, part-time work on (sometimes) renewable contracts extends for far longer than they anticipated when choosing to make academia a career. As austerity measures and assessment frameworks combine with an established culture of competition, recent graduates are told to expect between two to five years of employment in precarious conditions, stringing together fellowships as a means of material survival and CV building while publishing, proposing and applying in hopes of attaining more permanent and lucrative positions. Importantly—and for some, shockingly—these scholars emerge into a job market that not only presents limited opportunities for adequately paid full-time work, but also creates hierarchies among those vying for precarious part-time employment.

Upon meeting with a mentor one year after earning my doctorate, I explained how my then-present application strategy targeted entry-level lectureships across a limited number of disciplines, from Gender Studies to politics, anthropology and sociology. With a PhD in Gender Studies, an MA in Near and Middle Eastern Studies and a BA in Women's Studies, I understood interdisciplinarity to be a strength that would widen rather than restrict my opportunities; however, thus far my applications had yielded nothing. Clearly and kindly, I was told that the lack of response was less tied up with disciplinary rigour and more connected to the relative stage at which fellow applicants were submitting their scholarship, experience and plans for consideration—while I had one year as a Teaching Fellow and two peer-reviewed published articles behind me, others were likely to have been building their profiles over a minimum of three years, with more publications and hours spent in the classroom.[4] Thus advised, I re-calibrated my strategy to target temporary fractional positions, applying for Teaching Fellowships and Research Assistantships rather than the full-time permanent lectureships for which I now understood my fellow applicants to be more qualified, by virtue of time forcibly spent in precarious conditions.

While postdoctoral research fellowships provide a limited number of recent graduates with two to three years of respite from the precarity of higher education,[5] for many the years immediately post-PhD unfold in a manner similar to my own experience—patching together part-time temporary work that provides important experience and (theoretically) time to develop publication records and future research plans, entailing long working hours for meagre pay. Forebodingly, Rosalind Gill (2009: 232) writes, "Precariousness is one of the defining experiences of contemporary academic life—particularly, but not exclusively, for younger or "early career" staff (a designation that can now extend for one's entire "career," given the few opportunities for development or secure employment)." Significantly, this situation should not be viewed as inherent to academia as a competitive field or career path, but as intrinsically linked to the processes and logics set into motion by neoliberalism.

In the context of higher education, the precarity experienced by early career academics reflects the emergence of neoliberal thinking as a dominant political—and educational—philosophy. Ongoing in the United Kingodm since the mid-1970s (Radice 2013: 407–408, 411), the rise of neoliberalism has resulted in the treatment of knowledge "as a marketable commodity" regarded as best approached through practices of financial management (Radice 2013: 412). As Hugo Radice (2013: 412) highlights, this shift toward marketisation and commodification within higher education reflects and compounds movement away from an understanding of knowledge as a collective social endeavour. Linked to the cultural changes that construct the "free individual" as model citizen, UK universities increasingly constitute sites in which academics view themselves as atomised "workers," monitored and rewarded by the larger system (Radice 2013: 415).

Critically, these transformations—the production of a "knowledge economy" (Radice 2013: 408) and the rise of the autonomous individuals therein—are key to the proliferation of casualisation within academia, now characterised by a preponderance of temporary part-time contracts, many of them teaching-only (Gill 2009: 233; Kendzior 2012; Calkin 2013). As recent studies of higher education reveal, processes of marketisation and commodification fashion self-governing subjects who internalise and accept the logics of neoliberalism within their profession, managing and disciplining themselves while effectively regularising the field (Gill 2009: 231; Radice 2013: 415–416). Here, "[...] new and emerging forms of discipline ... operate as technologies of selfhood that bring into being the endlessly self-monitoring, planning, prioritising 'responsibilised' subject required by the University" (Gill 2009: 231).

So not only do early career academics encounter neoliberal logics, systems and practices as they enter academia through university classrooms (Gill 2009; Kendzior 2012; Calkin 2013), but they also become participants in the process of "subjectification" (Althusser 1971; Foucault 1988). As an ideology, neoliberalism fashions "good subjects," interpellated into the system "[...] *as a (free) subject in order that he shall submit freely to the commandments of the Subject, i.e. in order that he shall (freely) accept his subjection*, i.e. in order that he shall make the gestures and actions of his subjection 'all by himself'" (Althusser 1971: 56).[6] Within higher education the production of good subjects breaks and precludes solidarities, compounding the shift from education as a collective endeavor to knowledge as an (individualised) economy. Fundamentally changing the environment into which recent graduates seek entry, neoliberalism intensifies competition to the extent of undermining the attachments and relations that make collective action possible (Gill 2009: 235; Radice 2013: 416). Thus what constitutes ultimate "success" within higher education increasingly emerges as a full-time permanent contract awarded to a "good subject" who dutifully reproduces the logics of neoliberalism, both within and without her classroom.

For many feminist early career academics, this seeming complicity constitutes a significant obstacle to long-term achievement, as much of our work interrogates the sites and logics through which power is produced and maintained. However, neoliberalism more immediately presents emerging feminist scholars with troubling tensions within our classrooms, the very sites through which we gain a footing in academia and come to understand ourselves as educators whose political, personal and professional praxis are intertwined. The following section explores these tensions through a consideration of my own classrooms, revealing how neoliberalism poses particular challenges to feminist critical pedagogy.

Tensions in/of the Classroom[7]

As proponents of critical pedagogy highlight (Freire 1996 [1970], 1998; hooks 1994; Darder 2002; Evans 2005), neoliberalism indeed constitutes a significant force shaping practices and philosophies of education, whether in primary schools or universities. Considering how today's "knowledge economy" (Radice 2013) takes shape through material practices, early in the development of critical pedagogy Paulo Freire (1996 [1970]: 53) outlined the production of a "banking system" through which "education ... becomes an act of depositing." Here, as Freire (1996 [1970]) writes—

> [...] the scope of action allowed to the students extends only as far as receiving, filing and storing the deposits. They do, it is true, have the opportunity to become collectors or cataloguers of the things they store. But in the last analysis, it is the people themselves who are filed away through the lack of creativity, transformation, and knowledge in this (at best) misguided system.

Neoliberal processes of subjectification, then, pertain not solely to those many early career scholars who enter academia as teachers, but also to the students present in our classrooms. This capacity to transmit ideology is perhaps the most insidious aspect of the neoliberal knowledge economy— in fashioning subjects, teachers and students alike, who accept the world as it is, neoliberalism constitutes an "immobilizing ideology" (Freire 1998: 26–27, 126) that thwarts resistance and transformative action.

However, action, resistance and transformation are precisely what practitioners of critical pedagogy seek to foster within the spaces of their classrooms. Indeed, while Freire (1996 [1970], 1998) details the mechanisms and logics through which neoliberal education gains purchase, the main thrust of his work aims at subverting this very system. In practicing and teaching resistance, practitioners of critical pedagogy contest the "taming" capacity of ideology, (re-)positioning education as a "form of intervention in the world" (Freire 1998: 113, 90–91). As advanced by feminist scholar, educator and activist bell hooks (1994: 2, 7), feminist critical pedagogy takes up this charge as a radical practice of engagement. For hooks (1994: 2, 14), devotion to learning constitutes a "counter-hegemonic act" that challenges not only the neoliberal banking system of education, but also inequalities based on race, gender, sexuality, nationality and class. Through impelling teachers and students to acknowledge difference and interrogate its relationship to power, the feminist classroom becomes a space of shared knowledge production, creating and sustaining a political community (hooks 1994: 8).

Contesting the fragmentation and atomisation of neoliberalism while at the same time drawing attention to difference and power, critical pedagogy takes shape within feminist classrooms as an ethics, politics and practice that promotes a particular mode of intervention in the world. Rather than striving to reinforce domination, here education might become "a practice of freedom" (hooks 1994: 4), fostering resistance and transgression without eliding the ways in which power distinguishes and differentiates. Yet critical approaches to education do not solely challenge power, whether on broad or more nuanced scales—as Freire (1998: 91) writes, "[...] this type of intervention ... implies both the reproduction of the dominant ideology and its unmasking. The dialectical nature of the educational process does not allow it to be only one or the other of these things." Then as early career feminist scholars "teach to transgress" within their classrooms, to a degree we inevitably reproduce the very relations and conditions that we seek to contest.

This dynamic has indeed characterised my experiences as a feminist educator, first as a Graduate Teaching Assistant and more recently as a Senior Teaching Fellow. Initially, I became aware of the tension inherent in my pedagogical practice not in relation to neoliberalism, but through a discussion of power and violence. Through sometimes difficult interactions, during my time as a GTA I realised that while we might aid our students in fashioning analytical and political tools with which to identify and challenge power, at the same time we unexpectedly reproduce forms of violence within our very classrooms.

For many students in the MA Gender Studies core course, tensions arose with the introduction of Gayatri Chakravorty Spivak's (1994) article "Can the Subaltern Speak?" Centred on the political and methodological question of voice, in tutorial sessions we discussed whether Spivak's query might concern not the ability of the subaltern to speak, but rather whether we listen—"(what) can we hear?" Despite the difficulties of the article's language, many of our students deftly connected the politics of discourse, reception and representation to material realities, seeing personal experiences reflected or complicated by Spivak's critique. For some, privilege loomed large; by virtue of race, class, education and geopolitical location they have access to and currency within prevailing hierarchies of knowledge and power. For others, marginalisation, invisibility and silencing rang true; through different circumstances, they understand themselves and their communities as unable—though not unwilling—to participate in the conversation.

Across these varying terms of recognition, engagement with "Can the Subaltern Speak?" (Spivak 1994) raised the spectre of epistemic violence and consequently shifted the focus of our students' critiques and interventions. Having spent the previous weeks working through foundational (Western) approaches to gender including naturalisation and biological determinism, psychoanalysis, materialist critiques, postmodernism and post-structuralism, postcolonial scholarship now directed attention to the effects of the relationship between power and knowledge. In grappling with the questions of who is "subject to" and "subject of" knowledge, students use the language of epistemic violence to locate and challenge power not only within the academe, but also within our course. Designed to provoke questions around agency, structure, voice and privilege—including within feminist movements and bodies of knowledge—the core theory course traces the circulation and function of power at micro-, meso- and macro-levels across diverse contexts. Yet as our students highlight, at the same time as we unmask power and aim to foster resistance, we risk reproducing epistemic violence. Devoting a series of focussed sessions to African, Asian and Middle Eastern contexts "after" a term of Western theory and replacing exams with short weekly papers still evaluated on the basis of standardised marking criteria, we transgress particular limits while reproducing others. Thus while student critiques testify to the relative success of our critical pedagogical practices—underlining how our classrooms become open sites of engagement, exchange and action—they also reveal the extent to which we continue to fall short of our political, personal and professional ideals.

These tensions and dynamics continue to inform my experiences as an educator, though as a Senior Teaching Fellow the embeddedness of my pedagogical practices has become apparent in ways that resonate more clearly with the challenges of neoliberalism. Now responsible for convening the MA Gender Studies core course, my reorganised syllabus and addition of less formal writing assignments go some way in mitigating the epistemic violence unintentionally experienced by students in the course. However, at the same time I have become more deeply implicated in the relations of power underwriting neoliberalism as a dominant ideology, largely through my precarious position as a part-time fractional member of staff. While I urge students to take up the critiques of transnational feminist scholars who identify and challenge neoliberal logics and global capitalism (Grewal and Kaplan 2000; Mohanty 2003; Mama 2011), my very presence within the classroom reinforces the inequitable relations and conditions in question. Like many feminist early career scholars, I might contest the "banking system" of neoliberal education (Freire 1996 [1970]) through fostering engagement and action, but at the same time I somehow reproduce the deeper ideology through my assent to the current terms of academia, as outlined above. The challenge, then, is how to understand our seemingly hypocritical actions as we teach to transgress in neoliberal education.

"Bad Subjects," Radical Potential

Rather than positing stakes in which feminist early career academics either assent to the demands of neoliberalism or leave higher education with our ideals intact, after five years of learning and practicing critical pedagogy I suggest that we might understand our actions not as a "choice" between complicity or resistance, but as a worthwhile struggle to carve out a new space within academia. In drawing attention to power, structure, agency and resistance in our classrooms, yet remaining entangled within their tensions, we effectively undertake a mode of bargaining that positions us both inside and outside the system—in this, we are poised to disrupt.

As scholars of critical pedagogy make visible, resistance to neoliberal education is not an endpoint, but rather an ongoing unfinished process (Freire 1970, 1998; hooks 1994; Darder 2002; Hey 2015; Leany and Webb 2015; Pryor 2015). Whether fostering critical thinking as a practice of difference and hope (Danvers 2015), reasserting sociality as a mode of everyday political interruption (Leaney and Webb 2015) or generating new publics through our visions of feminist futures (Hey 2015), the location of early career academics on the "front lines" of the classroom enables us to intervene precisely where neoliberalism takes root as an ideology. Yet recalling Freire's (1998: 90–91) important caution, these acts of intervention will reproduce the dominant ideology at the same time as interrogating it—our entanglement is a necessary element of the struggle. However, rather than regretfully acknowledging our implication in the production and maintenance of power and teaching in spite of this tension, we might practice transgression through fully occupying and embodying the seeming grey zone in which we operate. In doing so we may take up positions as wilful "bad subjects" (Athusser 1971; Ahmed 2010), incompletely interpellated into the system and willing to cause its obstruction. While ideology fashions "good subjects" who work "all by themselves" to reproduce the wider structure and its logics, as described above in relation to neoliberal education, it simultaneously produces "bad subjects," or those who apparently fail to work as such (Althusser 1971: 55). Then the process of subjectification should be understood as a site of contestation as much as regulation, as instances arise in which individuals are indeed hailed by ideology, but only incompletely so. Like resistance, subjectification is an uncertain and unfinished process, constituting and conditioning the subject but not determining her (Foucault 1988: 50–51; Youdell 2006: 517; Freire 1998: 26). As Judith Butler (1995 cited in Davies 2006: 426) asserts, "[T]o claim that the subject is constituted is not to claim that it is determined; on the contrary, the constituted character of the subject is the very precondition of its agency."

By understanding ourselves as conditioned but not determined by neoliberalism, as agential despite constraints, we as feminist early career academics might use our position as "bad subjects" to craft more targeted and enduring interventions in the classroom and beyond. In keeping with the dialectic inherent to education, our actions will transgress particular limits while necessarily obeying others, entangling us with power and complicating our understandings of resistance. As Freire (1998: 91) reminds us—

> It is a fundamental error to state that education is simply an instrument for the reproduction of the dominant ideology, as it is an error to consider it no more than an instrument for unmasking that ideology, as if such a task were something that could be accomplished simplistically, fundamentally, without obstacles and difficult struggles.

In committing to the act of struggle and deliberately embodying our location inside yet outside ideology, we might realise the radical potential of our pedagogical practices. For many of us, the classroom remains a space of possibility (hooks 1994: 27, 207)—however, here our teaching might enable transgressions not despite, but rather "through" embeddedness in power. Following the imperatives of critical pedagogy and feminist politics (Mohanty 1989; Freire 1998; hooks 1994), as educators we must be willing to take risks, to expose our vulnerabilities as a means of being fully present within our learning communities (hooks 1994: 213). This means allowing our students to witness our struggles as part of our pedagogical practice, and bringing these tensions into the discussions that unfold within our classrooms (Freire 1998: 95). Through actions in and out of the classroom, students may take part in the conversation about precarity, acting as full partners in the practice of education. We might begin within the space of a lesson, identifying the multiple forces that shape our learning communities, from everyday questions of access and voice, to the broader relationship between students and instructors, to the structure and aims of the university as an institution. Once named and unpacked in the classroom, these forces might be contested on wider political scales as an act of community—here struggles and interests emerge as interconnected, breaking down the perceptions of difference and hierarchies of power that obstruct collective action. As such, we cannot allow neoliberalism to enter our spaces of education solely as a constitutive or conditioning power—instead we must act willfully as bad subjects, "[...] not only being willing not to go with the flow, but also *being willing to cause its obstruction*" (Ahmed 2010).

Then the task confronting feminist early career scholars is in part explaining how to understand struggle and bargaining as crucial aspects of resistance, as integral to the always-unfinished process and practice of transgression. Our embeddedness in the structures and logics of neoliberalism need not be a sign of complicity, but might constitute the very means through which we are able to practice engaged pedagogy as a radical form of intervention in the world. In this endeavour, the ability to wilfully embody our positions as "bad subjects" becomes an expression of political activism, rather than defeat or depression. By taking up positions inside yet outside ideology, presenting this position coherently to our students and encouraging engagement in a collective struggle, we do not accept the conditions of precarity in which many early career academics presently feel entrapped—rather, these pedagogical practices might enable us to become agents of the very transgression we teach.

NOTES

1. After a series of strikes and negotiations, UCU members voted to accept a final offer of a two per cent pay rise from August 2014, in addition to the one per cent offered from August 2013; see UCU (2015).
2. Throughout the 2013–14 campaign, the SOAS Student Union officially supported the actions of UCU members; see Kush (2013).
3. As Tariq Barkawi (2013) highlights, performance in the REF is directly linked to university and departmental funding.
4. Interlocutor anonymised; personal communication 20 February 2014.
5. Within the context of UK academia, postdoctoral research fellowships have grown increasingly competitive. For example, in 2013–14 Clare College (Cambridge) received 230 applications for one Junior Research Fellowship; during the same year, 325 applicants bid for three Junior Research Fellowships at Peterhouse (Cambridge). See Grove (2014) for further rates of application.
6. Emphasis in original.
7. The analysis presented in this section draws from an earlier paper written for the 2013 meeting of the International Studies Association (ISA). My thanks go to Nadje Al-Ali and Mark Douglas for their critical feedback on the material presented at that time.

REFERENCES

Ahmed, S. (2010, Summer). Feminist Killjoys (and other willful subjects). *The Scholar and Feminist Online*. [Online] Issue 8.3. Available from: http://sfonline.barnard.edu/polyphonic/print_ahmed.htm. Accessed 9 June 2015.

Althusser, L. (1971). *Essays on ideology*. London/New York: Verso.

Barkawi, T. (2013, April 25). The neoliberal assault on education. *Al Jazeera*. Available from: http://www.aljazeera.com/indepth/opinion/2013/04/20134238284530760.html. Accessed 15 May 2015.

Calkin, S. (2013, November 1). *The academic career path has been thoroughly destabilised by the precarious practices of the neoliberal university*. [Online]. Available from: blogs.lse.ac.uk http://blogs.lse.ac.uk/impactofsocialsciences/2013/11/01/precarity-and-the-neoliberal-university. Accessed 15 May 2015.

Danvers, E. (2015, April 17). *Rethinking critical thinking in higher education: Foregrounding difference*. Annual meeting of the British Sociological Association.

Darder, A. (2002). *Reinventing paulo freire: A pedagogy of love*. Boulder: Westview Press.

Davies, B. (2006, September). Subjectification: The relevance of Butler's analysis for education. *British Journal of Sociology of Education, 27*(4), 425–438.

Evans, M. (2005). *Killing thinking: The death of the university*. London: Continuum.

Foucault, M. (1988). An aesthetics of existence. In L. Kritzman (Ed.), *Michel Foucault—Politics, philosophy, culture: Interviews and other writings 1977–1984* (pp. 41–53). London: Routledge.

Freire, P. (1996 [1970]). *Pedagogy of the oppressed* (M. Bergman Ramos, Trans.). London: Penguin Books.

Freire, P. (1998). *Pedagogy of freedom: Ethics, democracy and civic courage* (P. Clarke, Trans.). Lanham/Boulder/New York/Oxford: Rowman & Littlefield Publishers, Inc.

Gill, R. (2009). Breaking the silence: The hidden injuries of neo-liberal academia. In R. Ryan-Flood & R. Gill (Eds.), *Secrecy and silence in the research process: Feminist reflections* (pp. 228–244). London: Routledge.

Grewal, I., & Kaplan, C. (2000, Autumn). Postcolonial studies and transnational feminist practice. *Jouvert: A Journal of Postcolonial Studies, 5*(1). Available from: http://english.chass.ncsu.edu/jouvert/v5i1/grewal.htm. Accessed 17 May 2015.

Grove, J. (2014, November 6). Hundreds of PhD students chasing every early career post. *Times Higher Education*. Available from: https://www.timeshighereducation.co.uk/news/hundreds-of-phd-students-chasing-every-early-career-post/2016799.article. Accessed 17 May 2015.

Hey, V. (2015, April 17). *Dissident daughters? The psychic life of academic feminism*. Annual meeting of the British Sociological Association.

hooks, b. (1994). *Teaching to transgress: Education as the practice of freedom*. New York/London: Routledge.

Jump, P. (2013, September 26). Twenty per-cent contracts rise in run-up to REF. *Times Higher Education*. Available from: https://www.timeshighereducation.co.uk/news/twenty-per-cent-contracts-rise-in-run-up-to-ref/2007670.article. Accessed 15 May 2015.

Kendzior, S. (2012, August 20). The closing of American academia. *Al Jazeera*. Available from: http://www.aljazeera.com/indepth/opinion/2012/08/2012820102749246453.html. Accessed 15 May 2015.

Kush. (2013, November 14). SOAS staff strike over pay. *SOAS Spirit*. [Online]. Available from: http://soasspirit.co.uk/news/london/soas-staff-strike-over-pay. Accessed 10 May 2015.

Leaney, S., & Webb, R. C. (2015, April 17). *The neoliberal doctoral student? Sociability and the possibilities of everyday political interruptions*. Annual meeting of the British Sociologial Association.

Mama, A. (2011). What does it mean to do feminist research in African contexts? In *Feminist theory and activism in global perspective: Feminist review conference proceedings* (pp. e4–e20). Available from: http://www.palgrave-journals.com/fr/conf-proceedings/n1s/full/fr201122a.html. Accessed 17 May 2015.

Mohanty, C. T. (1989). On race and voice: Challenges for liberal education in the 1990s. *Cultural Critique, 18*(14), 179–208.

Mohanty, C. T. (2003). 'Under Western Eyes' revisited: Feminist solidarity through anticapitalist struggle. In *Feminism without borders: Decolonising theory, practicing solidarity.* Durham/London: Duke University Press.

Morgan, J. (2015, March 12). Universities warned over breaching consumer law. *Times Higher Education.* Available from: https://www.timeshighereducation.com/news/universities-warned-over-breaching-consumer-law/2019064.article. Accessed 5 Jan 2016.

Press Association. (2014, January 15). University staff to strike over 1% pay offer. *The Guardian.* Available from: http://www.theguardian.com/education/2014/jan/15/university-staff-strike-pay-offer. Accessed 10 May 2015.

Pryor, J. (2015, April 17). *The making of the neoliberal academic: The state, the market and the PhD.* Annual meeting of the British Sociological Association.

Radice, H. (2013). How we got here: UK higher education under neoliberalism. *ACME: An International E-Journal for Critical Geographies, 12*(3), 407–418.

Ratcliffe, R. (2015, November 2). The teaching excellence framework: Can higher education up its game? *The Guardian.* Available from: http://www.theguardian.com/education/2015/nov/02/teaching-excellence-framework-university-tef-student-data-higher-education. Accessed 5 Jan 2016.

Sedgi, A., & Shepherd, J. (2012). Tuition fees 2012: What are the universities charging? *The Guardian, 23* June 2011. Available from: http://www.theguardian.com/news/datablog/2011/mar/25/higher-education-universityfunding. Accessed 12 May 2015.

Shaw, C. (2013, October 30). University staff: Why we are striking. *The Guardian.* Available from: http://www.theguardian.com/higher-education-network/blog/2013/oct/30/university-staff-why-we-are-striking-higher-education-pay. Accessed 10 May 2015.

Spivak, G. C. (1994). Can the Subaltern speak? In P. Williams & L. Chrisman (Eds.), *Colonial discourse and post-colonial theory: A reader* (pp. 66–111). New York/London: Harvester/Wheatsheaf.

UCU. (2015). *HE national negotiations 2013–15 & 2014–15.* Available from: http://www.ucu.org.uk/index.cfm?articleid=6759. Accessed 10 May 2015.

Youdell, D. (2006, September). Subjectivation and performative politics—Butler thinking Althusser and Foucault: Intelligibility, agency, and the raced-nationed-religioned subjects of education. *British Journal of Sociology of Education, 27*(4), 511–528.

Embracing Vulnerability: A Reflection on my Academic Journey as a Japanese Early Career Feminist Academic Abroad

Misato Matsuoka

INTRODUCTION

There has been increasing awareness in academia that there is a lack of job security for PhD holders due to heightened competition and lower demand (*The Guardian* 2014).[1] In the age of "massification, marketisation and internationalisation" (Barcan 2013, p. 6), the environment has become especially challenging for feminist early career researchers. As an international feminist academic in the United Kingdom, I reflect in this chapter on my own academic and pedagogical experiences, underscoring both the difficulties and opportunities I have encountered in my career. Embracing the vulnerability, or "precariousness" (Gill and Donaghue 2016), involved in being a feminist early career academic abroad, this reflection illustrates my own personal and academic journey which nurtured my strong aspiration to become a researcher in the discipline of political science and international relations (IR) as well as establishing my feminist identity in the period of neoliberalisation and globalisation. In this chapter, I first explore the nature of feminism itself within the IR framework. This is widely debated in the fields of political science and IR, so it is important to examine various aspects of feminism and pro-

M. Matsuoka (✉)
Tokai University, Tokyo, Japan

© The Author(s) 2017
R. Thwaites, A. Pressland (eds.), *Being an Early Career Feminist Academic*, DOI 10.1057/978-1-137-54325-7_13

vide a rationale as to why I can be regarded as a feminist. I also discuss the concept of "research as praxis," which may help explain the ways in which I have engaged with research. Secondly, I explain how my personal background has shaped my feminist identity. Born to a Japanese family in the United States and having moved to Japan at an early age, my feminist identity developed gradually, although not necessarily in the ideological sense. This discussion of my personal and family background lays important groundwork for understanding the concept of cultural capital[2] that is discussed subsequently. I then go on to describe my academic journey, beginning with my undergraduate studies, during which I learned about political science and IR through an "English as a Medium of Instruction" (EMI) program in Japan. I explain why I found the subject of IR attractive as well as the obstacles I encountered in researching it, noting along the way that it was some of the more unconvincing aspects of this discipline that actually encouraged me to engage more deeply with it. Thirdly, I identify the challenges that an international feminist early career academic might face when trying to forge a career in the United Kingdom during the current periods of neoliberalisation and globalisation. I conclude by discussing the future aims of my academic career while highlighting the ways in which I have attempted to develop my academic portfolio in both research and teaching.

Feminist or Not?

Whether I can be considered to be a feminist or not has been a major question regarding my identity. As I have read and listened to the discourse found in the academic literature as well as within the social and political movements of feminism themselves, I have ceaselessly considered the question of whether I am or should be regarded as a feminist, especially since my research is located in the disciplines of political science and IR. Feminism began with the first-wave movements in the nineteenth and early twentieth centuries, when it was associated with suffrage and voting rights. Second-wave feminism arose in the 1970s, focusing mainly on women's social issues. This also led to the emergence of radical feminism in the late 1980s and 1990s who "see the primary goal of feminism as freeing women from the imposition of so-called 'male values', and creating an alternative culture based on 'female values'" (Willis 1984, p. 117). Some scholars argue that we are now in the age of "post-feminism", believing that we live in an era marked not by feminist failings, but rather by feminism's success. This point of view applies particularly to younger women "who are thought to benefit from the women's movement through expanded access to employment and education and new family arrangements but at the same time do not push for further political change" (Aronson 2003, p. 904). It is also worth noting that an increasing amount of feminist-related literature also recognises a variety of feminisms that stem from the diverse experiences of each individual based on location, age, and environment. As Sassoon (2000) points out, "rich feminist literature which has placed gender on the intellectual agenda is underpinned by the daily experience of millions of women" (Sassoon 2000, p. 62). It is also argued that "although some critics associate this fragmentation with modern feminism, feminists have always emerged from diverse cultural and political perspectives and focused on issues germane to the time and location they inhabit" (Pilcher and Whelehan 2004, p. 50). Considering the widening scope of feminism, I can describe myself as feminist with strong consciousness of the challenges that have arisen due to neoliberalism and globalisation, as explained later in this chapter.

Research as Praxis

My engagement with Gramscian theory in my research has further shaped my identity as a feminist researcher. As Ledwith (2009) notes, Gramsci's theory of hegemony "offered feminists a conceptual lead on the *personal as political*" (p. 686).[3] Considering my role as an academic researcher, the concept of "research as praxis" (Salamini 1981; Lather 1986) is useful in explaining how my academic journey has intertwined with my identity as a feminist. According to Lather (1986), "praxis-oriented inquirers seek emancipatory knowledge. Emancipatory knowledge increases awareness of contradictions hidden or distorted by everyday understandings, and in doing so it directs attention to the possibilities for social transformation inherent in the present configuration of social processes" (p. 259). She also notes that "not only must theory illuminate the lived experience of progressive social groups; it must also be illuminated by their struggles" (Lather 1991, p. 55).[4] The idea of research as praxis is taken into account throughout this chapter by discussing my research, which has focused on the periods of neoliberalisation and globalisation. It may be a helpful conceptual tool in considering the ways in which I have been educated, harnessed cultural capital, and developed my research activities.

Journey into Academia: Becoming a Japanese Feminist Researcher

Realizing My Feminist Identity

My identity as a feminist emerged from my personal experiences, beginning in childhood. Born to a Japanese family living abroad, I grew up in the United States until the age of 9. During this time I developed my Japanese identity as well as my gender identity as a female in a multicultural environment, but these identities also conflicted with my personal ideal of being more vocal. Specifically, although I have rarely experienced overt discrimination, I have struggled internally with an inferiority complex due to being a small and reticent Japanese (or Asian) girl, who appears to be voiceless and to not have any opinions, even though I actually did have opinions that I kept to myself.[5] Another experience which enabled me to realise my feminist identity came after moving to Japan, where I experienced a different form of frustration, this time due to a patriarchal environment which discouraged women from pursuing independent careers, encouraging them to become housewives instead.[6] While it is not exceptional globally, it is worth pointing out that few women in Japan reach senior positions in the male-dominated institutions, including higher education.[7] Historically speaking, men were the only members of the university academic profession in academic research-centred teaching from the establishment of the Tokyo Imperial University in 1886 until the end of the Second World War (Kimoto 2015).

Despite these difficulties, I was determined to advance my career in academia for the following reasons: Firstly, due to my struggles during my childhood in the United States, I was keen to overcome my inferiority complex and perceiving myself as a powerless, quiet Japanese woman. This desire drove me to become more enthusiastic about research and teaching activities in higher education, where I found more space for creativity for both students and teachers, and which I believed could be a platform to empower myself, especially through research as praxis. Secondly, the influence of my mother, an academic herself, is undeniable. She became a model for me to follow and an ideal to strive for. Having seen her cope with the demands of research and teaching while also doing the household tasks, my own desire to become a researcher grew. In Japan, the assumption is that only a genius can become an academic researcher.[8] Therefore, it became my challenge to overcome these stereotypes about academia and strive to be successful in this male-dominated world. Thirdly, in line with the previous points, I have a desire to become an example of a working woman in Japan. Living in an environment where society pressures women to become housewives (Ryan 2015) has further strengthened my resolve to work in academia. This can be regarded as a way of overcoming gender stereotypes in Japan, and it can be considered a form of research as praxis in my role as a feminist researcher.

Harnessing Cultural Capital During My Undergraduate Education

Stemming from my upbringing abroad, I knew that English was an indispensable tool for the dissemination of knowledge. This encouraged me to pursue my undergraduate education at an institution in Japan that offered an "English as a Medium of Instruction" (EMI) program.[9] In Japan, English is viewed as a "global" language, and it "is often seen as a resource that can contribute to personal, social and economic development in a range of diverse contexts.... Due to these associations, the learning of English in many contexts is viewed as a means of increasing one's social and cultural capital" (Erling and Seargeant 2011, p. 2).[10] Within this environment, I had a strong interest in enhancing myself by acquiring high-level English ability as a form of cultural capital, and the prospect of working in academia in the future further motivated me to acquire academic skills in and through English.[11] My improved English proficiency gave me access to a wider variety of resources and also allowed me to disseminate my findings to a larger audience via presentation and publication. Further, it enabled me not only to obtain a PhD degree but also to actively attend international academic conferences and engage in teaching activities in the United Kingdom. Moreover, the ways in which I approach my research and teaching were largely influenced by the liberal arts education I received during my undergraduate and graduate studies. This is where I first acquired not only my knowledge of political science and sociology/anthropology, which I majored in, but also other academic disciplines, including literature and art history, which broadened my perspective and my approach to research and encouraged me to continue researching politics and IR in an interdisciplinary manner.

Doctoral Education in the United Kingdom

I decided to pursue my PhD in the field of politics and IR in the UK. It is worth noting that feminist struggles exist within this discipline. For instance, Hooper (2001) remarks that the male dominance of the IR field "seems a particularly appropriate site for an investigation into masculinities, and particularly into their dominant, or 'hegemonic,' forms" (p. 5). Blanchard (2003) also notes that "national security discourses are typically part of the elite world of masculine high politics" (p. 1289). With these characteristics of the IR field in mind, my PhD thesis examines the US-Japan alliance through the neo-Gramscian framework in an attempt to answer the research question, Why is the US-Japan alliance being strengthened, and how might this be related to the concept of hegemony? By adopting this alternative IR approach to the US-Japan alliance, I attempted to broaden our understanding about security and IR rather than restricting it to narrow political considerations. Although this should be and often is the attitude of most academic researchers in general, it can also be regarded as an example of research as praxis—rather than limiting myself to the mainstream understanding of the US-Japan alliance, my research attempts to explain political dynamism in a broader context. In this way, completing my PhD degree in the United Kingdom can be seen as a platform for me to pursue my research activities in the areas of security studies, politics, and IR in an emancipatory and empowering way.

FUTURE CHALLENGES FOR FEMINIST EARLY CAREER ACADEMICS WORKING ABROAD: NEOLIBERAL AND GLOBALIZED MOMENTS

Getting a job in academia is becoming far more challenging for international feminist early career academics in the United Kingdom, especially when one has just received a PhD and has few research and teaching experiences, not to mention the obstacles presented by visa restrictions.[12] Furthermore, the phenomenon of neoliberalisation that is occurring in higher education raises the bar that much higher.[13] Aware of the increasing difficulty of forging an academic career in the United Kingdom, I devoted much time and energy to enhancing my research and teaching credentials in the context of UK academia.[14] Regarding research, I have attempted to broaden the scope of understanding within my discipline about IR and security issues, drawing from my own undergraduate and postgraduate education as well as my research experiences as an early career fellow at an institution where interdisciplinary research was encouraged.[15] My teaching activities have also helped me to put my research expertise into action—I have taught modules on global governance and international political economy since completing my PhD. Still, as a result of not being able to obtain an academic posting in the United Kingdom, I was left with no alternative but to return to my home country of Japan.

Female early career academics may face more challenges than males due to neoliberalisation and globalisation trends in higher education, and Japan is no exception. Kimoto (2015) reveals that "women's sense of belonging to the university structure has become even weaker than that of men. This suggests that women, more than men, consider recent university reforms to be negative" (p. 98) and "university management has not necessarily gone in the direction that members of faculty had hoped, leading to a breakdown in the sense of community" (p. 100). As Yamanoi (2015) remarks, "Although mobility seems to be growing thanks to the introduction of the fixed-term system as opportunity, such an unregulated fixed-term system, in tandem with the tenure system, would never contribute to the welfare of the academic profession" (pp. 53–54). These developments demonstrate the difficulties faced by female academics in Japan, especially early in their careers, in developing their academic careers under these challenging circumstances. Furthermore, non-native English speakers have additional obstacles related to accessing English-language education, which is becoming stratified in Japan due to the neoliberalisation of education (Brinton 2011; Horiguchi et al. 2015). As Kitamura (2011) remarks, English proficiency attainment is increasingly stratified in terms of not only generation but also class and gender through the marketisation of English education, affecting "especially women with ambitions for upward mobility through the cultural capital of English skills" (Kitamura 2011; Horiguchi et al. 2015, p. 3).

Conclusion: Enriching Experiences as a Feminist Early Career Researcher

Although as a feminist early career researcher abroad I have encountered many obstacles to succeeding in the United Kingdom, I have continually made efforts to overcome these challenges and remain in academia. This chapter describes how my feminist identity grew out of my personal experiences and shaped my academic journey. Patti Lather encourages feminist scholars to think about how to use research as praxis to challenge common sense (Lather 1986, 1991). Rosalind Gill also provides encouraging advice about how to manage academic life in the neoliberal period, which reminds me of the importance of research as praxis. As she notes, "we often draw no distinction between our work and ourselves...I believe that we could substitute 'academic' for 'creatives' in this powerful life" (Gill 2010, p. 241). Yet, in the neoliberal context, she also argues that "the lack of resistance to the neoliberalization of universities is partly a result of these divisive, individualizing practices, of the silences around them, of the fact that people are too exhausted to resist and furthermore do not know *what* to resist or *how* to do so" (Gill 2010, p. 241).

For me, illustrating and sharing my journey as a feminist early career researcher in this chapter is my way of explicitly revealing my resistance to the forces of neoliberalisation. Viewing my own research as praxis, I have attempted to challenge the mainstream understanding about security and IR which may still be prominent in certain countries, including Japan. International Relations does not need to be defined as a narrow subfield in politics, but rather should be viewed as an interconnecting constellation with cultural, social, economic, and linguistic implications. This perspective stems from my experiences in a liberal arts educational environment, where I encountered various fields, all of which continue to influence my ideas about politics and remain useful in thinking about IR today. Although feminist early career researchers often find themselves in a vulnerable position with few academic experiences, especially when attempting to forge a career abroad, their identity can also be used as an opportunity to enrich their academic research and teaching portfolio. In my own personal experience, it has been challenging to get a paid academic position in the United Kingdom for various reasons, including the small number of publications I possess. However, having gained an understanding of those difficulties, I have been enhancing my research and teaching skills based on my undergraduate, graduate, and postgraduate experiences. Regardless of the challenges which female scholars may face, the only thing that I can do as a feminist early career researcher is to continue conducting research as praxis while linking my personal, educational, research, and teaching experiences. This is perhaps one of the most effective and practical ways that women can empower themselves and improve their position in society.

NOTES

1. It is argued that "neoliberal academia is producing new forms of insecurity that hamper sharing and exchange, but instead push us to work harder, sell ourselves better and engage in competition rather than collaboration" (Bal et al. 2014; Gill and Donaghue 2016, p. 43).

2. Stemming from Pierre Bourdieu's notion, the concept of cultural capital has been discussed in a range of different policy fields (Bennett and Silva 2006).

3. In relation to the hegemony of masculinity, Ledwith also notes that the patriarchal worldview can be regarded as "common sense," where the political, economic, and social status of women is "diminished and exploited" (2009, p. 686).

4. This idea is also reflected in Bakker and Gill's (2003) notion that "the making of history involves the dialectic of political agency and the formation of new potentials of power" (p. 24).

5. This "silence" is directly related to the discussions of silence in the context of neoliberal academic environments (e.g., Ryan-Flood and Gill 2010), although I would argue that it applies here in the general sense as well.

6. This might be influenced by "the reconstruction of the 'Japanese family'...that reinforced a gendered division of labour in which women bore increased responsibility for taking care of those who need help" (Mikanagi 1998, p. 182) in the 1980s.

7. In line with the previous note, the traditional notion of motherhood remains influential in Japan.

8. Simonton (1999) explains that Japanese culture discourages female participation in competition due to the Confucianist hierarchical view. However, Confucian-influenced thinking is also pervasive in the context of academic culture, where it works to suppress the opening up of opportunities for the majority of people.

9. Such programmes have been introduced in part due to the Japanese government's recent push to "globalise" higher education through prominently visible governmental initiatives such as the "Global 30" project, although other factors are also at play (e.g., Horiguchi et al. 2015).

10. Kubota (2011) explains how English is used for instrumental purposes in Japan.

11. This also relates to the concern within the IR discipline that non-Western perspectives tend to be hidden unless they are written or spoken about in English (Acharya and Buzan 2007).
12. I was fortunately able to extend my Tier 4 visa for an additional year, but this was still too short a period in which to make the sort of distinctive academic achievements that are required for academic positions.
13. The Research Excellence Framework (REF) and the Teaching Excellence Framework (TEF) can be regarded as examples of neo-liberalisation in higher education.
14. I obtained a teaching certification called "PGA: Teaching and Learning in Higher Education," which is accredited by the Higher Education Academy (HEA) and may contribute to my future teaching activities.
15. For instance, during this fellowship I launched an interdisciplinary research project entitled, "Hello Kitty and International Relations" in order to elicit various ideas and approaches toward exploring the relevance of "Hello Kitty" in the context of IR.

REFERENCES

Acharya, A., & Buzan, B. (2007). Why is there no non-Western international relations theory? An introduction. *International Relations of the Asia-Pacific, 7,* 287–312.

Aronson, P. (2003). Feminists or "Postfeminists"? Young women's attitudes toward feminism and gender relations. *Gender & Society, 17*(6), 903–922.

Bakker, I., & Gill, S. (2003). *Power, production and social reproduction: Human in/security in the global political economy.* London/New York: Palgrave-Macmillan.

Bal, E., Grassiani, E., & Kirk, K. (2014). Neoliberal individualism in Dutch universities: Teaching and learning anthropology in an insecure environment. *Learning and Teaching, 7*(3), 46–72.

Barcan, R. (2013). *Academic life and labour in the new university: Hope and other choices.* London: Ashgate.

Bennett, T., & Silva, E. B. (2006). Introduction cultural capital and inequality: Policy issues and contexts. *Cultural Trends, 15*(2–3), 87–106.

Blanchard, E. M. (2003). Gender, international relations, and the development of feminist security theory. *Signs, 28*(4), 1289–1312.

Brinton, M. (2011). *Lost in transition: Youth, work, and instability in postindustrial Japan.* Cambridge: Cambridge University Press.

Erling, E. J., & Seargeant, P. (2011). *English and development: Policy, pedagogy and globalization.* New York: Multilingual Matters.

Gill, R. (2010). Breaking the silence: The hidden injuries of neo-liberal Academia. In R. Ryan-Flood & R. Gill (Eds.), *Secrecy and silence in the research process: Feminist reflections* (pp. 228–244). New York: Routledge.

Gill, R., & Donaghue, N. (2016). Resilience, apps and reluctant individualism: Technologies of self in the neoliberal academy. *Women's Studies International Forum, 54,* 91–99.

Hooper, C. (2001). *Manly states: Masculinities, international relations, and gender politics.* New York: Columbia University Press.

Horiguchi, S., Imoto, Y., & Poole, G. S. (2015). *Foreign language education in Japan: Exploring qualitative approaches.* Netherlands: Sense Publishers.

Kimoto, N. (2015). Gender bias: What has changed for female academics? In A. Arimoto, W. K. Cummings, F. Huang, & J. C. Shin (Eds.), *The changing academic profession in Japan* (pp. 89–102). Switzerland: Springer International Publishing.

Kitamura, A. (2011). *Eigo wa Josei wo Sukuuno ka [Will English Save Japanese Women?].* Tokyo: Chikuma Shobo.

Lather, P. (1986). Research as praxis. *Harvard Educational Review, 56*(3), 257–278.

Lather, P. (1991). *Getting smart: Feminist research and pedagogy within the postmodern.* New York: Routledge.

Ledwith, M. (2009). Antonio Gramsci and feminism: The elusive nature of power. *Educational Philosophy and Theory, 41*(6), 684–697.

Mikanagi, Y. (1998). Japan's gender-based social security policy. *Japan Forum, 10*(2), 181–196.

Pilcher, J., & Whelehan, I. (2004). *50 key concepts in gender studies (Key concepts).* London: Sage.

Ryan, K. (2015). *Poll: Japanese women don't want to lead* [Online]. Available from: http://thediplomat.com/2015/07/poll-japanese-women-dont-want-to-lead/. Accessed 20 Aug 2015.

Ryan-Flood, R., & Gill, R. (2010). *Secrecy and silence in the research process: Feminist reflections.* London/New York: Routledge.

Salamini, L. (1981). *The sociology of political praxis: An introduction to Gramsci's theory.* London: Routledge & Kegan Paul.

Sassoon, A. S. (2000). *Gramsci and contemporary politics: Beyond pessimism of the intellect.* New York: Routledge.

Simonton, D. K. (1999). *Origins of genius: Darwinian perspectives on creativity.* Oxford: Oxford University Press.

The Guardian. (2014). *Academics anonymous: So many PhD students, so few jobs.* May 23.

Willis, E. (1984). Radical feminism and feminist radicalism. *Social Text, 9/10,* 91–118.

Yamanoi, A. (2015). Mobility. In A. Arimoto, W. K. Cummings, F. Huang, & J. C. Shin (Eds.), *The changing academic profession in Japan* (pp. 41–77). Switzerland: Springer.

'I'm an Early Career Feminist Academic: Get Me Out of Here?' Encountering and Resisting the Neoliberal Academy

The Res-Sisters

Introduction: Navigating the Academic Jungle

Being an early career female and feminist academic in these times can be tough. We face the marketisation and privatisation of higher education, the entrenchment of accountability cultures, and the growing casualisation and intensification of academic labour. Recent data on UK higher education provides a dismal picture for women, and Black and Minority Ethnic (BME) women in particular. A total of 71.2% of professors are white males, 20.3% are white females, but only 1.6% are BME women (Equality Challenge Unit 2014: 276; Alexander and Arday 2015). Not only are women (and especially BME women) under-represented in senior positions, they are also paid less, and are more likely to be found on casual contracts (Equality Challenge Unit 2014; JNCHES 2015; Savigny 2014).

The *Res-Sisters* are Jessie Abrahams, Cardiff University; Kim Allen, University of Leeds; Victoria Cann, University of East Anglia; Laura Harvey, University of Surrey; Sumi Hollingworth, London South Bank University; Nicola Ingram, Lancaster University; Kirsty Morrin, University of Manchester; Helene Snee, Manchester Metropolitan University; Annabel Wilson, Cardiff University.

Kim Allen (k.allen1@leeds.ac.uk) is the corresponding author.

Kim Allen (✉)
University of Leeds, Leeds, UK

© The Author(s) 2017
R. Thwaites, A. Pressland (eds.), *Being an Early Career Feminist Academic*, DOI 10.1057/978-1-137-54325-7_14

267

We find ourselves navigating an academic jungle where neoliberal values and processes permeate academic life. Tracing the embodied effects and affective cruelties of the neoliberal academy—including stress, shame, anxiety, guilt—Gill (2009) calls on academics to 'redress our own collective silence' about transformations in academic labour and how we might resist these (see also Gill and Donoghue forthcoming). Certainly, the conditions of academic labour and the inequalities these give rise to have long been subject to critique by feminist, working-class and BME scholars who have exposed the uneven power relations and processes of in/exclusion characterising academic life (e.g., Addison and Mountford 2015; Leathwood and Read 2013; Mirza 2006; Morley 1997; Reay 2000; Skeggs 1997; Taylor 2012). This work demonstrates how some academics are made to feel that they are outsiders, marked as 'bodies out of place' (Puwar 2004).

Contemporary academia demands a particular subject: enterprising, highly productive, competitive, always available and able to withstand precarity. But 'who' is this ideal academic? 'Who' can—and indeed wants to—play 'this' game? For those at the start of their career such questions have particular pertinence. In the context of the Research Excellence Framework (REF), increasingly competitive research funding and sometimes-brutal peer review, the early career academic is interpellated as a 'great mind' or a 'rising star'. She/he must win grants, achieve 'impact', satisfy students and impress peers through internationally leading publications. As Warner argues, 'young academics are slicing off their heels and cutting off their toes to fit into the glass shoe' (2015). Recent research suggests that the culture of 'publish or perish' is acutely felt by those at the lower rungs of the academic career ladder, with early career researchers reporting high levels of anxiety and a growing disillusionment with the profession (Mathieson 2015). At the same time, the casualisation of academic labour is highly gendered as 'subordinate workers, overwhelmingly women, service those who generate academic capital, overwhelmingly men' (Reay 2014). For marginalised 'Others', occupying the most precarious academic positions, contesting these demands and inequalities carries particular risks (Leathwood and Read 2013).

Set against this backdrop, this chapter contends with the pains and pleasures of carving out an academic career. It draws on the lived experiences of nine early career female academics working within the sociology and cultural studies of education and youth. Our name emphasises our shared occupational and political identities: as feminist academics engaged in and committed to *research*, *resistance* and *sisterhood*. We occupy a range of positions in relation to social class, race, ethnicity and sexuality as well as institutional location and contract type. As feminists engaged in critical theory and pedagogy, we are acutely aware of gender inequality and how this interacts with other categories to produce different experiences of in/exclusion. Ironically, we are confronted with these same forces within contemporary academia. We are simultaneously reflexive about, and constrained by, the intersectional inequalities that shape our sense of belonging within academia. We are also mindful of how we might be guilty of reproducing and sustaining the very systems that trouble us, where our 'manic productivity' (Hey 2004: 33), justified as a 'labour of love', may be evidence of our compliance with the demands of the neoliberal academy.

We share these professional–personal reflections on academia as a political and pedagogic imperative. As sociologists, we are committed to connecting individual struggles to societal issues of inequality and power. Such a commitment to connecting the personal to the political, to generating theory from 'ordinary' experiences, is also a feminist one: to quote Ahmed (2015) 'the everyday is our data'. While such autobiographical data has long been subject to derision, located as a less legitimate form of enquiry and self-indulgent naval-gazing, as feminists we reiterate its importance for understanding the lived experiences of gender, class and race oppression within higher education (Morley 1997).

In the spirit of feminist politics and consciousness-raising, this chapter is a necessarily and purposely 'collective' endeavour. Drawing on a tradition of feminist collective praxis as a space for generating change (see Mountz et al. 2015), this chapter seeks to be disruptive in and of itself; its 'collective' authorship is a political act of refusing the hyper-individualised and competitive modes of working that academia encourages. If the ideological devices of the neoliberal academy seek to constitute us as 'individual' subjects of knowledge, writing this as the 'Res-Sisters' is a form of counter-interpellation based on a feminist politics that emphasises our 'collective' identities. We wrote this chapter together, all contributing to the group discussion, writing and editing. Our approach is imbued with care and support for one another, allowing for members of the collective to have varying degrees of input at different times. No one is 'lead author'. This is a powerful and satisfying form of writing and thinking; our ideas are mutual yet also different and were often bounced off each other to construct new ones. Our sentences were initiated by some and finished by others.

In writing this chapter, our aim is not simply to break the silence about the difficulties of carving out an academic career. Crucially, we also attend to the passionate attachments (Leathwood and Hey 2009) that sustain us: the histories of feminist resistance that inspire us; the friendships we form and intellectual 'homes' we carve out; the practices of kindness, humour and inter-dependence that rub up against cultures of competition and individualism. The organisation of this chapter is underlined by a desire to steer the 'Feminist Killjoy' (Ahmed 2010) in us to positive and productive ends. Thus, we move beyond identifying and critiquing the forms of exclusion we encounter to offer suggestions for how early career academics may challenge the neoliberal university and occupy academia 'differently', adding to the voices of other academics endorsing collective strategies of resistance. These are summarised in a 'Manifesta' that concludes this chapter.

EXCLUSIONS AND INJUSTICES: BODIES OUT OF PLACE AND OUT OF TIME

To use the words of one Res-Sister, we feel we are 'neither one nor t'other': that we do not really fit. While our collective name emphasises our gender and feminist politics, our class and racial identities intersect with our positioning as women to create particular forms of exclusion. In line with the critical literature on belonging and exclusion in the academy, introduced at the start of this chapter, experiences of feeling 'a fraud', 'not good enough' and 'out of place' were vocalised by the collective in our group discussions. We described how we feel the whiteness, maleness and middle-classness of the academy in everyday encounters at conferences, in teaching rooms, in departmental meetings. At times we feel too feminine, not feminine enough, too working-class, too political, too black, too Northern, too urban, too Irish, too gay, too straight.

Perhaps we are also bodies out of time as well as bodies out of place. A key topic of our conversations has been the growing disjuncture between what we want from academia and what it demands from us. We find ourselves in academia through interests in, and commitments to, understanding and challenging inequalities. For all of us, our politics and intellectual passions are driven by personal experiences of injustice. However, we feel collectively that academia does not often provide us with the space or time to do what we entered this profession to do. The important aspects of our jobs—which we see as teaching and research committed to understanding and challenging social injustices—are increasingly sidelined by endless bureaucracy. We find ourselves caught up in recreating the very structures we wish to challenge.

As early career researchers we are under pressure to enhance 'productivity', measured by 'outputs'—the cold, clinical term for our carefully crafted writing and ideas (Warner 2015). While this process affects all academics, it feels as though early career academics are particularly punished by this shift towards commodification. We are trying to establish careers in an arena where competitive individualism is valued, where people spend years trying to land secure contracts, many of our contemporaries writing in their spare (unpaid) time to enhance their employment prospects. Increasingly, early career academics are living precariously on a patchwork quilt of short-term research contracts and crumbs of hourly-paid teaching. In this environment, competition and measurable outputs (publication and grant applications) are a means of survival. Caught up in these unfortunate shifts, we are being crushed by the very career we know should be liberating. We find ourselves forced to work in circumstances that are not of our making, in a system that we are simultaneously critiquing and (re) producing.

Added to this frustration is that we often find ourselves silenced when we speak of these things to senior management. We are told that it has always been this way, that we are naïve in our critique or that we should count ourselves lucky. We are left feeling like ungrateful daughters. Such practices cause us to question our very being and right to exist in academia. We are expected to cope with the spiralling demands of the job, not to question them. To critique feels tantamount to admitting that we are struggling and are not up to the job: that we are simply just not 'good enough' or 'tough enough'. Indeed, as Gill and Donoghue (forthcoming) argue, even when institutions acknowledge the stress and anxiety associated with academic work, the solutions offered 'remain locked into a profoundly individualist framework that turns away from systemic or collective politics to offer instead a set of individualised tools by which to "cope" with the strains of the neoliberal Academy'.

Furthermore, as class, gender and race inequality are increasingly discounted as tired concepts, 'reeking of old discredited metanarratives' (Reay 2000), to locate our frustrations within a broader context of inequality feels like a taboo. If we speak of sexism, racism or classism in the academy, we are met with 'rolling eyes' that instruct us to 'get over it' (Ahmed 2015). Indeed, even in spaces designed to officially 'represent' us, we can find ourselves frustrated, patronised by 'Union Man'[1], for whom gender discrimination in the academy is secondary to other 'battles'.

Trying to Escape? The Paradox of Exclusion

Contemporary academia is often positioned as progressive and inclusive with government and institutional policy espousing the benefits of a 'diverse' academic labour force. As young women, most of us the first in our families to attend a higher education institution let alone work in it, we may be seen as 'Top Girls' (McRobbie 2008): symbols of meritocracy and gender equality. Yet, as evidenced at the beginning of this chapter, there are endemic patterns of inequality across the sector. Whilst these injustices clearly exist, they are all too often silenced. Rather, a focus is placed on the fact that, whilst we may be in the minority, we are still here: we have 'arrived'. Even as institutions flaunt their commitments to equality, we are told to pipe down. Consequently, and as discussed above, there is little space for our experiences of marginalisation to be spoken beyond personal emails or hushed conversations at conferences. Even writing this chapter can feel like an indulgent act.

Talking about feelings of exclusion and injustice makes those in power feel uncomfortable. Yet paradoxically, through our classed, gendered and raced bodies, some of us find our 'difference' being used by our institutions as a token, symbolic of 'progress'. We may have 'made it' in the academy, but we often feel that we must change, or at least be grateful for the opportunity we have been given. Indeed, the appearance of 'non-traditional' subjects in higher education—as students and academics—is often celebrated as a symbol of meritocracy and ticket to upward social mobility. Such discourses painfully inscribe higher education as being a process of escaping one's working-class roots and become 'middle class' in a pursuit of self-betterment (Loveday 2014; Reay et al. 2009). We are not allowed to remain too working-class or too black. Rather we must adapt to 'fit in'. Many of us have felt such pressures in subtle and everyday practices of hostility—where our accents or style of dress raise eyebrows among colleagues. These painful processes generate feelings of anger, self-doubt and insecurity (Addison and Mountford 2015; Reay 2000; Skeggs 1997).

We are part of the game but we do not want to play by its rules. We suffer from a 'divided habitus' (Reay et al. 2009): internally we are conflicted. At times there is an overwhelming feeling that we just want to get out—to exclude ourselves from that which we are already excluded (Bourdieu

1984). Despite these feelings of frustration and discomfort, we feel a responsibility to 'stay put': to represent those who are not as privileged as us and enforce change from the inside.

FUGIVITY AND FIGHTING BACK: RESISTING AND (RE) OCCUPYING THE ACADEMY

At first glance, the neoliberalisation of academia appears to have taken root as 'common sense'. However, in the spaces between the publication targets, income generation and appraisals, one can find disagreement and discontent with the current state of affairs as academics express their fears, anger and anxieties.

Loveday (2014) describes the way in which working-class academics feel 'fugitive' in the 'middle class' space of the academy, rather than expressing 'indebtedness' or gratitude for being 'allowed' to sit at the middle-class table of the 'real' academics. This concept offers us a useful tool to consider our own (differently) 'marginalised' positions in the university. It allows us to think through how, while we might feel pressured by the current systems to 'conform', we can simultaneously think, feel and act alternatively.

There is an interesting rhetorical move that happens in these discussions of academic fear and fugivity. Such anger and resistance is often prefaced or followed by a disclaimer about academia as a privileged space ('at least I have a job' and a professional career at that). Academic work 'is' often stimulating, rewarding, varied and interesting, and offers some level of autonomy (you get to do research, and write, and manage your own time to some degree). The image of the academic as engaged in deep thought, alone, is something many of us enjoy—losing ourselves in ideas, our own and others' 'light-bulb moments'. However, we have found that it is often in spaces of 'collective' work that we feel these pleasures most deeply: the feeling of critically battling with ideas 'with others', of being around people who share our passions and inspire us.

Although we consider ourselves 'outsiders within' (and 'captive'), this does not mean that we cannot contest and push the boundaries of the current agenda. We contend that it is these very pleasurable attachments and collective moments that enable us to occupy space differently within the neoliberal academy, working together to push back and 'irritate' the system. Next we identify some of the spaces we have purposefully created, sustained or been invited to participate in, and discuss their potential as sites of collective support and resistance.

(Re)creating Spaces

Space has been a vital component of feminist politics, with the creation of physical spaces of care and support central to many feminist movements (Mountz et al. 2015). The spaces we occupy are formed not only in the present moment but in collaboration with past ideas and struggles. We take inspiration from the feminists past and present who—rather than being 'grateful' for having been invited—refused to sit politely and quietly at the table of a male-dominated academia. As Hall described the feminist intervention in cultural studies, 'it was ruptural. ... As a thief in the night, it broke in, interrupted, made an unseemly noise, seized the time, [and] crapped on the table of cultural studies' (1992: 282). We find rich and invaluable resources in the feminist writing that has helped us understand the injustices we observe and experience; in the feminist activism that has challenged male-stream academia[2]; and in the continuing 'wars of attrition, attention and citation' (Skeggs 2008: 672) as feminist scholars have battled to gain recognition for feminist epistemological imperatives, stretching disciplinary boundaries in important ways[3].

Even in the creation of this chapter we have benefited from others creating platforms from which we can speak. These spaces do not need to have an 'end product', however. In a stance against outcome-based models, there are other spaces in which we find ourselves coming together as academics to share ideas, such as reading groups and loose collectives. These spaces are necessary, fruitful and should be 'occupied'. As one Res-Sister put it, 'It's like food, nourishment: being surrounded by people who are bright and sparky and get you and make you think differently'.

Macoun and Miller (2014) contend that such informal feminist spaces can provide both refuge from universities in which our ideas and presence are marginalised, and opportunities to think and read in ways that allow 'an unfinished' 'inconclusive' 'open and engaged' reading (Walker 2011: 266, cited in Macoun and Miller 2014: 292). These spaces create a sense of belonging and safety that can militate against the pressures of public academic life to present 'polished' ideas and 'certain knowledge'. For example, we have all supported each other by organising conference panels to present emerging ideas. The solidarity symbolised in our name is brought to life in these academic practices.

Where we experience exclusions within our universities, we are able to turn to supportive intellectual communities with other feminists across other institutional and geographic locations. This can happen in both physical spaces, and more intangible networked spaces online. Indeed, while social media presents its own challenges in further blurring the boundaries between work and home, and increasing demands of public-facing 'fast academia' (Mendick 2014), such platforms also offer spaces for solidarity, resistance, humour and informal discussions about our work. While the neoliberal university nods towards collaboration in research, the individualised targets against which we are judged can leave academics isolated and atomised. Not bound by physical proximity, these virtual spaces provide important ways of re/connecting.

In building solidarities and collectives as a response to the invisible and normalised 'cliques' of masculinised, middle-class and white academia, we must, however, be careful not to risk reproducing the very same unequal power relations and practices of exclusion we seek to critique. Critical reflexivity on the micropolitics of the spaces we occupy is crucial to ensuring that such spaces remain open and inclusive, generative of building new alliances and allegiances rather than closing down connections.

We next want to consider what practices take place within the spaces we currently occupy, and how such practices enable space for others. In doing so, we argue for the importance of a feminist ethics of collaboration, kindness and care in our work.

Feminism in Practice: Collaboration, Kindness, Co-Mentoring

Clegg and Rowland (2010) argue that kindness is a radical practice, subversive of the neoliberal university's rational, instrumental focus on income and metrics. While they focus on teaching and kindness towards students, we extend this to propose that relations of care towards colleagues are not only survival tactics but crucial in resisting imperatives of competition and individualism. Such practices help build alternative ways of doing academic work that recognise the importance of genuine collaboration in our thinking and writing (Gillies and Lucey 2007; Mountz et al. 2015).

In recent years, 'mentoring' has become incorporated into the accountability practices of higher education, with schemes matching junior staff with more established mentors working towards career-related 'goals' and 'outputs'. However, we are drawn through our own experiences to consider mentoring as a place of resistance through McGuire and Reger's (2003) conceptualisation of 'feminist co-mentoring'. Their work challenges the hierarchy of traditional mentoring models, in favour of a practice in which colleagues at any level mentor each other, drawing on their experiences and engaging with the emotional dimensions of our labour and wider lives. This model resonates with our own experiences of being supported by other (feminist) academics through official and unofficial practices of support: those who have used their positions of power and privilege to help us as early career academics. Even 'within' this collective, we recognise the invaluable support we provide each other and benefit from.

Salient to challenging the conventional notion of mentoring is the attempt to collapse the overt nature of hierarchies within a co-mentoring space (McGuire and Reger 2003). This allows for pastoral relationships to flourish but it also brings forward the importance of reflecting on our own positions of security and privilege within institutions. Ensuring that we create spaces to co-mentor should include not only colleagues, especially those who are more precariously positioned than us, but students too. This means not just supporting others at the individual level but engaging in collective action to improve our working environments. This is becoming increasingly difficult as universities begin to outsource teaching and funders push for greater 'value for money' and evermore precarious research contracts. However, there are ways to push back: being aware and critical of exploitative working arrangements normalised by senior management; fighting for more secure terms and conditions, pay and recognition; and not taking for granted the work of junior colleagues as teaching and research assistants.

Teaching and Transgression

Drawing inspiration from radical, engaged pedagogy, we argue that teaching, as with mentoring, can be appropriated as a space to 'engage' students' criticality in the world (Friere 2010; hooks 1994). In the United Kingdom, teaching occupies a contradictory position in the context of increasing competition between universities for funding. On the one hand, the National Student Survey (NSS) has become an ever-present metric of 'student satisfaction', feeding into league tables and providing a tool for performance management. Simultaneously, there have been significant changes to the allocation of doctoral research funding in the United Kingdom to selective universities, arguably exacerbating existing distinctions between institutions as either 'research' or 'teaching' focused. Combined with the heavy weight of REF results, teaching in research-intensive universities can often be positioned as a 'less prestigious' task. The marked growth of staff on teaching-only contracts has raised concerns that some universities are moving staff onto 'teaching only' contracts if their publications are deemed not of sufficient quality (Jump 2013; Locke 2014).

In this context, 'engaged pedagogy' can be seen as an act of resistance—teaching not 'from the top down, but...from the inside out...with the collaboration of the educator' (Freire 2010: 43), working upon ourselves as well as our students. Teachers must be actively committed to 'a process of self-actualization that promotes their own wellbeing if they are to teach in a manner that empowers students' (hooks 1994: 15). Our own teaching practices are based on a commitment to challenging the reproduction of privilege. This includes drawing on pedagogic approaches that create 'safe spaces' for students from non-traditional backgrounds or those who are less confident, so they can share their perspectives and experiences and have these recognised as 'valuable' and 'valid'. We challenge the status quo of curricula which reproduce hierarchies of knowledge such as changing course reading lists which are only full of 'old white men'.

In this next section we consider how, outside of the 'self' as an individual project, self-care is a necessary foundation for building resistance. For those who are already marginalised, bearing the extra weight of engaging in such resistant spaces is not only tiring but often not 'easy'. Critical consciousness can involve painful work in changing our own practices, understanding the world and challenging injustice (hooks 1994).

Self-Preservation as a Collective Responsibility

Whilst the 'resistant' efforts discussed here are vital, the 'preservation of self' is also important. This is not in an individualistic sense: preservation here means not self-promotion or entering into competition with others, but rather it simply means 'self-care' (Ahmed 2014; Lorde 1988). We argue for a more collective sense of 'self-care', which encompasses a feminist ethics of care (Mountz et al. 2015) that actively works towards supporting and reminding each other to 'take care'.

Academia is exhausting and pressured, filled with efficiency frameworks, tight publishing deadlines, the pressure of completing a PhD within the funded (or even unfunded) timeframe, undertaking all the 'career musts' in academia, negotiating what those 'career musts' are and pitting your principles against them. The acceleration of time in the neoliberal academy feels pervasive. The notion of 'slow scholarship' has been advocated as a valuable alternative to the temporal logics governing academic life (Mountz et al. 2015). We find ourselves tantalised by the idea of slow scholarship but highly frustrated: we catch a romantic glimpse of it in our fantasies as our bodies and minds are forced to lurch forward at lightning speed. We ask ourselves, Can we afford to 'go at our own pace' when there is an eager reserve army of academic labour waiting to replace us? And the answer in the neoliberal university is 'probably not'.

Our bodies are out of time with how we want things to be. Our experiences suggest that slow scholarship as an alternative way of 'doing' academia is unequally afforded. As Mendick (2014) warns, only some academic subjects are able to 'go slow', while others—those trapped in short-term and precarious contracts—are left not entrapped by fast academia and marked as Slow's 'Others'. We pose the question of whether it is possible to practice 'slow scholarship'. Even in writing this chapter—amongst the competing deadlines of marking, teaching and industrial dispute, and amidst the pressures and responsibilities of our 'outside' lives (pregnancies, caring responsibilities, relationship breakups, illnesses, and unpaid leave)—we continue to think about how we can forge ways of working that are kinder, but that recognise the difficulties (and sometimes impossibilities) of 'slowing down' when the world around us accelerates.

We occupy different positions within academia, some of us more securely employed than others. In practicing care for ourselves and each other, we have sought to acknowledge these inequalities between us while creating spaces to work together and support each other across our different positions, including collective panels at conferences, joint publications and edited collections, and informal co-mentoring networks such as reading groups and writing groups conducted in our 'spare time' that collectively support peers in navigating the demands of academia. These practices are based on values and agendas other than and outside of individual career advancement.

Finally, as well as helping support others, we also need to keep time to be mothers, carers, friends, daughters, sisters and, importantly, to be ourselves. Therefore in order to fully engage in these resistance practices, we also need to extend the kindness and support offered to students, colleagues, family and friends, to ourselves.

Conclusion: The Res-Sister Manifesta

We love our jobs yet often feel conflicted, excluded, frustrated, worn-down, guilty. In the process of writing this chapter together we have recognised that we are not alone. In raising our own collective feminist consciousness through the process of writing this chapter, we hope to contribute to an on-going feminist politics along with the other contributors to this edited collection.

Consciousness-raising is more than just recognising oppression; it is also 'a foundation for change' (Kamen 1991: 4). As such, we close this chapter by encouraging change through collective feminist action. Our Manifesta[4] is both a call to arms and a resource to help early career academics counter the pervasive logic of neoliberalism that sets us apart and instead bring us together for positive change.

Embrace Collectivity and Nurture Allies

Feminists are most powerful as a collective. We are stronger and louder together. We must remind ourselves that we are working in academia for the pursuit of knowledge and the pursuit of equality for all, not for our own career advancement. One of the greatest challenges that feminism has faced—in the academy and across social life—is the rise of neoliberalism and rampant individualism. Collectivity disrupts these forces, providing support networks and helping us to organise against institutional and societal injustices. We must recognise feminism as something you 'do', not just something you are, thus welcoming and nurturing allies and uniting across intersectionalities rather than pursuing divisive and separatist politics.

We must unite with our feminist colleagues and allies, especially supporting PhD students, in our academic practices—from writing to activism. We need to co-author papers, not only to provide a platform for others but also because we can learn much by working together. We therefore need to create spaces for collaborative and vertical working within our grant applications and module design, bringing in junior colleagues, not merely clinging to 'Profs'.

We must also form allegiances outside of academia, including artists, graduates and labour activists such as those campaigning against zero-hours contracts and unpaid internships.

Little Acts of Solidarity Make a Big Difference

Academia can be a lonely place, but it does not need to be. In the spirit of embracing collectivity we also call for embracing little acts of solidarity and everyday gestures of kindness that can contribute to big changes.

If a colleague looks stressed and unhappy, we must talk to them and see if we can help. If we are at a conference and spot a nervous-looking post-graduate student, we should chat with them about their research. When a fellow early career academic gives a paper and is met with silence, we should ask a helpful question. We should tell newer colleagues what we wish we knew when we were at their stage in our careers. We must share our networks with colleagues and students. If we are running events in the community, we must invite colleagues to join us. We can act as mentors to our students; we should encourage their passions.

Speak Out

Academia is not a level playing field and it is not a meritocracy. The toxic conditions that create such inequality, however powerful, can be challenged. We must stand together to oppose precarious contracts as they are normalised by our institutions (especially if ours are indefinite). We must stand up for PhD students, who are all too often asked to (over)work as unpaid teachers. We must call out the whiteness and the maleness of academia as it is manifest in institutional boards and other mechanisms of decision-making.

We must be active in creating spaces that foster inclusivity, solidarity and care. We must be vocal in our critique of the REF and emphasise its negative impacts. We can participate in and organise 'big' action such as strikes, as well as 'cause trouble' through everyday acts of disquiet and critique. We must also not stay silent when we hear 'one off' injustices. In big acts and in little acts we can resist the reproduction of an unfair and unjust system.

We must be aware of the difficulties of 'resisting' for those in more precarious positions. Acts of naming and calling out injustice need force behind them; they must be 'taken strategically and with the support of advocates who carry weight' (Puwar 2004: 155). If we are in positions of power and privilege we must take responsibility to be an advocate for others while remaining mindful that choosing silence itself may be a survival strategy rather than evidence of disempowerment or collusion with oppressive regimes (Parpart 2010).

Recognise Your Power and Privilege

We are fortunate in many ways as feminist academics. Unlike many of our sisters we have the privilege of a platform from which to speak. Some of us are privileged because of our whiteness, our class capital or by virtue of the institutions we work in. It is vital that we recognise the power and privilege we have, and use it to more egalitarian ends.

We must create spaces for marginalised colleagues to talk. If we are organising conferences, we must be sure to provide a platform for those voices too infrequently heard. When we are speaking and writing, we must acknowledge and accredit the voices of others. We must 'take people with us'.

Much consciousness-raising takes place in the classroom (Sowards and Renegar 2004) and so we must be sensitive in our teaching practices, creating opportunities for marginalised people(s) to be heard and valued.

Self-Care Is a Must

Feminism needs feminists with the strength to fight. We should strive to live by our principles and politics, but this must not come at the cost of our health and well-being.

At a time when our politics are so often undermined and demeaned, it could be easy to work ourselves into the ground trying to 'prove ourselves' as 'good enough' academics as well as 'proper' feminists. As we have discussed, the feminist ethics of care applies to how we treat ourselves as well as others and we must not beat ourselves up for not taking on every battle. We may be in a position where we would not feel safe, physically or emotionally, to call out the injustices we observe. We may be employed so precariously that 'rocking the boat' is too costly. We may be unwell or be too tired to fight. It is not the job of one person to solve the problems of the world: this is what makes the strength of the collective so important.

AND HAVE FUN!

There are many pleasures of being in academia. Have fun!

Acknowledgements This chapter is dedicated to our fellow Res-Sisters—past, present and future.

NOTES

1. 'Union Man' is a caricature we have invented who embodies characteristics common to academic Union Representatives we have encountered within academia. Union Man sees the world through a lens of masculinised labour struggle, where issues of gender inequality

within academia are often dismissed as a nuisance. See also @aca-
demicmale on Twitter for a similar parody of academia's dismissal of
women academics and gender concerns.

2. For example, the feminist collective FAAB (Feminists Against
   Academic Bollocks). See Reay (2014).
3. For more on the feminist politics of citation see https://woman-
   theory.wordpress.com/.
4. In using the term 'Manifesta' we borrow from other calls for collective feminist activism in and through our academic practice, namely,
   Savigny and Warner (2015) and Kearney (2013).

References

Addison, M., & Mountford, V. (2015). Talking the talk and fitting in: Troubling
the practices of speaking 'what you are worth' in higher education in the UK.
Sociological Research Online, 20(2), 4.

Ahmed, S. (2010). *The promise of happiness.* London: Duke University Press.

Ahmed, S. (2014). *Selfcare as warfare.* http://feministkilljoys.com/2014/08/25/
selfcare-as-warfare/. Accessed 21 Apr 2015.

Ahmed, S. (2015). *Living a lesbian life.* http://feministkilljoys.com/2015/02/26/
living-a-lesbian-life/. Accessed 21 Apr 2015.

Alexander, C., & Arday, J. (Eds.) (2015). *Aiming higher: Race, inequality and
diversity in the academy.* London: Runnymeade.

Bourdieu, P. (1984). *Distinction.* London: Routledge & Kegan Paul.

Clegg, S., & Rowland, S. (2010). Kindness in pedagogical practice and academic
life. *British Journal of Sociology of Education, 31*(6), 719–735.

Equality Challenge Unit (2014). *Equality in higher education: Statistical report
2014.* London: ECU.

Freire, P. (2010). *Education for critical consciousness.* London: Continuum (First
published 1974).

Gill, R. (2009). The hidden injuries of the neoliberal university. In R. Ryan-Flood
& R. Gill (Eds.), *Secrecy and silence in the research process* (pp. 228–244).
London: Routledge.

Gill, R., & Donoghue, N. Resilience, apps and reluctant individualism:
Technologies of self in the neoliberal academy. *Women's Studies International
Forum* (forthcoming).

Gillies, V., & Lucey, H. (Eds.) (2007). *Power, knowledge and the academy: The
institutional is political.* London: Palgrave Macmillan.

Hall, S. (1992). Cultural studies and its theoretical legacies. In L. Grossberg &
C. Nelson (Eds.), *Cultural studies.* London: Routledge.

Hey, V. (2004). Perverse pleasures—Identity work and the Paradoxes of Greedy
Institutions. *Journal of International Women's Studies, 5*(3), 33–43.

hooks, b. (1994). *Teaching to transgress. Education as the practice of freedom.* London: Routledge.

Joint Negotiating Committee For Higher Education Staff. (2015). *Gender pay working group report.* London: Universities and Colleges Employers Association. Available at: http://www.ucea.ac.uk/en/publications/index.cfm/njgender. Accessed 20 July 2015.

Jump, P. (2013). REF non-submission may have consequences, Leicester warns. *Times Higher Education.* August 8. https://www.timeshighereducation.co. uk/news/ref-non-submission-may-have-consequences-leicester-warns/2006343.article. Accessed 20 July 2015.

Kamen, P. (1991). *Feminist Fatale: Voices from the "twentysomething" generation explore the future of the "Women's Movement".* New York: Fine.

Kearney, M. C. (2013). *Feminist media studies Manifesta.* http://www.consoleingpassions.org/wp-content/uploads/2013/08/FMC-Manifesta.pdf

Leathwood, C., & Hey, V. (2009). Passionate attachments: Higher education, policy, knowledge, emotion and social justice. *Higher Education Policy, 22*(1), 101–118.

Leathwood, C., & Read, B. (2013). Research policy and academic performativity: Compliance, contestation and complicity. *Studies in Higher Education, 38*(8), 1162–1174.

Locke, W. (2014). *Shifting academic careers: Implications for enhancing professionalism in teaching and supporting learning.* York: Higher Education Academy https://www.heacademy.ac.uk/sites/default/files/resources/shifting_academic_careers_FINAL.pdf. Accessed 20 July 2015.

Lorde, A. (1988). *A burst of light, essays.* London: Sheba Feminist Publishers.

Loveday, V. (2014). Working-class participation, middle-class aspiration? Value, upward mobility and symbolic indebtedness in higher education. *The Sociological Review.* (Online First).

Macoun, A., & Miller, D. (2014). Surviving (thriving) in academia: Feminist support networks and women ECRs. *Journal of Gender Studies, 23*(3), 287–301.

Mathieson, C. (2015). *A culture of publish or perish? The impact of the REF on ECRs.* https://charlottemathieson.wordpress.com/2015/04/24/a-culture-of-publish-or-perish-the-impact-of-the-ref-on-ecrs/. Accessed 29 May 2015.

Mcguire, G. M., & Reger, J. (2003). Feminist co-mentoring: A model for academic professional development. *NWSA Journal, 15*(1), 54–72.

McRobbie, A. (2008). *The aftermath of feminism: Gender, culture and social change.* London: Sage.

Mendick, H. (2014). Social class, gender and the pace of academic life: What kind of solution is slow? *Forum: Qualitative Social Research, 15*(3) http://www.qualitative-research.net/index.php/fqs/article/view/2224/3694. Accessed 29 May 2015.

Mirza, H. S. (2006). Transcendence over diversity: Black women in the academy. *Policy Futures in Education, 4*(2), 101–113.

Morley, L. (1997). A class of one's own: Women, social class and the academy. In P. Mahony & C. Zmroczek (Eds.), *Class matters: Working class women's perspectives on social class* (pp. 109–122). London: Taylor and Francis.

Mountz, A., Bonds, A., Mansfield, B., Loyd, J., Hindman, J., Walton-Roberts, M., et al. (2015). For slow scholarship: A feminist politics of resistance through collective action in the neoliberal university. *ACME, International E-Journal for Critical Geographies*. http://www.researchgate.net/publication/275100129_For_Slow_Scholarship_A_Feminist_Politics_of_Resistance_through_Collective_Action_in_the_Neoliberal_University. Accessed 20 May 2015.

Parpart, J. L. (2010). Choosing silence. In R. Ryan-Flood & R. Gill (Eds.), *Secrecy and silence in the research process: Feminist reflections* (pp. 15–29). London: Routledge.

Puwar, N. (2004). *Space invaders: Race, gender and bodies out of place*. Oxford: Berg.

Reay, D. (2000). Dim dross?: Marginalised voices both inside and outside the academy. *Women's Studies International Forum, 23*(1), 13–21.

Reay, D. (2014, February 15). From academic freedom to academic capitalism. *Discover Society*.

Reay, D., Crozier, G., & Clayton, J. (2009). Strangers in paradise: Working class students in elite universities. *Sociology, 43*(6), 1103–1121.

Savigny, H. (2014). Women, know your limits: cultural sexism in academia. *Gender and Education, 26*(7), 794–809.

Savigny, H., & Warner, H. (2015). *The politics of being a woman: Feminism, media and 21st century popular culture*. London: Palgrave.

Skeggs, B. (1997). Classifying practices: Representations, capitals and recognitions. In P. Mahony & C. Zmroczek (Eds.), *Class matters: Working class women's perspectives on social class* (pp. 123–139). London: Taylor and Francis.

Skeggs, B. (2008). The dirty history of feminism and sociology: Or the war of conceptual attrition. *The Sociological Review, 56*(4), 670–690.

Sowards, S., & Valerie, R. (2004). The rhetorical functions of consciousness-raising in third wave feminism. *Communication Studies, 55*(4), 535–552.

Taylor, Y. (2012). *Educational diversity: The subject of difference and different subjects*. Houndmills: Palgrave Macmillan.

Walker, M. B. (2011). Becoming slow: Philosophy, reading and the essay. In G. Oppy & N. N. Trakakis (Eds.), *The antipodean philosopher: Public lectures on philosophy in Australia and New Zealand* (Vol. 1, pp. 268–278). Lanham: Lexington Books.

Warner, M. (2015). Learning my lesson: Marina Warner on the disfiguring of higher education. *London Review of Books, 37*(6), 8–14.

Conclusion

Rachel Thwaites and Amy Pressland

'There is now significant debate as to whether universities are in crisis, in demise, or merely being restructured to meet the needs of knowledge-based economies' (Blackmore 2002: 419). Written almost 15 years ago, Blackmore's statement still holds true for universities around the globe today. Globalisation is no longer a future possibility (or threat); it is the current status quo. The global educational marketplace, coupled with the now de facto neoliberal style of management in higher education (HE); the influx of ever-evolving new technologies in pedagogy; and increasingly mobile, agentic and demanding HE students, have all contributed to a dramatic change in how universities are run, experienced and perceived around the world. The 'traditional' university has had to keep up with these changes and as such has changed as a consequence. No longer are universities uniquely places for lengthy contemplation of theory in quiet library enclaves, or in-depth philosophical debate (Deem 1998); now as young people enter HE they are immediately bombarded with questions about their employability plans, their career-enhancing extra-curricular activities, and how specific course modules will help them get the job they

R. Thwaites (✉)
Canterbury Christ Church University, Canterbury, Kent, UK

A. Pressland
DB Cargo UK, Doncaster, Yorkshire, UK

© The Author(s) 2017
R. Thwaites, A. Pressland (eds.), *Being an Early Career Feminist Academic*, DOI 10.1057/978-1-137-54325-7_15

want, with less and less time spent on academic study. Students, as 'user–payers' are also now allowed to dictate how their universities are run, but not simply through membership in unions as was once the primary channel of student-management interactions; now the national and university-specific surveys (such as the National Student Survey [NSS] in the United Kingdom) which pepper every module and element of university life give students the opportunities to 'rate' the 'service' they are paying for, which in turn contributes to how universities are ranked nationally and globally.

Equally, academic staff are under increasing pressure to produce; to teach more exciting and 'rateable' modules, to publish world-leading articles, to attract multi-million-pound funding grants, to engage and collaborate with local communities, to disseminate their research to fellow academics and lay audiences, to be 'au fait' with multiple social media platforms and to provide round-the-clock pastoral care for sometimes very troubled young people. Furthermore, universities themselves are under far greater scrutiny from governments, funders and the public. The new corporate-managerialist environment (Johansson and Sliwa 2014; Lafferty and Fleming 2000) in universities provides a response, of sorts, to some of the external pressures now facing HE institutions. Equally, the neoliberal style of university management has provoked and embedded diverse and multifaceted pressures on academic staff and students alike.

The consequence of this shift in governance has had widespread consequences globally, to which the contributors of this collection attest. The corporatisation of HE institutions has put gender equity under threat again 'despite seemingly equity-oriented discourses' abounding across different sectors in society (Blackmore 2002: 420). Johansson and Sliwa (2014) argue that such 'equality initiatives' hide instances of inequality, rather than making them more apparent. Given that women tend to occupy the lower end of the academic workforce in larger numbers, the change in managerial style has led to much greater job insecurity—the precarity that many of our contributors describe. Short-term contracts at the beginning of one's academic career are now commonplace and have a profound effect on later development due to the inability to build a research profile, the lack of continuity in the delivery of teaching activities and the constant worry about 'the next job'. The insecurity around work is also due to the increased monitoring activities which are integral to a corporate-style of university management. Now, more than ever, academic staff are under intense scrutiny to produce and provide evidence for every aspect of their work, leaving little time to actually 'do' their jobs effectively.

Our contributors also describe how this precarity impacts not only one's academic career, but also one's personal life outside of academia and general well-being. Early career academics are putting their personal lives on hold—buying a house, having children—partly due to the insecurity of their working lives and the burdensome workloads which they carry. In many ways early career female academics could be said to be supporting universities as the foot soldiers of HE institutions, akin to the way in which feminists in the 1960s and 1970s described frustrated housewives as supporting the economy by providing a happy and healthy home and hearth for their salaried husbands. Given the strength of the testimonies provided in this collection, it is time we recognise the work done by early career (female) academics in universities globally. Moreover, the threat to gender equality is being held at bay, to an extent, by early career feminists who are critiquing, challenging and supporting one another; protesting, writing, teaching and existing in an environment which seeks to impose again the patriarchal hand of control over academics. The work of women in this book, and more widely, should be applauded.

As the chapters of this book show, being a feminist does add another layer of complexity in managing these concerning changes. One must navigate the complex practical and affective realities of holding onto a politics which demands transformation, equality, power-sharing and collectivity while also, to some extent at least, playing the neoliberal game. One's feminist and scholarly identity can seem to be at odds both as a researcher and teacher. The demands of the contemporary university, and its inequalities, can be hard to bear when one is looking for a space to work together for a better world. Yet, it is exactly this conflict, inequality and set of demands which can encourage feminist early careers to push for change, call out inequity and make a real difference to the institution, their own lives and the lives of their colleagues. We do not wish to be naïve: this effort is serious and needs to be collective rather than solitary, but as our chapters show we need not despair at the state of higher education currently and our efforts at change are not in vain.

Our contributors have provided fascinating, insightful, honest and detailed accounts from personal, empirical and theoretical perspectives of how early career feminist academics are experiencing the academy globally. As Blackmore (2002: 421) states, '[u]niversities themselves have always presented possibilities and problems for women'. It would seem from the chapters in this collection that universities continue to provide feminists with opportunities to resist and challenge the patriarchal structures under which they work and have studied. However, if we take the final chapter's Manifesta, composed by the Res-Sisters collective, we could argue that universities are also positive sites for feminists to continue to push the feminist agenda into the mainstream through creative, subtle and effective methods. Rather than feel dismayed at some of the examples of discrimination and sexism detailed in the pages of this book, we would like to encourage readers to be empowered by the stories here, to recognise their own stories and to use this collective consciousness to keep moving forward step by step. Indeed, as Blackmore (2002) argues, women in academia have been, and need to continue to be 'cultural change agents' in order to question dominant values and cultures that pervade universities globally. As feminists before us—and now with our colleagues across career stages—it is we who will create change through our research, teaching, engagement, interactions and activism, making it all the more gratifying as a result.

We hope that this collection will give rise to greater debate within academia about its own culture and the position, most especially, of early career academics, as well as the potential for change that feminism holds. In collaborating with our contributors to bring this book to fruition we feel a space has been opened up for change, to give people a sense of not being alone in their struggles but part of a more visible and vocal community, and a growing and continuing global conversation. The book speaks, most critically, to the need for collective change across the sector and the necessity for this change to begin now.

References

Blackmore, J. (2002). Globalisation and the restructuring of higher education for new knowledge economies: New dangers or old habits troubling gender equity work in universities. *Higher Education Quarterly, 56*(4), 419–441.

Deem, R. (1998). New manageralism' and higher education: The management of performances and cultures in universities in the United Kingdom. *International Studies in Sociology of Education, 8*(1), 47–70.

Johansson, M., & Sliwa, M. (2014). Gender, foreigness and academia: An intersectional analysis of the experiences of Foreign women academics in UK business schools. *Gender, Work and Organisation, 21*(1), 18–36.

Lafferty, C., & Fleming, J. (2000). The restructuring of academic work in Australia: Power, management and gender. *British Journal of Sociology of Education, 21* (2), 257–267 (*51,* 331–340).

INDEX

Note: Page number followed by n denote footnotes

© The Author(s) 2017

R. Thwaites, A. Pressland (eds.), *Being an Early Career Feminist Academic*, DOI 10.1057/978-1-137-54325-7